UNITY AND DIVERSITY IN
EUROPEAN CULTURE c. 1800

PROCEEDINGS OF THE BRITISH ACADEMY · 134

UNITY AND DIVERSITY IN EUROPEAN CULTURE c. 1800

Edited by
TIM BLANNING & HAGEN SCHULZE

Published for THE BRITISH ACADEMY
by OXFORD UNIVERSITY PRESS

Oxford University Press, Great Clarendon Street, Oxford OX2 6DP

Oxford New York
Auckland Cape Town Dar es Salaam Hong Kong Karachi
Kuala Lumpur Madrid Melbourne Mexico City Nairobi
New Delhi Shanghai Taipei Toronto

With offices in
Argentina Austria Brazil Chile Czech Republic France Greece
Guatemala Hungary Italy Japan Poland Portugal Singapore
South Korea Switzerland Thailand Turkey Ukraine Vietnam

Published in the United States
by Oxford University Press Inc., New York

British Library Cataloguing in Publication Data
Data available

Library of Congress Cataloging in Publication Data
Data available

Typeset by J&L Composition, Filey, North Yorkshire
Printed in Great Britain
on acid-free paper by
Creative Print and Design (Wales) Ebbw Vale

ISBN 0–19–726382–8   978–0–19–726382–2
ISSN 0068–1202

Contents

Notes on Contributors

Peter Alter is Professor of Modern History at the University of Duisburg-Essen, Germany. Among his books are *Nationalism* (2nd edn, 1994) and *The German Question and Europe: A History* (2000). He has edited *Out of the Third Reich: Refugee Historians in Post-war Britain* (1998) and *Der DAAD in der Zeit: Geschichte, Gegenwart und zukünftige Aufgaben* (2000). He is currently working on the life of Sir W. S. Churchill.

Tim Blanning is Professor of Modern European History at the University of Cambridge and a Fellow of Sidney Sussex College. He is also a Fellow of the British Academy. His most recent book is *The Culture of Power and the Power of Culture: Old Regime Europe 1660–1789* (2002). He is currently writing the volume on 1648–1815 for *The Penguin History of Europe*.

Hans Erich Bödeker is a Senior Research Fellow at the Max-Planck-Institut für Geschichte, Göttingen. He has published books and articles on the history of culture of the early-modern period. Currently he is engaged in a research project on the emergence of human sciences in the eighteenth and early nineteenth centuries.

Otto Dann was Professor of Modern History at the University of Cologne until his retirement. His recent publications include *Vereinsbildung und Nationsbildung* (2003) and commentaries on the historical writings of Friedrich Schiller.

John Deathridge is King Edward VII Professor of Music at King's College London. His latest publication is a new critical and documentary edition of Wagner's *Lohengrin*. He has translated the *Ring* for Penguin Classics and is currently writing a study of German music and its many 'lives' since 1750.

Silke Leopold is Professor of Musicology and a Member of the Zentrum für europäische Geschichts- und Kulturwissenschaften at the University of Heidelberg. Her most recent books are *Die Oper im 17. Jahrhundert*

(2004) and *Guten Morgen, liebes Weibchen: Mozarts Briefe an Constanze* (2005). She is currently preparing a *Mozart-Handbuch* for the Bärenreiter/ Metzler series.

Peter Mandler is Reader in Modern British History at the University of Cambridge and a Fellow of Gonville and Caius College. His most recent books are, as author, *History and National Life* (2002) and, as editor, *Liberty and Authority in Victorian Britain* (2006). A history of the idea of the English national character from Edmund Burke to Tony Blair is forthcoming.

Vincent Morley is Fellow of the Mícheál Ó Cléirigh Institute for the Study of Irish History and Civilization, University College Dublin. His most recent publication is *Irish Opinion and the American Revolution, 1760–1783* (2002).

James J. Sheehan is Dickason Professor in the Humanities and Professor of History at Stanford University. His most recent book is *Museums in the German Art World* (2000). He is now writing a book tentatively entitled 'The Monopoly of Violence: War and the State in Twentieth-century Europe'.

Hagen Schulze is Professor of Modern German and European History at the Free University, Berlin, and is Director of the German Historical Institute London. Several of his books have been translated into English, including *The Course of German Nationalism* (1991), *States, Nations and Nationalism: From the Middle Ages to the Present* (1998), and the best-selling *Germany: A New History* (2001).

Siegfried Weichlein is Privatdozent of Modern History at the Humboldt University at Berlin. He recently taught at the Ruhr-University Bochum, the University of Cologne, the Nikolaus-Kopernikus-University at Torun (Poland), and at the Free University, Berlin. His most recent book is *Nation und Region: Integrationsprozesse im Bismarckreich* (2004). He is currently finishing a book on 'Modern Nationalism in Europe' (forthcoming).

Introduction

TIM BLANNING & HAGEN SCHULZE

HELD AT CARLTON HOUSE TERRACE on 26 and 27 September 2003, the
conference on 'Unity and diversity in European culture, c. 1800' was a
joint initiative on the part of the British Academy and the German
Historical Institute London. It was designed to perform three functions:
to renew the cooperation between the two institutions begun by a joint
conference in 1997;[1] to bring together British, Irish, and German scholars working on the late-eighteenth/early-nineteenth century; and to discuss a topic of central importance to the historiography of the period.
That topic was the transition from the cosmopolitan culture of the
Enlightenment to the self-consciously national cultures of the nineteenth
century, that is to say the period often described by German historians
as the *Sattelzeit* (literally 'saddle period') straddling old regime and
modernity.[2]

The nine papers[3] were divided into three sessions. The first, chaired by
Tim Blanning (Sidney Sussex College, Cambridge), comprised James
Sheehan (Stanford) on art and its publics c. 1800, Silke Leopold
(Heidelberg) on the idea of a national opera c. 1800, and John Deathridge
(King's College London) on the invention of German music c. 1800. In
the second session, presided over by Hagen Schulze (German Historical
Institute London), there were three papers on political culture: by Peter
Alter (Duisburg) on the impact of Napoleon, by Siegfried Weichlein
(Humboldt University, Berlin) on cosmopolitanism, patriotism, and
nationalism, and by Peter Mandler on the cultural policy of the British
state in European perspective, 1780–1850. The third session, chaired by

---

[1] T. C. W. Blanning and Peter Wende (eds), *Reform in Great Britain and Germany 1750–1850*,
Proceedings of the British Academy, 100 (Oxford, 1999).
[2] Otto Brunner, Werner Conze, and Reinhart Koselleck (eds), *Geschichtliche Grundbegriffe.
Historisches Lexikon zur politisch–sozialen Sprache in Deutschland* (Stuttgart, 1972–97). See
Koselleck, 'Einleitung', 1: xv.
[3] Unfortunately, Hans Erich Bödeker (Göttingen) was prevented by illness from attending the
conference, but fortunately his paper could be published in this volume.

Proceedings of the British Academy, **134**, 1–4. © The British Academy 2006.

Roy Foster (Hertford College, Oxford), concentrated on the written word, with contributions from Otto Dann (Cologne) on the invention of national languages, Marilyn Butler (Exeter College, Oxford) on Maria Edgworth,[4] and Vincent Morley (University College Dublin) on representations of the past in Irish vernacular literature, 1650–1850. There were many constructive and often trenchant contributions from the large audience (about sixty people attended for all or part of the conference).

Predictably, agreement on the nature—or even the reality—of the *Sattelzeit* could not be achieved. However, consensus was reached on certain characteristics common to European culture during the period. Among other things, it was established that there was a marked decline in the degree and importance of patronage by the churches and the nobility, a development accelerated by the French Revolution and Napoleon, not least by their destruction of the Holy Roman Empire. There was a corresponding expansion in the role played by the anonymous public and the market. Otto Dann was not alone in drawing attention to the decline of international languages—French for elite and Latin for scholarly discourse—in favour of national vernaculars. Especially from the German contributors, the name of Herder and his 'individualising gaze' (Bödeker) was invoked, notably his rehabilitation of particularity. Peter Mandler summed up a common view when he identified a growing concern for the significance of the 'fine arts', as being conducive to social harmony, economic prosperity, and political stability. James Sheehan developed that further by outlining three characteristics of European culture established by 1800—the establishment of a difference in kind between artist and artisan, a recognition of the need for artists to be autonomous, and an acknowledgement of a public to which all art should be accessible.

The sharpest disagreement was over the nature of the nationalism that was developing so rapidly during the period, not just in the sense that national values were being asserted but also in the sense that identifiably national styles were becoming apparent. The German contributors, supported by John Deathridge, were at pains to stress the fictive, artificial nature of national identity and loyalty. Frequent tributes were paid to Eric Hobsbawm (who was in the audience) and his concept of 'the invention of tradition', whose influence was reflected in the titles of two of the papers. Silke Leopold wrote off the possibility of a German 'national opera' with a series of rhetorical questions:

---

[4] We regret that a publishable version of Marilyn Butler's paper was not available when we were finally obliged to go to press.

> We therefore need to reflect in a fundamental way on the question of what makes an opera into a national opera. Is it the origin of the composer? The genre? The language? The subject? The musical style? The singers' style of interpretation? Or all of these together? To anticipate, the hopelessness of finding a satisfactory answer to these questions reveals the whole dilemma faced by the concept of a national opera.[5]

It might be thought that she had missed one rather important—perhaps decisive—question, namely: was it the way in which it was *perceived* by contemporaries? Indeed, she herself conceded this point in answer to a question from the audience when she replied: 'I don't believe in a national opera but I believe in reception of operas as national operas.'

Perhaps because they are so acutely aware of the dangers of perverted nationalism, the German contributors were at pains to deny both the antiquity and the organic nature of nationalism. Coming from polities with a less guilt-ridden past, the British 'team', which typically consisted of two Americans (Sheehan and Mandler), an Irishman (Morley), and two English (Deathridge and Butler), were less inclined to stress the modernity of national identity. Vincent Morley, in particular, was able to demonstrate that the central characteristics of Irish nationalism—pride in a history that went back to the legendary Milesius, coupled with hatred of the English conquerors—drew on a long indigenous tradition of historical writing. As John Breuilly ruefully conceded, Morley's paper was 'uncomfortably fascinating' for modernists like himself. He found an escape route by asking whether those early Irish nationalists had a political programme for a unified and independent Irish state, which of course they did not. One way to resolve this apparent impasse was indicated by Otto Dann, when he concluded that by 1800 two specific meanings of 'national language' had become established: 'This notion signified either the language of a people or an ethnicity that was described as a nation or understood itself as a nation, or the language of a nation-state, which was politically legitimised to manage and supervise it.'[6] In other words, nationalism has both a cultural and a political meaning. Modernists would experience less difficulty in accommodating the manifold evidence

---

[5] See below, p. 23. The national response to the work at the centre of Silke Leopold's analysis—the opera *Günther von Schwarzburg* of 1777, with a libretto by Anton Klein and music by Ignaz Holzbauer—has been demonstrated by Jost Hermand in 'Die erste Nationaloper. *Günther von Schwarzburg* (1777) von Anton Klein und Ignaz Holzbauer', in Jost Hermand and Michael Niedermeier, *Revolutio germanica. Die Sehnsucht nach der 'alten Freiheit' der Germanen. 1750–1820* (Frankfurt am Main, 2002).

[6] See below, p. 132.

of the existence of 'nationalism before nationalism' if they could bring themselves to recognise that these two senses of the word are discrete; they are not two sides of the same coin but are alternatives, usually jingling about in the same pocket—but not always.[7] It might also prompt John Deathridge to think twice before saying, as he did in reply to a question: 'Of course the lovely thing about German music is that there is no such place as Germany.'

One further fundamental source of division concerned the interaction between one nation and another. The importance of the English 'other' in moulding Irish nationalism was made very clear by Morley. It was also stressed by Siegfried Weichlein in his discussion of Klopstock: 'His drama *Arminius* inaugurated a tradition of anti-French and anti-Roman poetry which explicitly heralded German liberty and "German virtues" against foreign cultural dominance. Klopstock became the "poet of the fatherland". Liberty had turned xenophobic.'[8] In a different context, Peter Mandler showed how an aversion to 'bureau and barrack', exemplified by Prussia, turned the British away from the state promotion of the arts. A cultural desert was not the result—on the contrary, there were probably more concerts performed before larger audiences in London than in any other city in Europe. What it did mean was that the initiative was taken by ordinary citizens and voluntary associations, although it has to be conceded that, especially in the provinces, gasworks and tramways were more likely to be the beneficiaries of private patronage than art galleries or orchestras.

Arguments about this and other aspects continued long after the formal proceedings of the conference had ended. This volume will convey some impression of the vigour and variety of the debates. The organisers take this opportunity to thank both the paper-givers and the audience for making it such a rewarding occasion. They also thank the British Academy, especially Angela Pusey, and the German Historical Institute for their material and moral support.

---

[7] T. C. W. Blanning, *The Culture of Power and the Power of Culture: Old Regime Europe 1660–1789* (Oxford, 2002), p. 16.
[8] See below, p. 93.

Art and Its Publics, *c.* 1800

JAMES J. SHEEHAN

BY 1800 THE MODERN ART WORLD was firmly in place. In order to provide us with a point of departure, let me begin by sketching the principal ingredients of what Paul Kristeller called 'the modern system of the arts'.[1] This system was—and is—composed of three interlocking elements, each one shaped by, and dependent upon, the others.

The first, obviously, is the concept of *art* itself, which by the last decades of the eighteenth century had come to include painting, sculpture, architecture, literature, music (and, sometimes, dance and garden design), which were clearly separated from jewellry-making, weaving, glassblowing, and similar crafts. The set of things called art was defined not by how they were produced but by how they were experienced—this is what M. H. Abrams identified as the shift from the 'maker's' to the 'perceiver's' perspective. The objects of art were made in quite different ways, but they were all experienced 'aesthetically', which, in Kant's famous definition, was the experience of delight without interest—that is, the pleasure in experiencing something for itself rather than its usefulness.[2]

The second element follows from the first: art is created by an artist, whose social position and character were to be clearly distinguished from the artisan's. Both artist and artisans make things, both have special skills, but the artisan uses his to make useful things, the artist to create beauty. Essentially, the difference between them is a difference of sensibility; the artist possessed distinctive qualities of mind and spirit, which some contemporaries called genius. To exercise their genius, artists had to be autonomous, free, outside of the usual restraints of society.

Art was public—and this is the third element in the system. To be public meant, of course, to be open and accessible, in theory at least, to

[1] Paul Kristeller, 'The Modern System of the Arts', in *Renaissance Thought and the Arts*, vol. 2 (New York, 1980), pp. 163–227.
[2] M. H. Abrams, 'Art as Such: The Sociology of Modern Aesthetics', in *Doing Things with Texts* (New York, 1989), p. 137; Kant, *The Critique of Judgment* (Oxford, 1952), p. 50.

Proceedings of the British Academy, **134**, 5–17. © The British Academy 2006.

everyone. *The* public was that audience of listeners, viewers, and readers who were willing and able to experience art for itself, as beauty, as disinterested delight. Here too it is important to note that the key ingredient in the definition is a distinctive sensibility. In his treatise on the fine arts published in 1746, Charles Batteux drew a parallel between 'genius', that is, the 'father of the arts', with which the artist created beauty and 'taste', which allowed art's audience to recognise its value.[3]

Aesthetic sensibilities depended on a dense network of institutions that made the public perception of art possible: theatres and concert halls, reading societies and libraries, periodicals and publishing enterprises. In the visual arts, the characteristic aesthetic institution is, of course, the museum, the place where the visual arts—which were increasingly limited to painting and sculpture—could be appreciated for themselves, separated from their original site and purpose. If we had the time, we could describe the unity and diversity of the visual arts in the eighteenth century by following the development of European art museums, which all shared certain assumptions about art's character and function, but were each shaped by a particular social and political environment. For our present needs, it is enough to say that by 1800 most major cities had a museum of some sort and virtually every major city wanted to have one.[4]

Let us now turn to the subject at hand: the condition of the visual arts at the beginning of the nineteenth century, which means, of course, the condition of the visual arts in the middle of the great revolutionary era that began in 1789.

In talking about the arts, a Tocquevillian sense of continuity between old regime and revolution is wholly appropriate. Like most of the revolution's impact on European life, in the art world it created little that was completely new; its impact was to accelerate and partially redirect forces that had been at work well before 1789. (To illustrate what I have in mind, consider the careers of two great painters who will often appear in what follows: while Jacques-Louis David and Francisco Goya were both deeply affected by the revolution, their artistic visions had been formed before 1789.)

The revolution certainly did not create the modern art world, but it did change it in several important ways. Three of these changes will be the

---

[3] Quoted in Larry Shiner, *The Invention of Art: A Cultural History* (Chicago, IL, 2001), p. 83.
[4] There is more on this in Sheehan, *Museums in the German Art World: From the End of the Old Regime to the Rise of Modernism* (Oxford, 2000).

subject of this paper. The first has to do with the social setting of art and artists, and especially with artists' changing relationship to patrons and the public. The second concerns the geographical location of art, particularly the shift in the visual arts' centre of gravity away from Italy to Paris, which would remain the artistic capital of Europe for the next century. The third theme—and the one most directly relevant to the subject of our conference—is about the complex relationship of national values and national themes to European art, especially painting.

Patrons and Publics

In his interesting book, *The Invention of Art*, the American philosopher Larry Shiner wrote: 'The key factor in splitting apart the old art system was the replacement of patronage by an art market and a middle-class public.'[5] There are, I think, a number of things about this statement with which we might quarrel, but I want to concentrate on the implications of the word 'replacement', which suggests that there are two alternative ways for art to be produced and consumed, one characterised by a direct, personal relationship between artist and patron, the other by an impersonal cash nexus in which artists produce art for members of a public they do not know and cannot see—let's leave to one side the issue of whether or not this customer belonged to anything that might be plausibly described as 'middle class'. It seems to me to be more analytically useful and historically accurate to imagine a continuum of relationships, ranging, on the one extreme, from patronage in its purest form, that is, when an artist worked full-time for a single individual, characteristically as a member of a ruler's court or aristocrat's household, and, on the other, to artists who made works and then sold them to strangers at an exhibition, gallery, or from their own workshops. In between, there is a series of intermediate conditions: for instance, there is what we might call serial patronage, in which an artist worked on a major project for a single patron and then moved on to work for someone else. And then there were those artists who combined a position at court with commercial activities, living from some combination of patronage and public. What really matters in these relationships is not the artists' formal position or source of income, but how free they are to make the kind of art they wanted. Both

---

[5] Shiner, *Invention of Art*, p. 7.

patron and market can restrict as well as enhance this freedom; it is a mistake to overestimate either the limitations imposed by patrons or the autonomy made possible by the market.

By the second half of the eighteenth century, patronage in its purest form was in decline almost everywhere. There were, to be sure, still a number of artists, such as Johann Christian Mannlich of Zweibrücken, who worked full-time for a single patron, but more and more produced works for several patrons or for both patrons and the market.[6] From 1750 to 1753, Giambattista Tiepolo, for instance, was contracted to work for the Prince Bishop of Würzburg, then returned to Venice to work on a variety of commissions before leaving to become the Court Painter in Madrid, where he died in 1770. In a certain sense, Tiepolo marketed himself, but only among the rather small group of patrons who could afford the kind of large projects at which he excelled.[7] On a rather more modest scale, Anton Graff was appointed Court Painter in Dresden in 1766 and spent the rest of his long life working for Saxony's ruling family and painting some 1,200 portraits of noblemen, intellectuals, civil servants, and businessmen.[8] One need only look at the self-portrait that Tiepolo prominently displayed in his frescos in the great stairway of the bishop's palace or at Graff's wonderful 1794 self-portrait at age 58 (now in Dresden) in order to realise that neither artist thought of himself as a humble artisan.

As patronage declined in the second half of the eighteenth century, there is no doubt that market relations became more important in the European art world. Printmakers fed the public's appetite for illustrations and reproductions; painters of landscapes, still lifes, and genre scenes sold their works to fit the tastes and requirements of a new public. London and Paris developed institutions in which thousands of people could view, discuss, and perhaps purchase original art works. Even some sculptors, for whom commissions and patronage were of obvious practical importance, learned to market their wares.[9] Jean-Antoine Houdon, for instance, became one of the best known and most successful artists of his

---

[6] Johann Christian von Mannlich, *Rokoko und Revolution: Lebenserinnerungen* (Stuttgart, 1966).

[7] See Peter Krückmann (ed.), *Der Himmel auf Erden: Tiepolo in Würzburg* (Munich, 1996).

[8] There is a good deal of information on the social world of German artists in *Briefe Daniel Chodowieckis an Anton Graff* (Berlin, 1921); see also the useful biographical information provided in Helmut Börsch-Supan, *Die deutsche Malerei von Anton Graff bis Hans von Marées, 1760–1870* (Munich, 1988).

[9] On the London art world, see David Solkin, *Painting for the Money: The Visual Arts and the Public Sphere in 18th Century England* (New Haven, CT, 1992); on Paris, Thomas Crow, *Painters and Public Life in Eighteenth-century Paris* (New Haven, CT, 1985).

day by producing a series of extraordinary portrait busts of Parisian notables, starting with Diderot in 1771 and including virtually everyone who mattered for the next two decades. By perfecting a method of producing casts of his portraits—he made over forty copies of his bust of Voltaire—Houdon was able to market his work from Virginia to St Petersburg. The revolution, by the way, was not good for Houdon; he continued to work but never had the same sort of success that he had enjoyed before 1789.[10]

The revolution accelerated the decline of patronage as a source of support for artists. In the first place, it destroyed a number of sources of patronage, such as the small courts in the western part of the Holy Roman Empire. Elsewhere, in Berlin for instance, the demands of war dried up a number of resources that might have been used to support artistic projects. But the revolution's most powerful impact on cultural institutions was in that cluster of measures conventionally called 'secularisation'. As Rudolf Schlögl argued in a recent *Bulletin* of the German Historical Institute, secularisation did not cause a decline of religious belief or practice, but it did transform the Church's position in European politics and society—and I would argue that among the most significant aspects of this transformation was the decline and in some places the destruction of the Church's centuries-old role as a patron of the arts.[11] Of course churches continued to be built and religious themes remained important for artists, but never again would Catholicism become the source and subject of Europe's greatest paintings and statues. In this sense at least it is perfectly justifiable to talk about cultural secularisation.

Although many sources of patronage disappeared after 1789 and the Church's role everywhere declined, other forms of patronage remained. Consider, for instance, the career of Francisco Goya. Born in 1746, Goya's earliest work was for churches and the local nobility in his hometown of Saragossa. He went to Madrid to prepare cartoons for the royal tapestry factory, for which he worked on and off for more than a decade. In 1789 he was made painter in the royal household by the new monarch, Charles IV. In 1798, the year he finally became First Court Painter, Goya did several portraits, a painting for the cathedral of Toledo, frescos for the

---

[10] On Houdon, see the catalogue of a major exhibition of his work edited by Anne Poulet (Washington, 2003) and Willibald Sauerländer, *Ein Versuch über die Gesichter Houdons* (Munich, 2002).

[11] R. Schlögl, 'Secularization: German Catholicism on the Eve of Modernity', German Historical Institute London, *Bulletin*, 35, 1 (May 2003), 5–21.

church of San Antonio, and completed work on his series of eighty etchings, printed as *The Caprices* in 1799. *The Caprices* were designed for the market but, after the venture failed, the king acquired the original plates in return for granting a royal pension to Goya's son—yet another instance of the complex interweaving of patronage and commerce. Goya grew rich from his various commissions, painted a great many deeply private and politically subversive works, but never severed his ties to the court: he worked for the Bourbons and then for Joseph Bonaparte, did an equestrian portrait of the Duke of Wellington (now in Apsley House) and a formal portrait of King Ferdinand VII when he was restored to power in 1814.[12]

Jacques-Louis David's career provides what the art historian Robert Rosenblum once called 'a close and often sinister parallel' to Goya's. David was two years younger than Goya and like him had developed his talent within the world of royal stipends and commissions. The picture that made his reputation, the *Oath of the Horatii* of 1785, was commissioned by the Administrator of Royal Residences. Like Goya, David made a good deal of money from his various works: he was paid the princely sum of 7,000 livres for his portrait of the chemist Lavoisier and his wife. And both men spread their loyalties across the political spectrum. David supported the revolution, was a member of the Convention and an organiser of revolutionary festivals; an early admirer of Bonaparte, he produced a series of paintings glorifying his victories, for which he was paid handsomely. In 1804, he became First Painter to the Emperor. Both men died in exile; Goya's was voluntary, David's was not.[13]

In one form or another, patronage survived well into the nineteenth century: a few artistically ambitious monarchs like Bavaria's Ludwig I continued to employ artists full-time, dress them in livery, and use them to design court festivals. For artists, like almost everybody else, a well placed patron could tilt the playing field towards their goal. But, overall, the dependent relationship between artist and patron that had characterised the old regime became increasingly rare, while an impersonal art market expanded. This did not, as we have seen, *create* the modern art

[12] See Robert Hughes, *Goya* (New York, 2003) for a stimulating recent account of his life and art.
[13] Robert Rosenblum, *Nineteenth-century Art* (New York, 1984), p. 50; on David and the revolution, see David Dowd, *Pageant-master of the Republic* (Lincoln, NB, 1948) and Warren Roberts, *Jacques-Louis David, Revolutionary Artist* (Chapel Hill, NC, 1989).

world, but it did change it in several important ways. To state one obvious example, the disappearance of the patron left the choice of subject-matter up to artists, granting them greater freedom as well as imposing upon them the burdens freedom always demands. This freedom intensified the impetus for innovation—to do something new, unexpected, attention-getting—and as a result greatly expanded the range of possible subjects and further weakened the established hierarchy of genres. The great beneficiary of these developments was easel painting, the most flexible and therefore the most marketable form of the visual arts, which became the nineteenth century's dominant mode of artistic expression. Artistic forms that depended on some form of patronage—murals, for instance—declined in popularity, as did sculpture. In 1800, the two most celebrated artists in Europe were Houdon and Antonio Canova; never again would sculptors achieve that kind of fame and pre-eminence.

Rome and Paris

The revolution accelerated the long process of decline that had gradually moved Italy from the centre to the margins of the European art world.

In 1797, for example, 28-year-old General Napoleon Bonaparte terminated the thousand-year history of the Venetian Republic. To be sure, by the 1790s, the creative energies that had animated Venetian painting throughout the century were virtually gone. The great master of the Venetian cityscape, Francesco Guardi, had died in 1793 at the age of 81. Giandomenico Tiepolo, Giambattista's eldest and most talented son, had returned to Venice from Spain. He died there in 1804. 'His drawings and frescos', wrote Jean Starobinski, 'show the almost limitless freedom of an art that confronts its own death; a strange combination of decline and frenzy.'[14] Nevertheless, Giandomenico's work is enough like his father's to remind us of how much was lost as this great era in European art came to a dispirited and depressing end.

More significant for the history of the European art world was the declining importance of Rome as a centre for the visual arts. Throughout the eighteenth century, Rome had attracted artists from all over Europe: Frenchmen like David, Spaniards like Goya, Germans like Raphael Mengs and Angelika Kaufmann, Americans like Benjamin West,

---

[14] Jean Starobinski, 'Venice at Sunset', in *1789: The Emblems of Reason* (Cambridge, MA, 1988), p. 27.

Scotsmen like Gavin Hamilton—all spent time there. Perhaps the most vital and cohesive group of Roman artists were the neo-classical sculptors around Antonio Canova, who had settled in Rome in 1781. This group included Johann Gottfried Schadow, who worked in Rome in the mid-1780s before returning to Berlin, Christian Daniel Rauch, who was there a decade later, and the Dane Bertil Thorvaldsen, who remained in Rome from 1797 to 1838. Rome was not just a giant museum, it was a thriving community of creative artists, who were drawn to the city not only for instruction and inspiration, but also to work and to have their work displayed and noticed. In 1785, for instance, David first showed his *Oath of the Horatii* in Rome before transporting it to Paris.[15]

Artists continued to go to Rome throughout the nineteenth century. It remained especially attractive to Germans: there were, for instance, around 130 German artists working there in 1830 when George Eliot's heroine Dorothea Causabon met some of them during her Roman sojourn—her contact with these German painters was, the reader will recall, one of the many, but perhaps not the greatest, of that lady's disappointments during her dismal honeymoon. An exhibition devoted to 'French Artists in Rome, 1803–1873', recently displayed at New York's Dahesh Museum, records Rome's persistent appeal for French painters. Nevertheless, the qualitative decline in Rome's place in the European art world is unmistakable. In comparison to the eighteenth century, the Roman artistic community was significantly less vibrant, creative, and innovative. Canova was not only the last great representative of the classical tradition in Italy, he was also the last truly great artist to make Rome his base. Like so much else about Italy in the nineteenth century, the art produced there was seen by many as an example of the sad contrast between past glories and present decadence. Henry James's 'The Madonna of the Future', published in 1873, is just one of the many literary explorations of this theme.[16]

Rome after 1800 declined not only in comparison to its own past but also in comparison to the new and undisputed centre of the nineteenth-century art world, Paris.[17] Here too we must be aware of continuities. Under the old regime, the French capital had had a vibrant artistic

---

[15] See, for example, the material in *Künstlerleben in Rom: Bertil Thorvaldsen (1770–1844): Der dänische Bildhauer und seine deutschen Freunde* (Nürnberg, 1991).

[16] *The Madonna of the Future and other Early Stories*, ed. Willard Thorp (New York, 1962). Arthur Danto borrowed James's title for his *Essays in a Pluralistic Art World* (2000).

[17] See, for example, W. Becker, *Paris und die deutsche Malerei, 1750–1840* (Munich, 1971).

culture, nourished by the patronage of court and church and encouraged by one of Europe's most active and discerning publics. Nowhere else in Europe can we find such an extraordinary array of talent in painting, sculpture, and architecture. Between 1789 and 1815, these achievements were amplified and extended by Paris's political pre-eminence, first as the site of revolutionary upheaval and renewal, then as the centre of the Napoleonic empire. From the start, these political transformations were closely tied to the visual arts. The revolutionaries wanted to use art, as David declared in 1793, 'to contribute powerfully to public instruction' and 'to help the progress of the human spirit'.[18] In addition to painting the one true masterpiece of revolutionary art, *The Death of Marat*, David devoted his talent to the revolutionary cause and then, as we have seen, became an important player in the great artistic drama around Napoleon, for whom the visual arts were an essential source of aggrandisement and legitimacy.

The most significant intersection of art and politics was the museum in the Louvre, which was surely the nineteenth-century art world's most influential institution. This is not the place to tell the story of the Louvre, its origins in the old regime, revolutionary transformation, and Napoleonic reconstruction. But it is necessary to emphasise the museum's extraordinary visibility as Napoleon and his artistic advisers filled it with treasures looted from all of Europe. From the turn of the century on, thousands of European artists made the pilgrimage to Paris to see what was, without doubt, the greatest collection of art in the world. Nowhere else was it possible to get such a powerful sense of western art's range and accomplishment, from the ancient world to the eighteenth century. Even when some of the loot was returned to its rightful owners after Napoleon's defeat, the Louvre remained an extraordinary collection. It was, Paul Cézanne wrote, 'the book from which we learn to read'—a source of inspiration, instruction, and intimidation for generations of artists.[19]

Nineteenth-century art was shaped by two powerful challenges: one was the need to respond to the unprecedented character of contemporary political and social change; the other was the need to come to terms with

---

[18] As quoted in Daniel Fox, 'Artists in the Modern State: The Nineteenth Century Background', *Journal of Aesthetics and Art Criticism*, 22 (1963), 139.

[19] Andrew McClellan, *Inventing the Louvre: Art, Politics, and the Origins of the Modern Museum in Eighteenth-century Paris* (Berkeley, CA, 1994); Cézanne quoted in Hans Belting, *The Invisible Masterpiece* (Chicago, IL, 2001), p. 206.

the sustaining but problematic legacy of art's own rich history. Paris was the capital of the nineteenth-century art world in large part because here, more vividly than anywhere else in Europe, the challenges of the present and the past could simultaneously be experienced.

Art and the Nation

The displacement of Rome by Paris leads us to my third and final subject, the relationship between art and the nation. For a conference on 'Unity and diversity in European culture', this relationship is clearly a centrally important theme, but also, I think, a painfully difficult and perplexing one.

There is no doubt that the unity of the European art world declined after 1800. The ebbing vitality of Rome as a centre for the visual arts surely contributed to this decline. After all, art in Rome had always been inherently and unavoidably cosmopolitan, not simply because it was produced by an international community of artists but because the city itself lacked a national identity—Rome was the source of the classical heritage, claimed by all Europeans, and the centre of the Catholic Church, still Europe's most universal institution. Except geographically, Rome was not really an Italian city. Paris, by contrast, was inherently and unavoidably French, the site of France's own distinctive history, the most powerful source of France's identity as a nation. Paris, of course, attracted foreigners but, however welcome they may have felt, however much at home, they remained foreigners among natives in a way that outsiders in Rome did not.

In the nineteenth century, it is much more difficult to find those cosmopolitan figures that were so common before 1800: artists like the Venetian Tiepolo, who did his greatest work in Würzburg and died in Spain, or the Saxon painter Anton Raphael Mengs, who spent most of his active career in Rome with long intervals in Madrid, or Angelika Kaufmann, born in Chur, active in Rome and then in London, where she became one of the first members of the Royal Academy, or—on a much lower level of accomplishment—Jean Pierre Antoine Tassaert, born in Antwerp, trained in Paris, and eventually an artist at both the French and Prussian courts.

Was the European art world's declining cosmopolitan unity replaced by national diversity? It is certainly not difficult to find voices proclaiming that it should be.

Throughout the revolutionary period, artists and writers on art called for the dedication of art to national purposes. 'Each of us [artists]', David wrote in 1793, 'is accountable to the fatherland for the talents which he has received from nature.'[20] As we have seen, David devoted himself to serving the French nation, both in its revolutionary and Napoleonic manifestations. In the process he became a much more self-consciously French artist.

Across the Channel, artistic patriotism lacked such revolutionary fervour, but it was prominent nonetheless. In 1802, for instance, an exhibiting society was founded in London with the title, 'The British School', organised to recognise and encourage British artists. In his opening address, the marine painter John Thomas Serres, one of the founders of the society, pointed out 'for the information of the younger admirers of the Fine Arts', that in different countries where art flourished, 'each possessed a different manner or style, and were particularly distinguished by the appellation of different schools'—such as, the Venetian, Flemish, Dutch, and French. England, he lamented, 'was not, at that time, considered worthy of being classed among them, although, in the minds of no mean judges, equally deserving', particularly, he added, in comparison to the French. The exhibiting society itself did not last long, but efforts to define and nourish a distinctively British school of the fine arts continued throughout the century.[21]

Nowhere were national aspirations for art more prevalent than in the German states, where the traumatic impact of the French revolution had encouraged a variety of efforts to use art to renew Germans' sense of national identity. Throughout the nineteenth century, some German artists felt it to be their special mission to express or encourage national consciousness, even to create a national art that could take the place of political nationhood. As the critic Rudolf Marggraff wrote in the 1830s, 'The work of art not only reveals, it also stimulates and enlivens the spirit of the Volk, and thus becomes . . . a means of cultivating the national spirit.'[22]

Most nineteenth-century observers shared Marggraff's conviction, and not only in Germany. Were they right?

[20] Fox, 'Artists', 139.

[21] Brian Allen, *Towards a Modern Art World* (New Haven, CT, 1995); John Barrell (ed.), *Painting and the Politics of Culture: New Essays on British Art, 1700–1800* (Oxford, 1992).

[22] Quoted in Klaus Döhmer, 'In welchem Style sollen wir bauen?', in *Architekturtheorie zwischen Klassizismus und Jugendstil* (Munich, 1976), p. 75.

Let us consider, for example, three great paintings, all done around the same time, and all inspired by national themes. Théodore Géricault's *Wounded Cuirassier*, which he showed in the Paris Salon of 1814, is a monumental painting of a single individual's fate; Géricault, who began his brilliant but tragically brief career glorifying Napoleon's military victories, depicts the hopelessness and confusion of a wounded man, isolated on the battlefield. C. D. Friedrich's *Chasseur in the Woods* also shows an individual soldier, in this case a dismounted French cavalryman standing in the snow and facing an impenetrable barrier of dark trees; a raven, the symbol of death, sits on a stump in the foreground, underscoring the viewer's impression that this chasseur will not leave the woods alive. Although this is one of Friedrich's few explicitly political pictures, painted during the French occupation of Dresden, the German struggle against Napoleon and the disappointing end of political reform often make an oblique appearance in his work. Finally—and by far the best known of the three—is Goya's *Third of May 1808*, one of the two works commissioned by the regency established in January 1814. The picture shows the execution of Spanish patriots by French troops; the executioners themselves are faceless instruments of violence, while their victims are individuals who respond in a variety of ways, from anger to acquiescence; the central figure raises his arms in a gesture that evokes Christ on the cross. Bodies in the foreground and a line of future victims to the side suggest that what we see is a single moment in time, one episode in history's brutal pageant.

Each of these paintings reflects the experience of the Napoleonic wars and in each the experience is seen from a particular national perspective. Géricault is a French, Friedrich a German, and Goya a Spanish painter. But just how they are French, German, and Spanish is, it seems to me, by no means clear. The distinctive power of each artist's personal vision is surely more striking than the national experience he reflects.

If we expand our purview to include a larger group of contemporary French or German or Spanish artists, we can't help but be struck by their diversity: is there, we must ask ourselves, some mysterious national communality—what Marggraff called the 'national spirit' that unites them? Or are some of them more genuinely national than others? These are the sort of questions to which straightforward empirical answers would seem hard to find. Despite what the apostles of cultural nationalism have insisted, culture rarely comes in national packages, and especially those forms of culture that are not rooted in language.

We can certainly understand why patriots hoped that they could use the visual arts on behalf of the nation: for centuries, painters and sculptors had been enlisted to enkindle faith and celebrate power, precisely that blend of religious fervour and political legitimacy that the nation hoped to inspire. And it is also easy to understand the appeal of the nation for nineteenth-century artists, who hoped that the nation would help them resolve the questions raised by the modern art world, questions about art's purpose, the proper place of the artist in society, the relationship of art to its public. They hoped that the nation could give art a purpose without compromising its special status, that it could give the artist a place that was free from both the restraints of traditional patronage and the insecurities of the market, and that it could close the gap between art and public by providing a common cause, a shared set of symbols, an integrating identity.

Nations, in Benedict Anderson's famous, and perhaps somewhat overused, phrase, are imagined communities—and no one imagined them with more expansive expectations than European artists. These expectations were rarely if ever met. Nationalism's history is a prolonged history of disappointment and disillusionment, and the story of art's relationship to the nation is no exception.

The Idea of National Opera,
c. 1800*

SILKE LEOPOLD

ON 29 AUGUST 1781 WOLFGANG AMADEUS MOZART in Vienna wrote a letter to his father in Salzburg, passing on the latest gossip about the opera. It concerned the singer Antonia Bernasconi, *née* Wagele, from Stuttgart, who had premièred the title role of Christoph Willibald Gluck's *Alceste* fourteen years previously, in 1767, in Vienna. Three years later she had left to sing all over Europe, but had now returned to Vienna for an annual fee of 500 ducats: 'I think that Count Dietrichstein, Master of the Horse and her protector, knew about it beforehand, and that Gluck also helped, so that he can perform his French operas in German . . . And so that she doesn't get 500 ducats for nothing, the Kaiser has, with great difficulty, been persuaded to perform Gluck's *Iphigenie* and *Alceste*—the first in German, the second in Italian.'[1]

Mozart was one of many composers who, during the last quarter of the eighteenth century, thought more and more about a German-language opera. With *Die Entführung aus dem Serail* (1782) and *Die Zauberflöte* (1791), he later provided the works without whose musical quality it would have been much more difficult for the German-language opera to establish itself next to the Italian and the French. His interest had been awakened in Mannheim where he had spent some time on the way to Paris between the end of 1777 and the beginning of 1778 in the hope of finding a position at the court of the Prince Elector Karl

---

* Translated by Angela Davies, German Historical Institute London.
[1] 'Ich glaub das graf Dietrichstein : der stallmeister : ihr Protector schon vorher davon gewust hat—und daß gluck : damit er seine französischen opern im teutschen aufführen kann : auch dazu geholfen hat . . . und damit sie die 500 dukaten nicht umsonst einnimmt, so hat sich : mit vieller mühe : der kayser bewegen lassen, die Iphigenie und Alceste vom gluck aufzuführen.— Erstere teutsch, und die zweyte Welsch.' Wolfgang Amadeus Mozart, *Briefe und Aufzeichnungen, Gesamtausgabe*, ed. Internationale Stiftung Mozarteum Salzburg, compiled by W. A. Bauer and O. E. Deutsch, commentary by J. H. Eibl, 7 vols (Kassel, 1962–75), no. 620, III, p. 153.

Theodor. The idea of a German national opera was intensively discussed in Mannheim, and also put into practice with Ignaz Holzbauer's setting of Anton Klein's libretto *Günther von Schwarzburg* (1777). Even Mozart, who had so far worked exclusively with the Italian opera, could not avoid the idea of a German-language opera, as he hoped to get a *Scrittura* in Mannheim: 'strange, if it were to be an opera. I can't get the idea of writing an opera out of my head: French rather than German, but Italian in preference to either German or French.'[2] As this letter to his father demonstrates, his preferences were clear. His first choice was an Italian opera; he would have agreed to a French one; but a German one was his last choice. When the Palatine court moved from Mannheim to Munich in 1778, the residents of Mannheim still had a German-language stage in the National Theatre, but it was the end of opera in Mannheim for the time being. In Vienna, Emperor Joseph II pursued the idea of a German-language opera in the form of an institution, which he founded, named *Nationaloperette mit dem Nationaltheater* (national operetta with the national theatre),[3] before abandoning it in favour of the Italian opera in 1783, while public interest in German-language opera declined to such a degree that Mozart commented, with undisguised sarcasm, to Anton Klein in Mannheim: 'if only there was a single patriot with us on the boards—it [the theatre] would have a different aspect!—but then, perhaps, the beautifully budding national theatre would thrive and blossom, and it would be eternal shame for Germany if we Germans were to start thinking seriously in German—acting in German, and even singing in German!!!'[4]

But what was a 'German' opera at the end of the eighteenth century? A German translation of Gluck's *Iphigenie auf Tauris*, a *Tragédie en musique* composed for Paris? Mozart's *Entführung aus dem Serail*, a 'Turkish' subject in the form of a *Singspiel*, modelled on the French

---

[2] '. . . absonderlich, wenn es eine opera wäre. Das opera schreiben steckt mit halt starck im kopf. französisch lieber als teütsch. italienisch aber lieber als teutsch und französisch.' Letter of 7 February 1778, in Mozart, *Briefe und Aufzeichnungen*, no. 419, II, p. 265.

[3] On this, see Helga Lühning, 'Das Theater Carl Theodors und die Idee der Nationaloper', in Ludwig Finscher, Bärbel Pelker, and Jochen Reutter (eds), *Mozart und Mannheim: Kongressbericht Mannheim 1991*, Quellen und Studien zur Geschichte der Mannheimer Hofkapelle, 2 (Frankfurt am Main, 1994), p. 91.

[4] 'wäre nur ein einziger Patriot mit am brette—es [das Theater] sollte ein anderes gesicht bekommen!—doch da würde vielleicht das so schön aufkeimende National=theater zur blüthe gedeihen, und das wäre Ja ein Ewiger Schandfleck für teutschland, wenn wir teütsche einmal mit Ernst anfiengen teutsch zu denken—teutsch zu handeln—teutsch zu reden, und gar teutsch—zu Singen!!!' Letter of 21 May 1785, in Mozart, *Briefe und Aufzeichnungen*, no. 867, III, p. 393.

Opéra comique? Although there is much to suggest that people were thinking about a national opera as early as the last quarter of the eighteenth century, conventional music history universally accepts that the national opera was a child of the nineteenth century. A glance at the contents page of Roger Parker's extraordinarily successful *Oxford Illustrated History of Opera,* published in 1994,[5] makes this clear. The chapters, written by different authors, are grouped as follows:

> 1: The Seventeenth Century. 2: The Eighteenth Century: Serious Opera. 3: The Eighteenth Century: Comic Opera. 4: The Nineteenth Century: France. 5: The Nineteenth Century: Italy. 6: The Nineteenth Century: Germany. 7: Russian, Czech, Polish and Hungarian Opera to 1900. 8: The Twentieth Century: to 1945. 9: The Twentieth Century: 1945 to the Present Day.

Nothing could more clearly illustrate the conviction that the idea of the national opera took hold in Europe during the nineteenth century than the way in which this book is structured. While the main question addressed to opera of the eighteenth century concerns genre, the dramaturgical differences between serious opera and comic opera, and the musical forms associated with them, for the nineteenth century the focus is on the national variants of opera. The structure of this book implies a break between the end of the eighteenth and the beginning of the nineteenth centuries which justifies this change of perspective within a book conceived of as a unit. Or is the perspective itself perhaps the problem? Is the German national opera, which composers and writers on music from Richard Wagner to Hans Pfitzner see as starting with Christoph Willibald Gluck's *Iphigenie auf Tauris* and Carl Maria von Weber's *Freischütz,* a historical reality or a historiographical construct? In order to answer this question we need to take a brief look at the situation of opera around 1800, for only in Germany, and not in the other two leading opera nations, Italy and France, can a development at this time be observed in which the idea of a national opera takes shape.

Italy, in any case rather averse to the national idea, was the motherland of opera, which had developed into an international musical genre in its own right from the middle of the seventeenth century. Opera was the most successful of all Italy's exports, having created jobs for thousands of Italian singers, instrumentalists, stage designers, etc. both at home and abroad. There was simply no reason to define the Italian opera in national terms and thus to remove it from the international repertory. Towards the

---

[5] Roger Parker (ed.), *The Oxford Illustrated History of Opera* (Oxford, 1994).

end of the eighteenth century, however, France, which for more than a century had been caught up in a Parisian *Sonderweg* isolating it from the network of European court operas on the Italian model, was just starting to catch up with the Italian opera in international terms. Here, too, the interest in a national opera was therefore limited. And, although Napoleon promoted works such as Gasparo Spontini's *Fernand Cortez* (1809) because this opera about a Spanish general's conquest of Mexico could be used effectively in the propaganda run-up to his own Spanish campaign, opera in general, with its ambivalent patterns of identification, did not lend itself to Napoleon's purposes. Of all the dramatic spectacles in Paris, Georges Touchard-Lafosse noted in 1846,[6] the opera was the one which paid the least homage to Napoleon's fame.

Thinking about a national opera presupposed not only a general discussion of the national idea, but also the desire to offer something unique and unmistakable as opposed to the international forms of opera. For a number of reasons, Germany was the place where, towards the end of the eighteenth century, these ideas found advocates. First, there was a well organised infrastructure plus the highest density of opera houses outside Italy. In Germany, the opera stages at the princes' courts were in competition not only with those at neighbouring courts, but also with commercial opera houses in the towns. And, second, opera offered growing patriotism and the idea of unification, which was being expressed more and more strongly, a platform on which to express political ideas in an artistic form. However, the development of German national opera was by no means as linear as the authors of the second half of the nineteenth century liked to think, as the two works already named as the progenitors of the German national opera make clear: Gluck's *Iphigenie*, a translation from the French, and Weber's *Freischütz*, a *Singspiel* modelled on the French *Opéra comique*.

The break between the opera of the eighteenth century and that of the nineteenth, documented in Parker's chapter division, is presented as follows in the historiography of opera. In north Germany and in Vienna, various attempts were made in the genre of the German *Singspiel* in the last third of the eighteenth century. In a parallel development, the German translation of Gluck's *Iphigénie en Tauride* (Paris, 1779), presented in Vienna in 1782, allowed the idea of establishing the German language in the heroic genre as well to mature. German themes such as

---

[6] Georges Touchard-Lafosse, *Chroniques secrètes et galantes de l'Opera, 1667–1845* (Paris, 1846), p. 87.

Faust (Louis Spohr, 1816), *Undine* (E. T. A. Hoffmann, 1816), and, finally, *Der Freischütz* (Carl Maria von Weber, 1821) then definitively prepared the way for the German national opera.[7] All this is true. Yet, if one asks what was German about these operas, the whole edifice begins to crumble. Nor are there any simple answers to the question of how specific this development was to the period around 1800. We therefore need to reflect in a fundamental way on the question of what makes an opera into a national opera. Is it the origin of the composer? The genre? The language? The subject? The musical style? The singers' style of interpretation? Or all of these together? To anticipate, the hopelessness of finding a satisfactory answer to these questions reveals the whole dilemma faced by the concept of a national opera.

At all times, the origin of the composer has played only a subordinate part. No one illustrates this better than Gluck. Born in Bohemia, he had made a name for himself all over Europe with Italian *Opera seria* before he wrote French *Opéras comiques* and Italian reform operas in Vienna, finally giving the French *Tragédie en musique* a boost in Paris. What was German about Gluck was, perhaps, his mother tongue, for which he naturally did not compose. But there are also prominent examples of the opposite case. Gasparo Spontini, for example, an Italian, wrote French operas in Paris, but in Berlin composed *Agnes von Hohenstaufen* (1829), a work that is counted as a milestone on the road towards a German national opera.

Nor does looking at genre take us much further in answering our question about the national opera. Until at least one generation after 1800, there was no such category as 'German opera'. The eighteenth century was shaped by *Opera seria* and *Tragédie en musique*, by *Opera buffa* and *Opéra comique*, and everything that was tried out in German lands was related to these models with their dramaturgical and musical features specific to the genre—the *da capo* aria and plot ensembles in the Italian opera, the *Divertissement* and the mixture of spoken dialogue and sung numbers in the French opera. The *Singspiel*, whose development Emperor Joseph II promoted with such concern in Vienna, was, ultimately, nothing more than a translation of the *Opéra comique* into the German language. Was this the decisive criterion for the German national opera after all?

---

[7] I mention merely Anna Amalie Abert, *Geschichte der Oper* (Kassel, 1994) and Barry Millington, 'The Nineteenth Century: Germany', in Parker (ed.), *Oxford Illustrated History of Opera*, as examples standing for many others.

In order to answer this question, we will have to look at the origins of the German-language opera. There had been operas which were sung in German since the seventeenth century, and from the start they displayed two specific features. Their dramaturgical and musical origins lay in Italy, and their artistic homelands were the Protestant areas of the Empire—Nuremberg, Dresden, Ansbach, and Hamburg. In the Catholic territories—in Vienna, Munich, and Düsseldorf—Italian opera was performed. The language of church services was also the language of the opera stage. From 1678, the year in which it opened, to 1738, when it closed, the Hamburg Opera House on the Gänsemarkt put on operas in the German language without anyone speaking of a national opera, although the works of Reinhard Keiser fulfilled all the criteria—operas such as *Störtebeker*, *Die Leipziger Messe*, and *Die Hamburger Schlachtzeit* dealt with a German subject in the German language. In musical and dramaturgical terms, these operas continued to be indebted to the Italian *Dramma per musica*.

One generation later, during the 1770s, a new interest in German-language opera arose, this time on the basis of the French *Opéra comique*. Numerous touring companies in Germany had this sort of opera in repertory, translated into German so that their middle-class audiences would be able to follow the plot. This was a quiet, pragmatic opera reform from below, as it were, unaccompanied by theoretical reflection and hardly noticed by cultural opinion-formers. The Palatine Prince Elector, Karl Theodor, brought these translated operas to court and initiated a discussion of opera and the German language, with the result that Mannheim briefly became a pioneer in the campaign for a German national opera.

Unlike most German princes, Karl Theodor had control over two theatres, with two regular seasons. The Court Opera in Mannheim was reserved, as was usual in central Europe, for Italian *Opera seria*; in the theatre at his summer residence, Schwetzingen, Karl Theodor, unconstrained by court ceremonial, gave free rein to his curiosity about everything that went by the name of 'opera' in Europe.[8] The summer programme for Schwetzingen reads like a *Who's Who* of European forms of opera: *Opera seria*, *Opera buffa*, *Opéra comique*, *Singspiel*, melodrama, and reform opera. Only the *Tragédie en musique*, which was hardly performed outside France, was missing from this collection. Thus it comes as

[8] The operas performed in Schwetzingen are introduced in detail in the chapter 'Opernrepertoire des Schwetzinger Schlosstheaters', in Silke Leopold and Bärbel Pelker (eds), *Hofoper in Schwetzingen: Musik, Bühnenkunst, Architektur* (Heidelberg, 2004), pp. 87–154.

no surprise that Karl Theodor did not oppose the suggestion to produce French *Opéra comique* in the German language. Egidio Romoaldo Dunis's *Les deux chasseurs et la lattière* presented as *Das Milchmädgen und die beiden Jäger* (1774); François-Joseph Gossec's *Le tonnelier* as *Der Faßbinder* (1774); and André Ernest Modeste Grétry's *Le tableau parlant* as *Das redende Gemählde* (1776)—all these could be seen in Schwetzingen, and encouraged the interest in trying out other operas in German as well.

The Prince Elector followed with interest what was happening at the opera in Weimar, for example, where Anton Schweitzer had created his *Alceste* in 1773 in collaboration with a touring opera company. In 1775 this *Alceste* was performed in Schwetzingen, providing further encouragement for an attempt to prepare the ground for a German opera. 'He therefore resolved to have large-scale German *Singspiele* with plots drawn from German history performed at his opera theatre, and will make a start with Holzbauer's *Günther von Schwarzburg*',[9] the director of the Vienna *Nationaloperette*, Heinrich Friedrich Müller, reported after an audience with Karl Theodor. *Günther von Schwarzburg* was premièred in January 1777, not in the comparatively private setting of the summer residence at Schwetzingen, but in Mannheim's more public Court Theatre. Anton Klein, Professor of Fine Arts at Mannheim, chose for his libretto in the German language a historical event in which an ancestor of Karl Theodor, the Count Palatine Rudolf, had taken one of the major parts. This selection of material was not unusual; the Italian opera, too, as will be shown below, had also produced historical references of this sort. What was new, of course, was that the heroes in *Günther von Schwarzburg* constantly spoke of *Volk* and *Vaterland* (fatherland).

Anton Klein was an inexperienced librettist.[10] In Mannheim he could count on first-class singers who had command not only of Italian, but also of German as their mother tongue. However, texts such as Günther's aria about love of mankind, which is highly patriotic but practically unsingable for Italians because of its irregular accent structure and its

[9] 'Er habe daher den Entschluß gefasst, auf seinem Operntheater große deutsche Singspiele aus der vaterländischen Geschichte darstellen zu lassen und werde mit Holzbauers Günther von Schwarzburg den Anfang machen.' Quoted from Friedrich Walter, *Geschichte des Theaters und der Musik am kurpfälzischen Hofe* (Leipzig, 1898), p. 269.

[10] The libretto of *Günther von Schwarzburg* is reproduced in Ignaz Holzbauer, *Günther von Schwarzburg: Singspiel in drei Aufzügen*, ed. Bärbel Pelker for the Heidelberg Akademie der Wissenschaften, Quellen zur Musikgeschichte Baden-Württembergs; Kommentierte Faksimile-Ausgaben, 1, 2 vols (Munich, 2000), vol. 2, pp. 162–210.

accumulation of umlauts and consonants, confronted even experienced
German singers such as the tenor Anton Raff with practically insoluble
problems:

> Menschenliebe ist der Grund und Stolz der Throne!
> Sie rief mich—sie! Mich leite ewig ihre Hand!
> Völkerheil sproß unterm Schatten meiner Krone!
> Völkerheil hebt Könige zum Götterstand![11]

It took all the art of the composer, Ignaz Holzbauer, to turn this libretto
into a convincing opera, and to breathe musically emotional life into the
academic and discursive texts. The music, however, was Italian through
and through, as even the passionate patriot Christian Friedrich Daniel
Schubart had to acknowledge: 'An excellent mind, whose music had its
own mark, although he did not hesitate to draw on gold from foreign
countries. Germanness, coloured with Italian charm, was, roughly speaking, its main musical character.'[12] Mozart, who heard *Günther von
Schwarzburg* a few months after its première in Mannheim, was enthusiastic about the music. On 14 November 1777 he wrote to his father:
'Holzbauer's music is very beautiful, but the poetry is not worthy of such
music. What amazes me most is that a man as old as Holzbauer still has
so much spirit. It is unbelievable how much fire there is in the music.'[13]

As a heroic opera with a tragic ending, *Günther von Schwarzburg*
remained unique in the history of the German national opera. One year
after its première, Karl Theodor, as Prince Elector of Bavaria, left
Mannheim to reside in Munich, where there was no interest in the German
opera in the context of the court. Holzbauer, who had not followed the
Prince Elector to Munich, made a second attempt to realise the idea of a
German opera. Taking a shortened German translation of Pietro
Metastasio's successful *Didone abbandonata* as his libretto, he composed
Tod der Dido for the National Theatre in Mannheim. It was to be the last
opera composed by the 67 year old, and also the end, for the time being, of

---

[11] Pelker edition (as in note 10), p. 188.
[12] 'Ein trefflicher Kopf, dessen Musik einen eignen Stempel hatte, wenn er gleich darin nicht
eigensinnig war, auch Gold aus fremden Ländern zu holen. Deutschheit, mit welscher Anmuth
colorirt, war ungefähr sein musikalischer Hauptcharakter.' Christian Friedrich Daniel Schubart,
Ideen zu einer Ästhetik der Tonkunst (Stuttgart, 1839). Quoted from Pelker edition (as in note
10), p. 223.
[13] 'Die Musick von Holzbauer ist sehr schön. die Poesie ist nicht werth einer solchen Musick. an
meisten wundert mich, daß ein so alter Mann, wie holzbauer, noch so viell geist hat; denn das ist
nicht zu glauben was in der Musick für feüer ist.' Letter of 14 November 1777, in Mozart, *Briefe
und Aufzeichnungen*, no. 373, II, p. 125.

the heroic opera in German. In Mannheim and everywhere else in the German territories, there followed translations of Italian or French operas, plus comic but inoffensive and undemanding *Singspiele* in German, performed by singing actors rather than acting singers. Mozart had already offered a fitting description in 1777, in the letter quoted above: 'Here there is a permanent German national theatre, as in Munich. German *Singspiele* are sometimes performed, but the singers are wretched.'[14]

Thus, in addition to the German language, it was the subject which played the main part in discussions of the German national opera. The fact that *Günther von Schwarzburg* also represented a milestone in the history of German national opera because it presented heroes from German history on the stage had already been noticed by one reviewer at the première: 'To put a hero from German history on the opera stage is a daring enterprise; but to perform it, as Prof. Klein has done, is to define an epoch in German literature.'[15] The review is mistaken, of course, in assuming that it was daring to use subjects from German history for opera. After all, Herman the Cheruscan had appeared as Arminio in Heinrich Ignaz Franz Biber's *Chi la dura la vince* as early as 1690, and then, on the basis of Antonio Salvi's libretto *Arminio*, repeatedly featured in new settings throughout the entire eighteenth century. The history of the Langobards provided a veritable treasure trove for seventeenth- and eighteenth-century librettists, as did the Ottonians, especially Otto II and his Byzantine consort Theophanu. Charlemagne was represented not only in the legendary subjects of Ariosto's *Orlando Furioso*, but also as a historical figure. However, long before *Günther von Schwarzburg*, these historical figures had not appeared on the opera stage merely as private individuals relating the vicissitudes of their lives, as shown by an opera which, like *Günther von Schwarzburg*, has connections with the Palatine court. The occasion for the performance in 1709 of Stefano Pallavicino's *Tassilone* in the setting by Agostino Steffani was a significant event: the Bavarian Prince Elector Maximilian II Emanuel had, in the War of the Spanish Succession, concluded an alliance with France against the Emperor. The Emperor had responded by withdrawing Maximilian's

---

[14] 'Hier ist eine teütsche National=schaubühne, die immer bleibt, wie zu München. Teütsche singspielle giebt mann bisweilen, aber die singer und singerinnen sind darbey Elend.' Letter of 14 November 1777, in Mozart, *Briefe und Aufzeichnungen*, no. 373, II, p. 125.

[15] 'Es wagen, einen Helden aus der teutschen Geschichte auf die Singbühne zu bringen, ist ein sehr kühnes Unternehmen; aber sein Unternehmen so ausführen, wie es Hr. Prof. Klein gethan hat, das heist in der teutschen Litteratur eine Epoche machen.' *Frankfurter gelehrte Anzeigen vom Jahr 1777*, 28 January 1777, p. 59. Quoted from Pelker edition (as in note 10), p. 229.

electorship and transferring it to Johann Wilhelm von der Pfalz. In order to celebrate this event in fitting manner, Pallavicino had investigated medieval history to find a parallel. He discovered the Bavarian Archduke Tassilo, who had allied himself with the Avars against Charlemagne, and had thus had to cede his dukedom to Charlemagne. In the opera *Tassilone*, he tries to prove his innocence by fighting a duel with Gerold von Schwaben, but loses. Thereupon Gerold receives Bavaria as a fiefdom and Charlemagne's daughter Rotrude as his wife.[16]

At first glance, the dramaturgy of *Günther von Schwarzburg* hardly differs from that of the *Tassilone* libretto just seventy years earlier. It concerns the election of the Emperor in 1349, at which Günther is set up as a rival king to Charles IV. Prince Elector Rudolf von der Pfalz favours Günther, but has no objections to his daughter, Anna, marrying Charles. Günther defeats Charles in battle. However, historical tradition is turned into opera only by the addition of an invented character, namely Charles's wicked mother, Asberta, who wants to dominate her son and therefore not only intrigues against Anna, but also poisons Günther. On his deathbed, Günther is reconciled with Charles, who promises to continue the work of peace.

If we take a second, closer look, however, the differences between *Tassilone* and *Günther von Schwarzburg* emerge clearly. They are to be found less in the dramaturgy than in the ideas which the protagonists represent. The fact that Gerold von Schwaben in *Tassilone* is a successful war hero provides the background to the story, but plays no part in the plot of the opera. The people appear only briefly as a rejoicing crowd; the political events do not happen for the sake of the people. There are no peasants on the chessboard of power. However, what Günther von Schwarzburg and Prince Elector Rudolf do, they do in the name of the people and for a fatherland that needs to be united. Words such as those which Günther speaks as he dies had never been heard on an opera stage before, whether German, Italian, or French:

> I am dying!—Charles!
> Rule—over free peoples!
> O Germany—Germany!
> How small—you are—divided by discord!
> How great—through—brotherly unity!
> Charles!—Rudolf!—my brothers!

---

[16] On the political implications of *Tassilone*, see Gerhard Croll, preface to Agostino Steffani, *Tassilone*, Denkmäler rheinischer Musik, 8 (Düsseldorf, 1958).

> More enervating—than discord—
> Is the proclivity for foreign manners—
> Proud—to be German—that is—your greatness![17]

These patriotic tones were enthusiastically received by the contemporary press. A reviewer writing in the *Mannheimer Zeitung* on 6 January 1777 wrote: 'Germany is proud of the general and enthusiastic applause which *Günther von Schwarzburg*, the first German opera in terms not just of language but also of content to be performed on the Prince Elector's court opera stage, today elicited from every connoisseur and non-connoisseur (to the extent that their hearts were in tune with average human feeling). A large audience of locals and non-locals was all feeling, all ear; in every eye one could see a patriotic indignation about the former taste for foreign *Singspiele*.'[18] And, also in 1777, Philipp Jakob Moureaux wrote in his Mannheim letters: 'I have great hopes of *Günther*, and in the name of all Germans who love their fatherland, I thank the prince who has revived an old German hero and presented him to his nation again.'[19]

But how could this patriotism be expressed in music? In other words, were these sorts of words set differently from the usual opera libretti? The question of whether music can be political, patriotic, or in any way ideological, goes far beyond the scope of this essay. Here I shall restrict myself to asking whether Holzbauer found a musical language for the idea of national opera that was different from that of his other operas. The answer is a simple 'no'. There is nothing patriotic or heroic about

---

[17] 'Ich sterbe!—Karl!
Herrsch—über freie Völker!
O Deutschland,—Deutschland!—
Wie klein—bist du—zertheilt durch Zwietracht!
Wie groß—durch—Brüdereinheit!
Karl!—Rudolf!—meine Brüder!
Entnervender—als Zwietracht—
Ist Hang zu fremder Sitte—
Stolz—deutsch zu seyn—ist—eure Größe!' Pelker edition (as in note 10), p. 209.
[18] 'Stolz sey Deutschland auf den allgemeinen enthusiastischen Beifall, welchen heute Günther von Schwarzburg, die erste nicht nur der Sprache, sondern auch dem Inhalt nach Deutsche Oper auf der Kurfürstlichen Hofsingbühne jedem Kenner, und Nichtkenner (wenn anderst sein Herz nur zu einem mittelmäsigen Menschengefühle gestimmt war) entlockte. Eine Menge fremder und einheimischer Zuschauer war ganz Empfindung, ganz Ohr; in jedem Auge las man einen patriotisch glühenden Unwillen über den ehmaligen Geschmack an ausländischen Singspielen.' Ibid., p. 230.
[19] 'Ich verspreche mir auf diese Art alles von Günther, und danke im Nahmen aller Deutschen, die ihr Vaterland lieben, dem Fürsten, auf dessen Ruf ein alter deutscher Held aus seiner Asche auflebt und seiner Nation wieder vorgestellt wird.' Ibid., p. 232.

Günther's death scene. He dies a very private, almost religious death, and even the musical setting of the people's reaction, 'The hero of the fatherland is dying!', testifies more to quiet grief than to patriotic revolt.

If we also consider the arias of the patriotic hero, we are almost tempted to ask whether Holzbauer even noticed that the German national opera was here knocking on the door of the genre. The arias use the same musical means as those of his Italian operas—dance rhythms, virtuoso coloratura passages, tender *Siciliani*. Perhaps the only aria which spreads a little patriotic atmosphere is that of the Prince Elector Rudolf in the scene in which Günther is crowned King of the Germans, in Act II, Scene 5. However, this aria could equally well fit into a normal *Opera seria*, in which any king or emperor is crowned.

> When the silver of your hairs
> Adorns helmet and brows;
> Think of the springtime of your years
> Germany was blessed by that!
>
> You mighty Teutons!
> Behold your ruler! your name is great!
> You rulers on your thrones!
> Behold your leader! your name is great!![20]

The aria is in two parts. The first part is set in the courtly rhythm of the minuet; the orchestra is dominated by the woodwind. The second part, by contrast, employs the traditional musical attributes of the ruler, drums and trumpet, to underline the patriotic sentiment, but the music, again, does not differ from that of any *Opera seria*.

However, what really does distinguish *Günther von Schwarzburg* from the traditional *Opera seria* is the register of the voices for which it is scored. Since the second half of the seventeenth century, the heroes of Italian *Dramma per musica* had generally been high voices, mostly sung by castrati, but often by women. The rulers who headed the hierarchy of roles, such as Titus in Mozart's *La clemenza di Tito* (1791)—the older,

---

[20] 'Wenn das Silber deiner Hare
Helm und Stirne schmückt;
Denk des Frühlings deiner Jahre:
Deutschland ward durch ihn beglückt!

Ihr mächtigen Teutonen!
Seht euren Herrscher! euer Nam ist gros!
Ihr Herrscher auf den Thronen!
Seht euren Führer! euer Nam ist gros!' Pelker edition (as in note 10), p. 187.

wiser, mild kings—were generally tenor roles in eighteenth-century *Opera seria*. Basses, such as the Count Palatine Rudolf in Holzbauer's *Günther von Schwarzburg*, were practically unknown in *Opera seria*. In the middle of the eighteenth century, a debate had flared up in Germany about whether heroic roles should be composed for high or for low voices. Johann Adolf Scheibe expressed it most clearly in his *Critischer Musikus*, published in 1745. Alexander the Great, he pointed out, had not conquered the world with a bunch of women. Therefore, he argued, the heroic roles in opera should also be sung by men's voices, which must be recognisable as such. And he turned it into a national argument by suggesting that the Germans were better supplied with men's voices than the Italians, certainly with tenors, but especially with basses. In Germany, according to Scheibe, opera should therefore make more use of deep voices.[21]

If we now look at *Günther von Schwarzburg*, it is striking that all the men's roles are written for men's voices: the two rivals, Günther and Charles, are both tenors, while the Count Palatine and Anna's father is a bass. On closer inspection, however, this has less to do with the opera *Günther von Schwarzburg* than with the specific situation in Mannheim. If we look at other, Italian operas performed in Mannheim during the 1770s, we notice that men's voices are given more weight than was the norm in contemporary Italian operas in other places. This was to do not primarily with patriotism, but with the fact that Mannheim had engaged two outstanding singers, the tenor Anton Raff and the bass Ludwig Fischer, and that they had to be occupied.

The problem of voice register leads us to the final factor under consideration as a possible criterion for national opera—interpretation, a seemingly subordinate point which proves, on closer inspection, to be of great importance. Throughout the whole of Europe, opera singers were trained in Italian-style singing and sang in Italian or Latin, regardless of their own mother tongue. Outside the Protestant church, singing in the German language had little chance of establishing itself. Frederick II of Prussia compared the singing of a German woman to the whinnying of

---

[21] On this in detail, see Silke Leopold, 'Not Sex but Pitch: Kastraten als Liebhaber—einmal über der Gürtellinie betrachtet', in Hans-Martin Linde and Regula Rapp (eds), *Provokation und Tradition: Erfahrungen mit der Alten Musik, Festschrift* for Klaus L. Neumann (Stuttgart, 2000), pp. 219–40.

his horse,[22] and Christian Friedrich Daniel Schubart, too, called German 'the language of horses'.[23] There were very few opera singers who could speak German; Mannheim, with its permanent musical ensemble at court, was an exception. Mannheim's singers, both male and female, were almost all German-speaking—in addition to Anton Raff and Ludwig Fischer, there were also Franziska Danzi and the female members of the Wendling family. Although they were used to singing in Italian, they were capable of delivering German spoken parts perfectly. With their assistance, it was much more possible to embark upon the risky business of an opera sung in German which demanded much greater artistry than the small, undemanding, and technically simple ariettas typically found in *Singspiele*.

Thus, if a prize were to be given for an attempt to write a German national opera before 1800 and even until well into the nineteenth century—regardless of the fact that this did not signify the automatic invention of a German national music—then Anton Klein's libretto for *Günther von Schwarzburg* deserves it. But how could it happen that after a few much discussed performances in Mannheim and elsewhere it was forgotten after 1785, and, even more strikingly, that it found no imitators? How, on the other hand, could it be that the German translation of Gluck's *Iphigenie auf Tauris* was so successful in Vienna in 1782 that contemporaries and later historians of opera saw it as representing the start of the German national opera, even though it was a French work on a theme drawn from mythological antiquity? In both cases, the answer may lie more in its reception than in the work itself. The publicity surrounding *Günther von Schwarzburg* and the patriotic noises made by reviewers quickly died down, and when the Prince Elector's court moved to Munich the platform upon which the idea of a national opera could have developed further disappeared. Vienna, by contrast, with its various public theatres, with an Emperor who considered opera in German important, offered the new idea of German-language opera so much space that it found an audience there, in the national theatre and later in the suburban theatres. Yet historical coincidence probably also played a part in deter-

[22] See Charles Burney, *Tagebuch seiner Musikalischen Reisen, vol. 3: Durch Böhmen, Sachsen, Brandenburg, Hamburg und Holland: Aus dem Englischen übersetzt*, trans. J. J. Bode (Hamburg, 1773), p. 76.
[23] Christian Friedrich Daniel Schubart (ed.), *Deutsche Chronik auf das Jahr 1775* (Ulm/Augsburg, 1775), p. 702.

mining the musical and dramaturgical character of German national opera as a model. On 12 September 1781 Mozart wrote to his father:

> I think I wrote to you last time that Gluck's *Iphigenie* is being performed in German, and *Alceste* in Italian. I would have been happy if either *Iphigenie* or *Alceste* had been performed alone—but both, I will tell you the reason. The person who translated Iphigenie into German is a splendid poet, and I would have been happy to give him my Munich opera to translate. I would have completely changed the role of Idomeneo, and written a bass part for Fischer, and made several other changes, and made it more French in style. Bernaskoni, Adamberger, and Fischer would have sung with the greatest pleasure—but as they have two operas to learn, and such tedious ones, I have to excuse them. And a third opera would have been too much anyway—[24]

It is unimaginable what the history of the German national opera might have been if its musical and dramaturgical model had been Mozart's *Idomeneo* instead of Gluck's *Iphigenie*.

[24] 'ich habe ihnen glaube ich schon lezthin geschrieben daß die Iphigenie teutsch und Alceste welsch vom Gluck aufgeführt wird . wenn die Iphigenie oder Alceste allein aufgeführt würde, wäre es mir schon recht, aber alle beyde, ich will ihnen die ursache sagen. der die Iphigenie in das teutsche übersezt hat, ist ein vortreflicher Poet, und dem hätte ich recht gerne meine Oper von München zum übersetzen gegeben—die Rolle des Idomenè hätte ich ganz geändert—und für den fischer im Baß geschrieben—und andere Mehrere veränderungen vorgenommen, und sie mehr auf französische art eingerichtet.—die Bernaskoni, Adamberger und fischer hätten mit grösten vergnügen gesungen—da sie aber nun 2 opern zu studieren haben—und so mühsame opern—so muß ich sie entschuldigen—und eine 3.te opera wäre ohnehin zu viel—' Letter dated 12 September 1781, in Mozart, *Briefe und Aufzeichnungen*, no. 624, III, p. 157.

The Invention of German Music, *c.* 1800

JOHN DEATHRIDGE

ARNOLD SCHOENBERG ONCE SPOKE FAMOUSLY OF HIS INVENTION of 'the method of composition with twelve tones related only to one another', as the discovery of 'something which will assure the supremacy of German music for the next hundred years'.[1] By 'German music' he meant the music of J. S. Bach and the so-called first Viennese School (Haydn, Mozart, Beethoven) and everything that followed on from it: Schubert, Schumann, Brahms, Wagner, Bruckner, Mahler, and of course himself. The construction of a musical culture, especially one vaulting together German and Austrian traditions as if they were identical, can itself be seen as an invention which began its course around 1800 and eventually, in the spirit of the French Revolution and German Romanticism, developed an ambition for universal sovereignty. But how did the generally inclusive habits of composers in German-speaking countries in the eighteenth century, who did not hesitate to adopt diverse musical styles from other countries in Europe, turn into something called German music in the nineteenth century that was decidedly exclusive? And who were its inventors?

The bizarre and unpredictable musical terrain around 1800 is by now well traversed. Important books by Andrew Bowie[2] and Lydia Goehr[3] started mapping it out in new ways in the early 1990s. And there have been some notable adventures in it since, especially Christine Lubkoll's authoritative study of music as myth in German works of literature published towards the end of the eighteenth century and at the beginning of the nineteenth.[4] Lubkoll shows just how critically important music turned out to be as an idealistic model for authors like Tieck, Brentano,

[1] Josef Rufer, *The Works of Arnold Schoenberg: A Catalogue of his Compositions, Writings and Paintings*, trans. Dika Newlin (London, 1962), p. 45.
[2] Andrew Bowie, *Aesthetics and Subjectivity: From Kant to Nietzsche* (Manchester, 1990).
[3] Lydia Goehr, *The Imaginary Museum of Musical Works* (Oxford, 1992).
[4] Christine Lubkoll, *Mythos Musik: Poetische Entwürfe des Musikalischen in der Literatur um 1800* (Freiburg im Breisgau, 1995).

Proceedings of the British Academy, **134**, 35–60. © The British Academy 2006.

Kleist, E. T. A. Hoffmann, and others, though this does not necessarily mean, as Adorno pointed out long ago, that the model was equally valid for musicians.[5] In a brilliant book, *Absolute Music and the Construction of Meaning*, Daniel Chua has traced the emergence of the *idea* of absolute music at the beginning of the nineteenth century. In essence he explores a paradox: the history of absolute music that claims to have no history, which 'means that absolute music can only have a history when it is no longer absolute music'.[6] I do not myself believe that for its creators absolute music was quite the historical *tabula rasa* its later admirers claimed it to be, but it is a nice idea and in terms of Enlightenment rationality Chua has plenty of astonishing things to say about it. Finally, Berthold Hoeckner in his study *Programming the Absolute* does for absolute music what the American minimalists did for authoritarian avant-garde music in the 1970s and 1980s: he explores an essentially Teutonic claim for musical universality (originating around 1800) and by taking it down from its pedestal distances it with elaborate hermeneutic strategies as a past phenomenon of history—'the moment of German music'[7]—from which we are compelled to move on, necessarily, I assume, with utterly different aesthetic premises.

I have learned a great deal travelling on this high road of philosophy and aesthetics. Here I want to try a more haphazard route, a bit lower down in the terrain perhaps, but one where I believe German musicians and music historians around 1800 actually operated, trying to puzzle out where they were, where they were going, and above all how they stood in relation to the music of other countries. The road I have chosen, therefore, does not even begin in 1800, or for that matter in Germany or Austria. Indeed, part of my point is that, from the moment of its inception as an idealistic notion, German music took its bearings from non-German countries in a spirit of assimilation or opposition—and vice versa. 'Can one be a maker of music *without* being German?', Thomas Mann once asked.[8] At first sight the question seems almost stupefyingly arrogant. The more one tries to disentangle the ideological threads of German music going back to its inception as a patriotic and essentially

---

[5] Theodor W. Adorno, *Sound Figures*, trans. Rodney Livingstone (Stanford, CA, 1999), p. 114.
[6] Daniel K. L. Chua, *Absolute Music: And the Construction of Meaning* (Cambridge, 1999), p. 3.
[7] Berthold Hoeckner, *Programming the Absolute: Nineteenth-century German Music and the Hermeneutics of the Moment* (Princeton, NJ, and Oxford, 2002), p. 2.
[8] Thomas Mann, *Pro and contra Wagner*, trans. Allan Blunden with an introduction by Erich Heller (London and Boston, MA, 1985), p. 57. The question is from Mann's book *Reflections of a Non-political Man* (1918).

fictional concept with manifold non-German resonances, however, the more labyrinthine and subversive that question appears.

I

The year is 1948, and the place the Soviet Union. Andrey Alexandrovich Zhdanov, Joseph Stalin's famously repressive cultural secretary, has just engineered what is probably the most terrible document in the history of twentieth-century music: the notorious 'Resolution of the Central Committee of the Communist Party' on the opera *Velikaya druzhba* ('The Great Friendship') by Vano Muradeli (1908–70).[9] Muradeli's mediocre opera was only an excuse for the declaration of a pernicious all-out war in classic Zhdanovian mould against Formalism, Naturalism, Modernism, Decadence, and above all the best Soviet composers of the time: the 'comrades' Shostakovich, Prokoviev, Khachaturian, Shebalin, Miaskovsky, and others. They were all accused of 'anti-democratic tendencies which are alien to the Soviet people and its artistic tastes' and their music condemned as a demonstration of 'the negation of [the] basic principles of classical music'.[10]

At the same time an interesting document was discovered in the archive of the Music Conservatoire in Odessa. This was the manuscript of the previously unknown Symphony no. 21 in G minor by Nikolay Dmitriyevich Ovsyaniko-Kulikovsky (1768–1846), a Ukrainian landowner figure well known in Odessa in the early nineteenth century.[11] Ovsyaniko-Kulikovsky, according to scholarly research, had written the symphony in 1809 and presented it to his new serf orchestra, which premièred it at the inauguration of the Odessa Theatre the following year. Its discovery in 1948 caused a furore in the midst of Stalin's growing Soviet-style heritage industry because it was the long-sought proof that symphonies had been composed in Russia as early as Beethoven's time. The early history of the symphony was from now on just as much a Soviet as a German affair. It mattered little that Ovsyaniko-Kulikovsky's symphony was more in the style of Haydn than Beethoven. The important

[9] Translated in Nicolas Slonimsky, *Music since 1900*, 4th edn (London, 1972), pp. 1358–62.
[10] Ibid., pp. 1359–60.
[11] Allan Ho and Dmitry Feofanov (eds), *Biographical Dictionary of Russian/Soviet Composers* (New York, Westport, CT, and London, 1989), pp. 182–4. Thanks to Gerard McBurney for drawing my attention to Ovsyaniko-Kulikovsky.

thing was that it was early enough to prove the origin of a tradition previously thought to be solely German.

The symphony was performed in Odessa and Kiev and printed by the State Publisher in Moscow in a version for modern orchestra arranged by A. G. Svechnikov. The printed score was the basis of at least two dissertations in the early 1950s by Soviet musicologists; and a recording of a performance of it under the direction of the great Russian conductor Yevgeny Mravinsky was issued in 1954, coupled with Shostakovich's Fifth Symphony.[12] The purpose of the coupling is clear: to present one of Shostakovich's most famous symphonies no longer simply as a masterly product of the progressively minded communist project, but also as a classic in its own right with a national pedigree deeply rooted in the first decade of the nineteenth century, and by implication (because the number of the Ovsyaniko-Kulikovsky symphony is quite high) the eighteenth as well.

The only trouble with this proof of a link between Soviet music and the classical tradition of the German symphony is that it turned out to be a fake. Ovsyaniko-Kulikovsky the ebullient landowner was real enough in early nineteenth-century Odessa. But of Ovsyaniko-Kulikovsky the composer there is no trace: he wrote not a single note and was probably incapable of even reading a musical score. The real author of the symphony was the archivist of the Odessa Conservatoire who 'discovered' it, Mikhail Emmanuilovich Gol'dshtein (1917–89)—also well known in 1948 in Soviet circles as a composer and violinist, who had had to endure criticism of his work on Ukrainian folk music from the Soviet state because he was a Jew and hence without the authentic national identity required for such research. In the early 1950s, Gol'dshtein was forced to admit that the Ovsyaniko-Kulikovsky symphony was a joke played on the Soviet government to get his own back, when one of the musicologists doing research into the composer—by now well known as one of the founding fathers of Soviet music—asked to see the original manuscript.

The important point is that the authorities officially refused to acknowledge Gol'dshtein's confession, and even appointed a worthy Ukrainian composer and teacher at the Kiev Conservatoire called Gleb Taranov (1904–89) to decide the matter. His verdict was inconclusive; indeed, it had to be, as the work had already served for too long, despite insiders in on the joke, as a cornerstone of official ideology, which is why it enjoyed a surprisingly long life, even until as late as 1980 in the *New*

---

[12] Issued in 1996 on CD in the second volume of the Mravinsky edition: BMG-Melodiya 74321 29459-2.

Grove Dictionary of Music and Musicians, where Ovsyaniko-Kulikovsky is still being described, without any sign of tongue in cheek, as one of 'a number of outstanding composers' who 'were active in the nineteenth century'. Indeed, his Symphony no. 21 is singled out for special praise because it 'shows advanced compositional technique' and a structure 'closely' resembling Haydn.[13]

II

The Ovsyaniko-Kulikovsky case is a minor example of a tradition that needs to exist in the minds of its public recipients, even though it never really did in history, or at least not in the form that some would like to imagine. In David Cannadine's landmark article on the British monarchy in Eric Hobsbawm's and Terence Ranger's *The Invention of Tradition* we find a description of something not dissimilar, albeit on a vaster scale. Cannadine shows that the ceremonial pomp of the British royal weddings, funerals, coronations, and, most regularly of all, the opening of parliament is largely a Victorian and Edwardian invention, even though the enaction of these rituals still somehow gives the impression of stretching back into the grey mists of Britain's distant past.[14] My favourite in this marvellous book is Hugh Trevor-Roper's exposure of the Scottish Highland tradition as a myth, a key part of which is the kilt. The kilt turns out to have been the idea of a Quaker from Lancashire called Thomas Rawlinson in the first part of the eighteenth century and (not unlike the Ovsyaniko-Kulikovsky symphony) came to be regarded as a foundational artefact, even though it was in reality quite modern, and moreover had not even been invented by a Scot.[15]

While I do not want to suggest a wholesale application to German music of Hobsbawm's and Ranger's *Invention of Tradition*—music by its very nature tends to fulfil its social task less visibly, or should I say less audibly, than most arts—the idea that such invented traditions provide a sense of much needed identity with certain rituals in a turbulent present

[13] Stanley Sadie (ed.), *The New Grove Dictionary of Music and Musicians*, 20 vols (London, 1980), vol. 19, p. 407.
[14] David Cannadine, 'The Context, Performance and Meaning of Ritual: The British Monarchy and the "Invention of Tradition", *c.* 1820–1977', in Eric Hobsbawm and Terence Ranger (eds), *The Invention of Tradition* (Cambridge, 1983), pp. 101–64.
[15] Hugh Trevor-Roper, 'The Invention of Tradition: The Highland Tradition of Scotland', ibid., pp. 15–41.

by evoking memories of an imagined glorious past, which at the same
time guarantee an assured repetition well into the future, is not inappro-
priate. Public ritual and predictable cycles most memorably marked by
German music began in Germany in the nineteenth century with the
inauguration of the annual Lower Rhine Music Festivals founded in the
late 1810s,[16] and later with the obligatory performances on Good Friday
of J. S. Bach's *St Matthew Passion*. Still later after the First World War,
Wagner's *Parsifal* was added to the *bürgerlich* Good Friday ritual as well,
notwithstanding its creator's conviction that it was against 'the whole
historical phenomenon of Christianity'.[17]

   The marked suitability of German music to do cultural work in the
name of the past in order to stabilise uncertain life in the present is not
without precedent in Britain too. The huge success of Henry Wood's
famous yearly Promenade concerts in the first fifty or so years of their
existence from 1895 right through to the early 1940s was due in no small
part to German music and the way it was programmed. In 1935 and 1936,
to take two years at random, Monday night was always Wagner Night,
Wednesday night was always a Bach or Brahms Night, and Friday always
Beethoven. Tuesday could either be Mozart or Haydn, or devoted to the
'New German School', while what was left of the rest of the week was
given over to 'others', i.e. mixtures of Russian, French, Italian, English,
and Finnish music, and, interestingly, German moderns like Schoenberg,
who were not seen to belong in the same Augustan stable as their
predecessors.

   A related observation can be made about Britain's longest-running
classical music programme 'Composer of the Week'. For its sixtieth
anniversary in 2003, Paul Donovan compiled a league table of composers'
appearances, noting the surprising consistency of the list in view of the
many people involved in producing the programme over the years.[18] J. S.
Bach was top with a total of seventy-one weeks, 'one whose music can be
relied upon to convince people that God exists' (Donovan)—a not
insignificant comment, as we shall see. Beethoven, Haydn, and Mozart
came equal second with sixty-nine weeks each, then Handel with sixty-

---

[16] For details, see E. A. Hauchecorne, *Blätter der Erinnerung an die fünfzigjährige Dauer der
Niederrheinischen Musikfeste* (Cologne, 1868); and C. H. Porter, 'The New Public and the
Reordering of the Musical Establishment: The Lower Rhine Music Festivals, 1818–67', *19th-
century Music*, 3 (1979–80), 211–24.
[17] Letter to Hans von Wolzogen (17 January 1880), *Selected Letters of Richard Wagner*, trans.
and ed. Stewart Spencer and Barry Millington (London and Melbourne, 1987), p. 899.
[18] Paul Donovan, 'Roll Over, Beethoven', *Sunday Times 'Culture'* (10 August 2003), 14–15.

eight, Schubert with sixty, and Schumann with fifty-nine. The striking point, not made by Donovan, is that the top seven places were occupied by German and Austrian composers.

III

The year is 1792, and the place London. On 31 January, the *Morning Chronicle*, then one of England's most important newspapers, published a report on a musical caricature then circulating in private circles in the capital. 'This admirable piece of humour', it said, 'is a lampoon on the taste which the Germans have introduced, for trick, artifice, surprize, and difficulty, instead of simplicity and nature.'[19] The caricature consisted of two contrasting pieces of music, the one composed in a supposedly German style and the other in an Italian one. The title (see Figure 1) is in French and in translation reads: 'Two trios in different styles by a dilettante from Amsterdam'. The Amsterdam publishing house 'Jaque Vanderbouzzen' is also a pure invention, possibly a humorous allusion to the fact that Europe's then most illustrious book on music, Jean-Jacques Rousseau's *Dictionnaire de musique*, whose sentiments about the superiority of Italian music over that of the 'north' are reflected in the satire, had seen one of the first of its many publications in Amsterdam in 1768.[20]

What clinches the satire, however, is the vignette on the title-page. Here is how the *Morning Chronicle* describes it:

A balance and scales are held by the Deity.—In the one scale are the simple notes—in the other a vast number of notes covered with flowers.—The three simple notes weigh down the multitude, while, from the sky, Beams of Genius illuminate them, and below a Band of Loves accompany on the violin, the flute, &c. in a gay landscape, where doves coo, and lambkins gambol. The other scale is enveloped in gloom, while under it a band of German figures, with immense hats, are bursting their cheeks in blowing the bassoon, the horn, &c.—a peacock is singing on a tree—a bear beats time, and there is a full chorus of frogs.[21]

[19] *Morning Chronicle*, no. 7066 (London, 31 January 1792). The full article is cited with the inaccurate date January 1793 in H. C. Robbins Landon, *Haydn in England 1791–1795* (Bloomington, IN, and London, 1976), pp. 126–7.
[20] Jean-Jacques Rousseau, *Dictionnaire de musique*, 2 vols (Amsterdam, 1768). The Amsterdam publisher was Marc Michel Rey.
[21] *Morning Chronicle*, no. 7066.

Figure 1.   Title-page of 'Two trios in different styles by a dilettante from Amsterdam', apparently
published by Jaque Vanderbouzzen, 1792 (British Library, London).

It is a nice visual image of how German music, warts and all, was
perceived at the time, and also, perhaps more importantly, what it was felt
not to be.

    The music itself reinforces the image. The Italian style (see Figure 2,
bottom half) is presented in well balanced long and short notes with a

Figure 2.   Notation of 'Two trios in different styles by a dilettante from Amsterdam', apparently
published by Jaque Vanderbouzzen, 1792 (British Library, London).

sense of spaciousness and clarity. The notation of the German music, on
the other hand, looks crabbed, with lots of little notes, mostly short in
duration and comically overburdened with dots and slurs (Figure 2, top
half). The German music is also written in the then relatively rare key of
C sharp minor and provided with an amusingly abstruse Italian tempo

marking 'Andante non troppo Allegro a suo Comodo ma con Moto e Dolcezza'—an uncanny premonition of some of Beethoven's later habits of notation and instruction about performance, incidentally, including the encyclopaedic tempo direction 'Andante con moto assai vivace quasi Allegretto ma non troppo' at the start of his Mass in C major, op. 86. In contrast to this supposedly German penchant for complexity, the Italian music sounds in a crystal-clear C major and is given the perfectly under-standable and straightforward tempo 'Andante'. As the *Morning Chronicle* observes:

> The one has all the perplexity of the modern German; the other all the tender-ness of the Italian. It is just possible for a dexterous Musician to play the one, and every body may play the other.[22]

By no means for the last time in the history of German music, a musician well versed in the arcane technical art of music that only experts can ever hope fully to understand is pitted against the idea of an art of music that is meant from the start to be accessible to all.

The author of the satire is anonymous. The *Morning Chronicle* haz-ards the probably correct guess that it was the Italian composer and famous violinist then resident in London, Felice Giardini (1716–96). The caricature's target, on the other hand, is perfectly clear: it was undoubt-edly the music of Joseph Haydn who was in London in 1792 enjoying a huge success with his concerts in Hanover Square. Not so well known now is the fact that by this time Haydn had met with stiff opposition from a not disreputable party of Italian musicians in London. That is not sur-prising, as the music of the Italians and their many imitators had long since been the most celebrated and performed in the concert life of the capital. The *Morning Chronicle* even speaks of inevitable open warfare, but with the gently admonishing caveat: 'If we are to have war, let us have war with wit in it.'[23]

And indeed it was not long before the oppressed, too, declared a war of wit against the oppressor. Shortly after the appearance of the 'Two trios' by the alleged dilettante from Amsterdam, August Frederic Christopher Kollmann (1756–1829), a German organist and music theorist who came to London in September 1782 as organist and school-master of the Royal German Chapel at St James's Palace, devised an ingenious counter-image and had it engraved in copper. Part of it was

---

[22] *Morning Chronicle*, no. 7066.
[23] Ibid.

Figure 3.   Engraving published in the Leipzig *Allgemeine musikalische Zeitung*, 1799, in response to the 'Two trios' (*AmZ*, 30 October 1799). By permission of the Syndics of Cambridge University Library.

later published in Germany in the Leipzig *Allgemeine musikalische Zeitung* in 1799, and that image has been reproduced several times since.[24] What has not always been made entirely clear, however, is that it is a specific response to Giardini's satire. The Italian sun is now the German

[24] *Allgemeine musikalische Zeitung*, ii/5 (30 October 1799), cols 103–4 (hereafter *AmZ*). See also Hans-Joachim Schulze (ed.), *Dokumente zum Nachwirken Johann Sebastian Bachs 1750–1800* (Kassel, 1972), p. 586; Hans T. David, Arthur Mendel, and Christoph Wolff (eds), *New Bach Reader: A Life of Johann Sebastian Bach in Letters and Documents* (New York, 1998), p. 374; Matthew Head, 'Music With "No Past?" Archeologies of Joseph Haydn and *The Creation*', *19th-century Music*, 23, 3 (Spring 2000), 195.

sun (see Figure 3). And at the centre of that sun is none other than J. S. Bach, immediately surrounded along the edges of a triangle by Handel, Haydn, and the Berlin composer Carl Heinrich Graun (1703–59), one of Friedrich II's favourite composers and his Kapellmeister, which partly accounts for his prominence here. Mozart occupies one of the sun's inner fourteen rays along with Christoph Willibald Gluck (1714–87), Georg Philipp Telemann (1681–67), Carl Philipp Emanuel Bach (1714–88), and others, while the outer rays carry the names of minor figures like Carl Friedrich Abel (1723–87), Karl Ditters von Dittersdorf (1739–99), Johann Nikolaus Forkel (1749–1818), and Johann Joachim Quantz (1697–1773).

The bottom half of the copper engraving was never published and is now lost. According to Forkel's description of it in the *Allgemeine musikalische Zeitung*, however, under the sun was originally a cowering Italian owl, unable to stand the light streaming forth from the composers of Germany. And interestingly, especially in the light of ensuing arguments about potency made on behalf of German music in its battles for supremacy in late nineteenth-century Europe, an Italian capon (that is, a rooster that has been castrated to improve the quality of its flesh for food) is seen at the side of the image facing a German rooster in war-like posture.[25] The implication of the image is clear: corpulent and above all neutered and unable to give issue, the Italian capon is no match for its German antagonist, who is slimmer, more manly, potent, spiritually healthy, and more than ready to spread its kind throughout the world.

IV

The year is 1800, and the place Leipzig. The *Allgemeine musikalische Zeitung*, founded three years previously by Breitkopf & Härtel—a publishing firm that was to play a major role in the coming nineteenth century in establishing a German musical canon with collected editions of nearly all its major composers—is already being recognised in German-speaking countries, and even at a modest international level, as the journal at the centre of a new awareness of German music's historical significance. Copies of the journal were being sold in London in 1800 by

---

[25] *AmZ*, ii/5 (30 October 1799), col. 104: 'Unter der Sonne befindet sich eine italienische Eule, die das Licht deutscher Komponisten nicht vertragen kann; auf der Seite aber ein italienischer Kapaun und ein deutscher Hahn, in einer Stellung, als wenn sie eben einen Kampf mit einander beginnen wollten.'

the bookseller Henry Escher of Gerard Street, and the inventor of the war between the Italian capon and the German rooster beneath the blazing 'sun' of German music, A. F. C. Kollmann, received his copy, as many other German and Austrian musicians abroad doubtless did as well, directly from Leipzig.[26]

For the 24 December 1800 issue of the *Allgemeine musikalische Zeitung*, the editor of the journal, Johann Friedrich Rochlitz (1769–1842), who for another eighteen years was to establish it as the foundation-stone of the ideological edifice of German music, commissioned an article from Johann Friedrich Christmann (1752–1817) to mark the passing of the old century—in some, but by no means all, circles then generally deemed to end with the dawning of the 01, and not the double zero. Summoning all his experience as a writer on music theory, as a composer of church and chamber music, and, perhaps most significantly, as a Protestant priest, Christmann lost no time in launching into a mock oration to the passing century that continued Kollmann's theme of potency versus impotence with an almost ghoulishly sardonic reference to the ban on castration of boy sopranos imposed by the Jacobins after the invasion of Italy by Napoleon in 1796, though the practice had in fact been in decline for some time. Addressing the eighteenth century as if it were a cherished friend just recently deceased, he wrote:

> What glory you won for yourself in the final years of your sublunary government by sweeping away the method of inoculating the *genitalia* of a soprano voice in the hands of a miracle doctor from Bologna . . . in the torrent of the Enlightenment and the Revolution, and by teaching those people on the other side of the alps at last that it is cleverer to stay unmutilated for the sake of the kingdom of heaven on earth than it is to undergo a mundane operation in which you get chopped up so that you can become a seraphim of the true kingdom of heaven.[27]

Christmann's subtext of course is that (Catholic) Italian music has no future. It is mired in heavenly pleasure, itself reliant on the mutilation of

---

[26] See Michael Kassler (ed.), *English Bach Awakening: Knowledge of J. S. Bach and his Music in England* (Aldershot and Burlington, VT, 2004), p. 404.

[27] Johann Friedrich Christmann, 'An das scheidende Jahrhundert', *AmZ*, iii/13 (24 December 1800), col. 204: 'Welchen Ruhm erwarbst du dir, daß du in den letzten Zeiten deiner sublunarischen Regierung die Methode, durch die Hand eines Bolgnesischen Wunderarztes eine Sopranstimme auf die *genitalia* zu inoculiren, . . . mit dem Strome der Aufklärung und der Revolution hast dahin reissen lassen und die jenseitigen Bewohner der Alpen endlich belehrt hast, daß es klüger sey, um des irdischen [*sic*] Himmelsreichs willen, unverstümmelt zu bleiben, als sich diesseits schon durch eine solche Operation zum Seraph des wahren Himmelreiches schnitzeln zu lassen!'

male genitalia, and hence without issue. It is morally dubious, decadent, gone. Only (Protestant) German music on *this* side of the Alps is sobre enough to keep body and soul intact in order to produce true patriotic descendants who will fulfil its great promise in the new century.

The images of war and suspect decadence used to defend German music at the beginning of the new nineteenth century, not to say the ironical, sardonic manner with which they are presented, are reminiscent of Thomas Mann's *Reflections of a Non-political Man*, where he speaks of 'the spirit that informed the *Lohengrin* Prelude' finding 'itself at war with the international smart set'.[28] Mann plays such a dizzy literary game with musical and social images to defend German anti-internationalism that one can only speak with Friedrich Schlegel of a 'military language of art'[29]—a phrase coined by Schlegel already in 1798. And Mann's diaries also show that he closely followed the cunningly targeted arguments against the Italian composer Ferrucio Busoni in Hans Pfitzner's 1918 essay *Futuristengefahr* ('Danger of the Futurists'), which rely for their effect on abuse hurled at non-German musical thinking with stereotypes that had already begun to emerge more than a century previously. Like Kollmann and Christmann before him, Pfitzner simply reverses Rousseau's claim about the inherent superiority of Italian music over that of the 'north' and speaks instead of the 'music of the north' being 'warmer than that of the south',[30] adding perhaps more ominously that music for the Italian Busoni, who in Pfitzner's perception becomes uncannily like Christmann's 'miracle doctor from Bologna', is not something that is emotionally potent that comes straight from the human heart like true German music, but a cold matter of rational thought and action.

Pfitzner added still more vitriol a year later when he launched another devastating attack on his musical enemies. This time his principal victim was Paul Bekker's lavish book *Beethoven*, which since its publication in 1911 had already sold 36,000 copies. Bekker was a successful writer on

[28] 'als Krieg wurde zwischen dem Geist des Lohengrin-Vorspiels und der internationalen Eleganz'. Thomas Mann, *Betrachtungen eines Unpolitischen*, with an afterword by Hanno Helbing (Frankfurt am Main, 1983), p. 79. See also Mann, *Pro and contra Wagner*, p. 56.

[29] 'militärische Kunstsprache'. [Friedrich Schlegel], 'Fragmente', *Athenaeum*, eds August Wilhelm Schlegel and Friedrich Schlegel, i/2 (Berlin, 1798), 197.

[30] Hans Pfitzner, 'Futuristengefahr', *Gesammelte Schriften*, 3 vols (Augsburg, 1926–9), vol. 1, p. i. 222. The essay was first published in the *Süddeutsche Monatshefte* (Munich, 1917) as a response to Ferruccio Busoni, *Entwurf einer neuen Ästhetik der Tonkunst*, 2nd edn (Leipzig, 1916). See also Marc Weiner, *Undertones of Insurrection: Music, Politics, and the Social Sphere in the Modern German Narrative* (Lincoln, NE, and London, 1993), pp. 35–71.

music and a powerful critic, who annoyed Pfitzner not only because he was Jewish and therefore strictly speaking not genuinely German, but also because he had committed the unforgivable sin of hurling Beethoven from his throne of lofty greatness and exceptional genius into the rabble of the aesthetically underprivileged. In other words, he had dared to make Beethoven popular. By vigorously promoting the view that, on the contrary, Beethoven's music should be reserved for the happy few who really understand it, Pfitzner unwittingly reinforced the idea of an opposition between a dark and wilful Germanic elitism and an approach to music more Italianate and accessible, which, as we have seen, the London *Morning Chronicle* had already correctly observed in Giardini's satire of 1792. Along with his unpleasant anti-Semitic views, too, Pfitzner mixed inflammatory words and phrases like 'musical impotence' or 'symptom of decay' into the very title of his book,[31] which were in fact headier versions of ideas and similar turns of phrase that had originated around 1800 in tune with a heightened politics of national identity rapidly spreading through German-speaking lands in opposition to the continuing resonance of the French Revolution across Europe. As Bekker noted in his vigorous response, aptly titled 'Impotence or Potency?', Pfitzner's public battle in the immediate aftermath of the First World War amounted not just to a debate about aesthetics or the validity of new trends in music, but to 'a political confession of faith',[32] which in the face of growing internationalism still insisted on the right to occupy the war-zone called German music.

Admittedly all we really have in 1800 is the attempted act of occupation or, to change the metaphor, sketchy plans in a drawing-board version of what was to become a powerful prototype. There were no systematic arguments, sophisticated analogies, or scurrilous ironies; only strong feelings and snatches of insight, hinting at most at a wobbly construct. Christmann in the *Allgemeine musikalische Zeitung* tells us, with carefully calibrated bitter-sweetness, of being overcome with powerful emotion at the passing of the old century. But he also begins to surround the eighteenth century's demise with an intuitive sense of death and melancholy—a suggestion of

---

[31] *Die neue Aesthetik der musikalischen Impotenz: ein Verwesungssymtom?* ('The New Aesthetic of Musical Impotence: A Symptom of Decay?'). After its first publication in 1919, the book was in heavy demand and reprinted with a short foreword by Pfitzner a year later. Six years after that, he revised the essay and provided another, far more extensive foreword. Both forewords and the revised essay can be found in Hans Pfitzner, *Gesammelte Schriften*, vol. 2, pp. 99–252.

[32] 'ein politisches Glaubensbekenntnis'. Paul Bekker, 'Impotenz oder Potenz? Eine Antwort an Herrn Professor Dr. Hans Pfitzner', *Kritische Zeitbilder* (Berlin, 1921), p. 313.

the death-devoted universe of some of the greatest German music to come. 'With sunken head', he wrote, again addressing the eighteenth century, 'I stand by your coffin and watch your fast approaching end full of sorrow.'[33]

This is indeed another central, if elusive strand in the intellectual support-system of German music's champions that resonates well into the twentieth century. It really begins with a piece in the *Allgemeine musikalische Zeitung* in 1800 by its editor Rochlitz called 'Monuments of German Composers',[34] which I can only describe as the start of a philosophical discourse about musical performance and death. There is already some divergence here, incidentally, from literary romantics like Novalis and the Schlegel brothers, who were fascinated with the fact that in developed music, as Adorno has pointed out, 'no event is purely itself, but receives its meaning from what is absent—from the past and the future—which it then influences in its turn'.[35] Thus Novalis could speak of music's 'indefinite animation of the spirit'[36]—the perpetual renewal of poetic feeling that language seems to have lost and the guarantee of the vitality of art in the future. At almost exactly the same time, however, Rochlitz spoke, more prosaically, but more powerfully, of the perpetual *disappearance* of music. Music is mortal, constantly vanishing, and hence at the same time conjures up the ambition to be immortal—an idea which presciently focuses on the serious value of monuments in the creation of a musical legacy for the future of the German nation. The fact of decay (*das Verwesliche*)[37]—the vanishing of the notes after each performance and the death of an important composer—is countered by permanence. The sounds of music and their constant passing away turn the passage of time into a fiction, something never really present. Only the imperishable, the monument, will enable German music to seize the

---

[33] 'Mit herabgesenktem Haupte stehe ich hier an deinem Sarkophage und sehe mit wehmuthsvollem Blicke dem schnellen Fluge deiner Vollendung zu.' *AmZ*, iii/13 (24 December 1800), col. 201.

[34] Friedrich Rochlitz, 'Monumente deutscher Tonkünstler', *AmZ*, ii/24 (12 March 1800), cols 417–23. Matthew Head has contextualised Rochlitz's contribution with a somewhat different emphasis to the way I am interpreting it here. I am nonetheless deeply indebted to his discussion of it in his article on Haydn's *The Creation* in *19th-century Music* (see note 24).

[35] Adorno, *Sound Figures*, p. 114.

[36] The extent to which Novalis (whose real name was Friedrich von Hardenburg) has influenced the customary literary emphasis placed on the history of German music around 1800 is demonstrated by the fact that the passage from which these words are taken is cited in extenso by Lubkoll and Hoeckner, apparently independently of each other, at the very beginning of their respective books, *Mythos Musik* and *Programming the Absolute* (see notes 4 and 7).

[37] *AmZ*, ii/24 (12 March 1800), col. 417.

historical moment. Only through this indestructible material presence of a national heritage can it hold on to music's perpetual withering away of the past.

Alas, this splendid argument did not quite match Rochlitz's four illustrations (see Figure 4). Indeed, compared to the mania for monuments of great German composers in the German Empire of Wilhelm II at the end

Figure 4.   Illustrations for Rochlitz's 'Monuments of German Composers', published in the *Allgemeine musikalische Zeitung*, 1800 (*AmZ*, 12 March 1800). By permission of the Syndics of Cambridge University Library.

of the nineteenth century,[38] they look sympathetically shambolic. The Haydn monument (Figure 4, top left) was erected by Count Karl Leonard von Harrach in Rohrau, the birthplace of the composer, much too soon in 1793, sixteen years before Haydn actually died, so that one could say, without excessive irony, that, at least for a time, he managed successfully to outlive his own immortality. (One side of the memorial was even left blank for the date of his death to be inserted later.) Mozart's monument in Tiefurt near Weimar (Figure 4, top right) really was built after his death. As Rochlitz rightly complained, however, it was constructed mainly of burnt earth and therefore hardly made to last; and indeed it has completely disappeared. Last in this not-yet-quite-stable pantheon of German musicians according to Rochlitz are the monuments for C. P. E. Bach planned for Weimar and Hamburg (Figure 4, bottom). But various bureaucratic difficulties got in the way, and they were never built.

The marks of death in these images of German music around 1800 express not only the fear of this music's final disappearance, but also the pessimistic view that a national music worthy of the name will only ever escape the dominance of musical foreignness with difficulty. It was not quite like this in other cultural walks of life where, as Tim Blanning has said, Enlightenment cosmopolitanism had long since been effectively banished with the liturgical repetition of the prefix 'National' in those endless composite nouns possible in German: *Nationalsprache* (national language), *Nationalcharakter* (national character), *Nationalgeschichte* (national history), *Nationalerziehung* (national education), and so on.[39] Of a *Nationalmusik*, there were as yet only sporadic, if distinct signs. The commonest line of thought about musical Germanness went like this: if something German is to be found in music, it is the thoroughness and good taste with which German composers are able to imitate and cultivate all possible foreign styles.

This discrete universalism was hardly enough for the inventors of a more idealistic German music around 1800: Christmann, Rochlitz, our German organist in London, Kollmann, and others to be heard in a moment. To introduce the new musical century in 1801 in the pages of the

---

[38] For a vivid documentation relating to Wagner, see Hartmut Zelinsky, *Richard Wagner: ein deutsches Thema* (Frankfurt am Main, 1976). Zelinsky omits to say that other composers in the pantheon of German music from Bach to Bruckner were subject in varying degrees to similar treatment.

[39] Tim Blanning, *The Culture of Power and the Power of Culture: Old Regime Europe 1660–1789* (Oxford, 2002), p. 260.

Allgemeine musikalische Zeitung, Rochlitz commissioned a still longer essay in several episodes on eighteenth-century German music from yet another clergyman, Pastor Johann Karl Friedrich Triest of Stettin (1764–1810). After some lengthy rhetorical strutting-around among high-minded generalites, Triest eventually arrives at the crucial question: 'Do the Germans have a music they can call their own and have they ever had it?'[40] Basically, his answer is 'no'. As usual among eighteenth-century thinkers, Triest's approach to history is taxonomic and not dynamic, or, in other words, mercifully free of the Hegelian and Left-Hegelian fetishism of 'progress' that plagues later nineteenth-century constructions of German music. Still, there is more than just a hint that the course of musical history in the eighteenth century has seen the ever-increasing decadence of foreign music—a decadence which *could* be overcome by German musicians if they remain true to their pedagogic, theological, and above all patriotic values.

Not unlike Giardini's satire, but with the opposite purpose, Triest proceeds, interestingly, to prescribe the desired features of a truly German music by comparing them with foreign models, i.e. by defining them precisely by what they are *not*. To take one example: in what he calls the second period of the eighteenth century, he claims in an imaginative footnote that German music resembled French–Italian landscape-gardening 'which pleases the eye at first with its precisely measured forms, but in minds and hearts soon gives rise to a certain emptiness'.[41] The obvious implication is that German music in this mode *also* had a certain emptiness, but could still learn something from the French–Italian way of doing things by laying claim to depth nonetheless. And in the third period of the eighteenth century, German music, again according to Triest, 'came to resemble *English* gardens, whose main feature is the concealment of artifice in great vast masses, which are also not seldom the background for the appearance of truly (and not merely seemingly) irregular or

---

[40] 'Haben denn die Deutschen eine eigenthümliche Musik und haben sie je gehabt?' Johann Karl Friedrich Triest, 'Bemerkungen über die Ausbildung der Tonkunst in Deutschland im achtzehnten Jahrhundert', *AmZ*, iii/15 (7 January 1801), col. 241. Triest's essay has been translated in its entirety by Susan Gillespie in Elaine Sisman (ed.), *Haydn and His World* (Princeton, NJ, 1997), pp. 321–94. The translations here are my own, though I have consulted Gillespie's with profit. For further discussion of Triest, see the important article by Bernd Sponheuer, 'Reconstructing Ideal Types of the "German" in Music', in Celia Applegate and Pamela Potter (eds), *Music and German National Identity* (Chicago, IL, and London, 2002), pp. 36–57.
[41] 'die durch abgezirkelte Formen dem Auge erst gefällt, aber auch bald eine gewisse Leere im Gemüthe verursacht'. *AmZ*, iii/26 (25 March 1801), cols 443–4.

baroque constellations'.[42] The message here is that German music does not need to hide the irregular and the Baroque-like in a mass of anonymity. Rather, it can integrate them into a whole that has been built up organically, so that it does not appear barbaric or pompous, but warm and harmonious.[43]

Not content with turning the German composer, on account of his propensity for inclusiveness, into a kind of head gardener in the big musical park of Europe, Triest cultivated a near perfect image of how German music *ought* to be by distancing it emphatically from the weaknesses of foreign music as he saw them—a veritable catalogue in fact: emptiness, incoherence, feeble structure, dainty elegance, lack of unity, sensuousness, over-ornamentation, harmonic shallowness, anonymous vastness, impoverished counterpoint, and so on. All of these, Triest implies, can be effectively kept at bay by hard work and the will to learn. The exclusive image also reserved a special place for instrumental music, 'given our naturally outstanding talent for it';[44] or, as the London *Morning Chronicle* put it more pejoritavely, the fact that 'the Germans have seen riot in their *instrumentalities*'.[45] And indeed by 1801 Lutheran observers like Daniel Jenisch (1762–1804) were already praising 'true instrumental music' with 'virile and rich harmonies' as an 'invention' of the Germans.[46]

The only thing missing was a composer who could sum up all the required prerequisites of the new doctrine, and moreover someone who lent himself to the idea of a new beginning, an antidote to decadence.

[42] 'ahmte den *englischen* Gärten nach, deren Hauptcharakter die Versteckung der Kunst in großen unübersehbaren Massen ist, doch auch nicht selten wirkliche (nicht bloß scheinbar) regellose oder barocke Zusammenstellungen zum Vorschein bringt'. *Am Z*, iii/26 (25 March 1801), cols 443–4.

[43] Triest's view has part of its pedigree in Goethe's now famous praise of the 'harmonising' Gothic in a pamphlet published in 1772 about the architecture of Strasbourg Cathedral, which in turn was an implicit rebuttal of Rousseau's condemnation in his *Dictionnaire de musique* of the harmony-obsessed music of the 'north' as a 'Gothic and barbarous invention' (*une invention Gothique & barbare*) compared with the natural melodic pleasure principle of the 'south'. See Rousseau, *Dictionnaire*, vol. 1, p. 383 and Johann Wolfgang von Goethe, 'Von deutscher Baukunst', *Sämtliche Werke nach Epochen seines Schaffens*, ed. Karl Richter with Herbert G. Göpfert, Norbert Miller, and Gerhard Sauder, 2 vols (Munich, 1987), vol. 1, pp. 415–23.

[44] 'Mit der Instrumentalmusik hat es, bey unsrer natürlichen hervorstechenden Anlage dazu, keine Noth.' *AmZ*, iii/25 (18 March 1801), cols 426–7.

[45] *Morning Chronicle*, no. 7066. Emphasis in the original.

[46] 'Die wahre Instrumental-Musik ist ein Werk ihrer Erfindung . . . Sie [die Deutschen] haben dem übrigen Europa gezeigt, daß eine männliche und reiche Harmonie . . . eine außerordentliche Berühmtheit verschafft.' Daniel Jenisch, *Geist und Charakter des achtzehnten Jarhhunderts, politisch, moralisch, ästhetisch und wissenschaftlich betrachtet*, 3 vols (Berlin, 1800–1), vol. 3, p. 429.

V

Triest and the other draughtsmen of the ideological construct the world has come to know as German music could not accurately predict the consequences of their ideas. The simple observation that these ideas eventually led to social rituals of a certain musical kind in the future—the first properly constituted collected edition of a composer's work in the middle of the nineteenth century, many concerts in that same composer's name performed like church services in the secular sphere, countless monuments to him, yearly music festivals dedicated to him, and the morally unambiguous foundation he gave to the enterprise calling itself German music—hardly makes it difficult to guess who was eventually chosen to represent this new beginning.

The chosen one turned out to be Johann Sebastian Bach, a composer deemed to have been pious, a master of harmony and counterpoint, pedagogically minded, and above all dead for half a century, unable to reply to the cultural standards in his name about to be set in stone for generations to come. A well known literary man-about-Germany, Christian Friedrich Daniel Schubart (1739–91), had already christened him in the mid-1780s the 'Orpheus of the Germans', and celebrated him as a 'genius of the highest calibre [whose] spirit is so individual, so gigantic, that centuries will be needed to catch up with him'.[47] The *Allgemeine musikalische Zeitung* chose to adorn its first year of issues in 1798 with a title-page dominated by an engraving of J. S. Bach based on a lost painting by Emanuel Traugott Goebel (1751–1813).[48] And Triest devoted an entire section of his discourse on eighteenth-century music to J. S. Bach, citing him as a German, who was 'the greatest, most profound musical harmonist of all times', surpassing 'everything that Italy, France, and England had done for *pure* music' and therefore a 'joy [. . .] for patriotic citizens of our fatherland'.[49]

---

[47] 'der Orpheus der Deutschen . . . war Genie im höchsten Grade. Sein Geist ist so eigenthümlich, so Riesenförmig, daß Jahrhunderte erfordert werden, bis er einmal erreicht wird.' C. F. D. Schubart, *Ideen zu einer Aesthetik der Tonkunst*, ed. Ludwig Schubart (Stuttgart, 1839), p. 107 [= *Gesammelte Schriften und Schicksale*, vol. 5].

[48] The frontispiece of the first volume of the *AmZ* is reproduced in Werner Neumann (ed.), *Bilddokumente zur Lebensgeschichte Johann Sebastian Bachs* (Kassel, 1979), p. 24.

[49] 'Und nun—welche Freude für einen patriotischen Bewohner unseres Vaterlandes, zu wissen, daß der größte, tiefsinnigste Harmonist aller bisherigen Zeiten, der alles, was Italien, Frankreich und England für die *reine* Musik gethan hatte, übertraf . . . ein Deutscher war!' *AmZ*, iii/16 (14 January 1801), col. 259.

And then came the epochal publication on J. S. Bach by Johann Nicolaus Forkel (1749–1818), the first ever book about the composer. It was published in 1802 and provided with a highly resonant second title: 'For patriotic admirers of genuine musical art'.[50] Bach is presented in the book as the summit of German music, which practically no one can conquer. And not surprisingly there are warm words pleading for recognition of this 'priceless national inheritance'. The knowledge and fostering of Bach's works, Forkel writes, and 'the preservation of this great man's memory is not just the concern of art: it is the *concern of the nation*'[51]— statements only possible because of the increasing national musical awareness of the German-speaking world at the end of the eighteenth century, which Forkel's little book embodied, and at the same time helped to promote.

Forkel's famous book on J. S. Bach is the first really significant document around 1800 marking the reversal of the relationship between the German and the non-German in music: the foreign is no longer to determine the national, the national now determines the foreign. Here we have the first real step towards the fake Teutonic musical universalism first promoted in the middle of the nineteenth century. Which is to say, in the name of progress, German music is all music: Berlioz, Liszt, Wagner— French, Hungarian, German. The national differences do not really matter. All of these composers wrote in the same universalist German spirit, according to the group's supporters, and the name they gave to their movement, the New German School, remains in the history books well into the twenty-first century[52]—a real consequence of the promotion of Bach at the beginning of the nineteenth as the representative of a national, and at the same time truly universal, music. Indeed, in outline the whole of German music already seems to exist in 1801: 'One thinks of the beginning of the world authority of German music,' Leo Schrade

---

[50] Johann Nicolaus Forkel, *Ueber Johann Sebastian Bachs Leben, Kunst und Kunstwerke. Für patriotische Verehrer echter musikalischer Kunst* (Leipzig, 1802).

[51] 'unschätzbares Nationalerbgut ... doch ist die Erhaltung des Andenkens an diesen großen Mann ... nicht bloß Kunst-Angelegenheit—sie ist *National-Angelegenheit*.' Forkel, *Ueber Johann Sebastian Bachs Leben*, pp. v–vi. Emphasis in the original.

[52] Even without much investigation of its ideological background in Richard Taruskin's otherwise critical and at times refreshingly revisionist *Oxford History of Western Music*, 6 vols (Oxford, 2004), vol. 3, pp. 416–28.

once wrote perceptively, 'includes Bach in the picture, and then believes that Bach himself had a decisive influence on that authority.'[53]

Let us imagine for a moment what Bach's reaction might have been if he had lived to see the emergence of Forkel's little book. (Had he lasted that long, incidentally, he would have been 117 years old.) What would he have said? Perhaps this: 'Me, the pinnacle of German music? Do these good people think I would have written my Italian Concerto, my French and English Suites, my Pièce d'Orgue and the Overture in B minor in the French manner, all for the glory of German music? Me, the inventor of instrumental music? What do they think I was doing spending all those hours studying Vivaldi concertos? Why did I spend so much time writing for voices? And why am I supposed to have been so stern? I am a fervent believer in God, it is true. But I am not pious like a monk. As for my being a symbol of patriotism, and one stoically pietistic to boot, that is just a war of words started by the German intellectuals against France—a rhetorical answer to the godless French Revolution. Anyway, these people do not know half my music.'

My posthumous Bach is right. Forkel's book lists only a smallish part of his output, most of it instrumental music. One knew the published *Art of Fugue*, a few keyboard pieces, the forty-eight Preludes and Fugues were circulating in manuscript, and only a privileged few, including Mozart when he discovered Baron van Swieten's manuscript collection in Vienna, had been able to study some of the choral music. (Forkel's book is dedicated to van Swieten.) My aged Bach also did not fail to notice the cultural–patriotic fictions that were beginning to surround his music and the gulf between that and what he had actually aspired to as a composer: the gulf, in other words, between construct and practice. Indeed, after the emergence of his choral works into the public domain later on, including Mendelssohn's famous revivial of the *St Matthew Passion* in 1829 in Berlin in the presence of Hegel, and in which Goethe in Weimar also took a more than passing interest, the gulf grew even wider.

There have been some notable collisions and collusions on the bridge across this gulf since the appearance of Forkel's work on Bach.

---

[53] 'Man denkt an ihre beginnende Weltgeltung, nimmt auch Bach in sie auf und glaubt nun, er selbst habe an dieser Weltgeltung bestimmend mitgewirkt.' Leo Schrade, 'Johann Sebastian Bach und die deutsche Nation', *Deutsche Vierteljahrsschrift für Literaturwissenschaft und Geistesgeschichte*, 15 (1937), 235.

Beethoven's *Missa solemnis*, op. 123, composed between 1819 and 1823, was surely intended at one level of its labyrinthine theological landscape as a monument to the idea of German music. Beethoven himself went out of his way to call it 'the *greatest* work'[54] he had written up to that point in his life; and its epigraph 'Von Herzen—Möge es wieder—zu Herzen gehen' (From the heart—may it again—return to the heart) is not unlike a remark in the first volume of Forkel's general history of music, 'Die Musik kommt aus dem Herzen, und geht in die Herzen' (Music comes from the heart, and goes to the heart),[55] which already suggests that there is a connection between Beethoven's and Forkel's ambitions on behalf of German music. Forkel never completed his history; but it is already clear in its first volume, published in 1788, that it was going to culminate in a patriotic bid for German music as a summation of the entire history of the art.

Despite the virtuosic fugal counterpoint in the 'Et vitam venturi saeculi' section of the Credo clearly modelled on Bach's *Art of Fugue*, and the audible struggle in supposedly German fashion to integrate irregular and sometimes deliberately jarring 'Gothic' musical features into an organically conceived harmonic background, however, Beethoven's *Missa solemnis* is also highly eclectic, borrowing freely from medieval, French, and Italian techniques of modal harmony, word-setting, vocal line, musical illustration, and colour, which on closer examination seem to collide with its more specific cultural purpose. The chauvinistic content of Wagner's *Die Meistersinger von Nürnberg* (the opera was first performed with huge success in 1868 in the years leading up to the Franco-Prussian War of 1870, starts with a fake Lutheran chorale, and ends with Hans Sachs's notorious speech about the supremacy of German art) is also made more complicated by the fact that for those with ears to hear the music frequently models itself audibly on non-German sources, including the Italian *bel canto* tradition in, of all things, Walther's Prize Song, the central musical 'number' of the whole work.

Indeed, the entire dramaturgy of *Die Meistersinger* colludes with a paradoxical idea, which is highly relevant to the present essay, even if it is borrowed wholesale from French Grand Opera: the invention of historical fiction using real historical sources. Sixteenth-century Nuremberg is recreated with innumerable bits of accurate archival detail just as sixteenth-

---

[54] Letter of 5 June 1822 to Peters. See Maynard Soloman, *Beethoven* (New York, 1979), p. 309.
[55] Johann Nicolaus Forkel, *Allgemeine Geschichte der Musik* (Leipzig, 1788), vol. 1, p. 71.

century Touraine and Paris are in Giocomo Meyerbeer's *Les Huguenots* (first performed in 1836). Indeed, the second act of *Die Meistersinger*, with its ingeniously constructed dramaturgy interweaving the exits and entrances of soloists, disparate crowds, a fighting mob, and last but not least the Night Watchman, is unthinkable without the specific model of the third act of *Les Huguenots*. Wagner was behaving in operatic practice like a well versed European, while at the same time promoting a phantas-magoria of German music which, as he knew perhaps more than any other composer in the nineteenth century, relied for its eloquence pre-cisely on its seamless absorption of different styles and techniques, whether German in origin or not, and an entirely imaginary recollection of a supposedly idyllic past inhabited by a key figure like Hans Sachs who really did exist, but not necessarily in the way a modern audience would like to see him.

I do not want to suggest, however, that J. S. Bach according to Forkel, or indeed Hans Sachs according to Wagner, were the Ovsyaniko-Kulikovskys of the future. Nor is it my intention just to observe that the many strands of the myth of German music that came to dominate the musical landscape of the nineteenth century and beyond were already in place around 1800: the image of a music potent enough to displace for-eign influence and yet absorb it discreetly in the name of a national ideal, a secular theology, a celebration of an imaginary new beginning of music, and at the same time an iconography of death. I also want to ask some more awkward questions. Has German music really underscored the so-called German *Sonderweg* (special path)—assuming such a thing exists for Germany alone—as faithfully as Bernd Sponheuer claims?[56] Or has its unofficial eclecticism and internationalism always been at odds with the supposedly inevitable German path against liberalism and democracy towards the catastrophes of the First and Second World Wars? Did the exclusive image of German music its inventors began to put on the drawing-board around 1800 not in fact conceal the inclusive instincts of German composers, which continued unabated? After all, the 'Two trios' by the dilettante from Amsterdam (see Figures 1 and 2) unwittingly sug-gest that the expansive tones in a spacious C major in the so-called Italian style are not such a great distance from the German style—in the world of Mozart's *Jupiter* Symphony, say, or one of his sonatas, not to mention the astonishing expansiveness of German music yet to be composed, such

---

[56] Bernd Sponheuer, 'Reconstructing Ideal Types', p. 54 (see note 40).

as the first movement of Beethoven's *Kreutzer* Sonata for violin and piano, op. 47, or, more famously, his *Eroica* Symphony, op. 55.

VI

I began with Schoenberg's bid to assure the world authority of German music for the next hundred years with his 'method of composition with twelve tones related only to one another'. The paradox remains to this day that the atonal and serial works on which his formidable historical renown for innovation hinges—the song-cycle *Book of the Hanging Gardens*, the piano pieces op. 33a, even his opera *Moses und Aron*—are precisely not the ones modern audiences have taken to their hearts. The question I would like to end with is this: did Schoenberg's insistence on the virtues of German music, its pedagogic fortitude, its secular theology, its confidence in dominating history, its emphasis on structure and musical logic (a term probably first introduced to musicology by Forkel incidentally), and above all its exclusionary bias mean that at last the prototype first envisaged by the inventors of German music around 1800 had come to fruition? No longer willing to tolerate the gulf between the way German composers and their followers tended to legitimise their music on the one hand, and the way they actually composed on the other, did Schoenberg at last close the gap between construct and practice? Did the composer who thought he embodied all the cultural–patriotic prerequisites invested in German music as it began to be defined around 1800, and carefully integrated their technical correlatives systematically into the fabric of his work, become a stumbling-block for audiences precisely because his music no longer thrived on the same tension? Was the provocative and fertile mismatch, in other words, still perceptible? Or did Schoenberg's ambition to assure the future of German music for the next hundred years ultimately fail because, ironically, it no longer sounded like German music?

Playing with the Nation: Napoleon and the Culture of Nationalism

PETER ALTER

AT THE END OF HIS STUDY OF NAPOLEON and his short-lived political comeback in March 1815, the well known German journalist and admirer of French culture, Friedrich Sieburg, simply stated: 'The man has commanded our continent, he still commands posterity.'[1] One may add, in his time the man also commanded the ideological environment which made nationalism grow and helped to turn the idea of the 'nation' into one of the most powerful political forces in the nineteenth and twentieth centuries. It would, of course, require a superhuman audacity to paint an adequate picture of Napoleon's impact on Europe as a destroyer and conqueror, as a moderniser and restorer, as a statesman and military genius, and so on.

I am not that ambitious. My few remarks are much more limited. I shall concentrate on one particular aspect, namely on Napoleon Bonaparte the nation-builder or, as some contemporaries and, later, historians liked to call him, the 'awakener' of peoples and nations. 'Napoleon's conquests, and the strong reactions they provoked in England, Spain, Germany, Poland, and Russia, intensified and diffused the civic ideas of national autonomy, unity, and identity across Europe and throughout Latin America.'[2] It is this aspect of Napoleon's historic

---

[1] Friedrich Sieburg, *Napoleon: Die hundert Tage* (Stuttgart, 1956), p. 413.
[2] 'Introduction', in John Hutchinson and Anthony D. Smith (eds), *Nationalism* (Oxford, 1994), p. 7. 'Napoleon hat Deutschland erweckt': Michael Freund, *Napoleon und die Deutschen: Despot oder Held der Freiheit* (Munich, 1969), p. 22. 'Ganz offensichtlich ist die Epoche der Französischen Revolution und des napoleonischen Empire in ganz Europa Schauplatz einer großen "Nationalisierungswelle", einer ersten wirksamen, wenngleich noch nicht massen- und dauerhaften Begründung nationalen Identitäts- und Gemeinschaftsgefühls': Reinhard Stauber, 'Nationalismus vor dem Nationalismus? Eine Bestandsaufnahme der Forschung zu "Nation" und "Nationalismus" in der Frühen Neuzeit', *Geschichte in Wissenschaft und Unterricht*, 47 (1996), 145–6.

Proceedings of the British Academy, **134**, 61–75. © The British Academy 2006.

impact which, more or less by accident, and only in a few instances deliberately, helped to spread a new political culture or, indeed, a new political
cult whose origins can be traced back to the French Revolution. This is
my first point, and I will briefly elaborate on it here.

The new political culture which arose out of the Revolution focused
on the concept of the democratic, sovereign nation as a novel political
and social unit for the organisation of society. In revolutionary France of
the late eighteenth century the new concept of the 'nation'—created or
invented—intrigued the intellectual elites and convincingly demonstrated
its formidable powers to mobilise and integrate large sections of society.
During Napoleon's reign over large parts of the Continent, and particularly towards its end, the 'nation' and its allegedly bright future conquered
the imagination of many Europeans, and continued to do so for more or
less 200 years, sometimes with felicitous, but more often with disastrous,
consequences.

This is, in retrospect, quite an amazing career for a term which, at that
time, was not new at all. However, in the course of the Revolution it was
given an explosive new meaning. When asked in 1789 what a 'nation' was,
one of the revolutionaries, the Abbé Sieyès, remarked that it was 'a body
of associates living under one common law and represented by the same
legislature'.[3] At first glance, this looked rather inoffensive. But if we
examine Sieyès's seemingly casual definition more closely, the 'body of
associates' saw itself as a political and social community of equal citizens
in possession of inalienable human rights who wished to decide their own
destiny. One of the leading ideologues of the Revolution, the former
lawyer Robespierre, affirmed in April 1793, less than a year before he was
executed, that oppression and the conquest of other nations were contrary to natural law. According to Robespierre, peoples had a right to self-
government and to be free of foreign domination in whatever shape:
'Whoever oppresses one nation declares himself the enemy of all the
others.'[4]

To cut a long story short, the 'nation'—democratic, sovereign, and
composed of free and equal citizens—became the battle-cry that the revolutionaries raised against feudal society, thereby destroying the basis

---

[3] Quoted in Elie Kedourie, *Nationalism* (London, 1961), p. 15. See also Peter Alter, *Nationalism*,
2nd edn (London, 1994), p. 40.

[4] Quoted in Florence Gauthier, 'Universal Rights and National Interest in the French
Revolution', in Otto Dann and John Dinwiddy (eds), *Nationalism in the Age of the French
Revolution* (London, 1988), p. 33.

which had traditionally legitimised rule. In other words, the revolutionary concept of society was that of a community of politically aware and self-governing citizens. This community was now considered the source of legitimacy for the exercise of rule; the 'nation' was, from now on, the sole repository of power. In Sieyès's classic formulation, the Third Estate had become the 'universal' class and identified itself with the sovereign 'nation'.[5]

The revolutionaries in France did not have any doubt whatsoever that in future the nation alone would exercise sovereignty in domestic as well as in external affairs. When the Prussian foreign minister of many years, Ewald Friedrich von Hertzberg, read the republican French constitution of September 1791 he no longer had any illusions about what a fundamental transfer of power had taken place. 'We are witnesses to the French Revolution', Hertzberg opined,

> in the process of which the French nation, enlightened and pushed forward by the new philosophers, wants to create the best constitution possible and even excel the English one by means of fusing monarchy and republic, or at least blending them together. The French assure all legislative powers to the nation and the executive powers to the king, however in such a way that the king remains subordinate to the representatives of the nation.[6]

So much for Hertzberg's perception of the Revolution and the influence of its 'new philosophers'. Years later, the eminent Prussian historian Leopold von Ranke asserted in his *History of England* that 'there is no single political idea which, in the course of the past centuries, has had an impact like the sovereignty of the people'.[7]

Now for my second point. The modern, free, and democratic nation, born in the Revolution, would not tolerate oppression or despotism in any shape or form. Consequently, the protagonists of the national concept were as opposed to monarchical rule in the style of the *anciens régimes* as they were to the tutelage of a nation by a foreign power or, even worse, by a dreaded universal monarchy pretending, since Napoleon's coronation in December 1804, to bring peace to Europe and with it the political achievements of the French Revolution. In 1792,

[5] Gauthier, 'Universal Rights and National Interest', p. 33.

[6] Hertzberg addressing the Berlin Academy on 6 October 1791. Quoted in Michael Hundt, 'Frieden und internationale Ordnung im Zeitalter der Französischen Revolution und Napoleons I. (1789–1815)', in Bernd Wegner (ed.), *Wie Kriege enden: Wege zum Frieden von der Antike bis zur Gegenwart* (Paderborn, 2002), p. 146.

[7] Leopold von Ranke, *Englische Geschichte vornehmlich im siebzehnten Jahrhundert*, 3 vols, 2nd edn (Leipzig, 1870), vol. 3, p. 328.

when the revolutionary wars began, there had been little nationalist spirit among the peoples outside France. But as the wars intensified, and especially under Napoleon's impact, the political climate in continental Europe changed. By 1807 most of the old regimes in Europe had been deeply shaken and battered, first by the Revolution and its shocking accompaniments, and then by Napoleon Bonaparte's radical transformation of the political map of the Continent. This, a time when old dynasties and people had been utterly humiliated by the conquering French, was the crucial moment when the new concept of the nation turned against its creators: the French in general and Napoleon Bonaparte in particular.

The older and much of the recent historiography on the rise of nationalism and national movements in post-revolutionary Europe is fairly unanimous in saying that Napoleon deliberately refrained from using the 'nation' as a political concept to revolutionise the European order of states. He also refrained from using the idea of the democratic nation to further his ambitions with regard to establishing a universal monarchy, legitimised by the wish of the peoples under its sceptre. Rather, the opposite seems to have been the case, for reasons which are not so obvious at first glance: Napoleon chose to contain the national idea and its dynamics whenever this was within his power.

However, as historical experience has shown again and again, attempts to exercise tight political control over events and developments, and ideas in particular, are not often successful. In fact, this is hardly ever possible. Much to the delight of the later historian there are always some ironic aspects to the story. Europe at the beginning of the nineteenth century was no exception. The charismatic Emperor Napoleon, as it turned out, became the catalyst in one way or another, and quite unintentionally, for the spread of the concept of the nation all over Europe at the height of his supremacy. Thus, contrary to his grand political design, Napoleon can be called 'nation-builder', and can be considered the godfather of the so-called 'national awakening' of the European peoples. The new concept of the nation was there—simply waiting, to put it in admittedly rather crude terms, to be picked up and instrumentalised by progressive writers, journalists, and academics sporting the idea of the sovereign nation, and by the organisers and leaders of national movements. It set in motion a triumphant procession of a new political culture unparalleled in the history of modern Europe. This new political culture is called either patriotism or, more appropriately, nationalism. It denounced foreign oppression and demanded freedom for individuals and peoples.

In the long run, and in retrospect, the adoption of the national principle seems to have benefited all Europeans, at least temporarily. Oppression by a dominant ethnic group, a foreign power, or a prerevolutionary monarchical regime sooner or later ended in the liberation and emancipation of the peoples, who founded their own sovereign nation-states. And 'in the beginning was Napoleon', to use the much quoted sentence with which Thomas Nipperdey opens his great work on nineteenth-century German history.[8] Napoleon Bonaparte became the liberator and nation-builder for some; the oppressor, the despot, the 'Corsican usurper' and 'scourge of God', the 'son of hell', or 'sublime monster' for others—but the rather unexpected catalyst and trigger for a new epoch in European history for all.[9] 'For all' includes the many historians who, soon after Napoleon's downfall and then for many decades to come, put pen to paper and wrote voluminous master-narratives for their 'reborn' nations, now allegedly free, united, and happy. That their frantic efforts were often marred by a mixture of facts, fiction, and myths is another story and need not be discussed here. Nor do we need to examine the readiness of the visual arts to take inspiration from historians' texts and create images which have sunk deeply into the collective memory of generations right up to the present.

Let us return to Napoleon Bonaparte, the catalyst and godfather of national movements all over Europe. If we accept the simple observation that nationally minded contemporaries and later historians alike almost unanimously accorded him the role of 'awakener' and nation-builder, then, on closer inspection, a few qualifications are necessary. In a political sense, Napoleon was undoubtedly the catalyst who, in his lifetime, prepared the ground for the breakthrough of the concept of the nation and, in its wake, the rise of national movements in many parts of Europe. However, this role took on a variety of shapes. Indeed, it was far from being uniform, deliberate, and monotonous. Mustering the better known cases of 'national awakening' and nation-building in the watershed years between the onset of the revolutionary wars in 1792 and 1814 when the peace conference assembled in Vienna, we can distinguish at least three

[8] Thomas Nipperdey, *Germany from Napoleon to Bismarck 1800–1866* (Dublin, 1996), p. 1.
[9] For Central Europe, see, e.g., Erich Pelzer, 'Die Wiedergeburt Deutschlands 1813 und die Dämonisierung Napoleons', in Gerd Krumeich and Hartmut Lehmann (eds), *'Gott mit uns': Nation, Religion und Gewalt* (Göttingen, 2000), pp. 135–56; Wulf Wülfing, '"Heiland" und "Höllensohn": Zum Napoleon-Mythos im Deutschland des 19. Jahrhunderts', in Helmut Berding (ed.), *Mythos und Nation: Studien zur Entwicklung des kollektiven Bewusstseins in der Neuzeit* (Frankfurt am Main, 1996), pp. 164–84.

categories or, perhaps more appropriately, three types of responses to the extraordinary challenge to political loyalties posed by Napoleon.

First, there were the European peoples under the direct rule of Napoleonic France, from the Netherlands to Nice and Savoy, and those who lived in French satellite states such as the Confederation of the Rhine, the Illyrian Provinces, or the Duchy of Warsaw, heavily dependent on, and subjected to, Napoleon's whims and favours. As the years went by some of them increasingly resented foreign domination. Their leaders, or, perhaps more precisely, marginal rather than substantial sections of their intellectual and political elites, began to speak of French oppression and tyranny, thus fanning a spirit of resistance among those who were being denied the very freedom and self-determination that the *grande nation* was proclaiming from the rooftops of Europe as the fruits of 1789. French expansionism and ambition to rule supreme let even surviving monarchical governments throughout Europe, so far dependent on Napoleon's goodwill and short-term political planning, appeal to the patriotism and national pride of the oppressed 'nation' to help repel the French drive for political hegemony. Examples from this category are, among others, Spain, Central Europe, and Italy.

My first example is Spain. Modern writers on nationalism and nation-building may find it hard to accept the interpretation of Spanish historians of the nineteenth and twentieth centuries according to which the riots in Madrid following 2 May 1808 stood for the rising of the 'Spanish nation' against Napoleon. What, they ask, did the term 'Spanish nation' mean in 1808, and who belonged to it? Nevertheless, the ensuing war of liberation against the occupying French armies (*la guerra de la independencia*) is rightly seen as a key event in Spanish history and the starting point of a new era in European history. For the first time the concept of the nation which refuses government based on the absolutist rule of a monarch, which upholds the guiding ideas of the French Revolution and wants them put into constitutional practice, and which repudiates political domination by expansionist France, became the powerful ingredient in a process which, for some good reasons, is labelled 'national awakening'.

My second example is Central Europe. The rather paradoxical constellation of political forces and aspirations in those years around 1807–8 is, of course, also clearly illustrated by the political situation in the German states at the beginning of the nineteenth century. On the one hand, the early national movement in Central Europe took its cue from revolutionary France and the ideas of human and civil rights, democracy, and peoples' sovereignty propagated there. Johann Gottlieb Fichte, Ernst

Moritz Arndt, Joseph Görres, Friedrich Schleiermacher, and others—all praised the achievements and glory of the French Revolution. Yet, owing to Napoleon's expansionism and oppression, the early German national movement and its leaders' agitation and rhetoric became heavily coloured by anti-French sentiment and, as recent research has once again pointed out, incorporated older traditions of patriotic feelings and cultural identities.[10] Consequently, the vision of a liberated, democratic, and politically united German nation was transformed into an effective weapon—perhaps *the* most effective weapon—against Napoleon's rule in Europe. Napoleon, in national rhetoric now the much despised enemy of the subjected nations, readily served to mobilise the people in a 'holy war' and to fuel the process of nation-building. Thus German national-ism, as is commonly observed, was 'triggered by Napoleon's oppressive rule and experienced its first powerful flowering in the wars of libera-tion'.[11] The hegemony of one country, the rule of one man over Europe with all its consequences for the peoples' own culture, language, identity, and political self-determination had clashed with the irresistible vision of a Europe of nations that upheld the principles of the French Revolution: liberty, equality, and fraternity.

My third example is Italy. In many ways, developments on the Italian peninsula were similar to those in Central Europe. There the incipient national movement, led by writers, scholars, and journalists such as Vittorio Alfieri, Vincenzo Cuoco, and Ugo Foscolo, acknowledged Napoleon's role as a moderniser but condemned him, at the same time, as the oppressor of the Italian people. Later historians more or less agree that Napoleon's rule in Italy was harsher than that of the Habsburgs or the Bourbons whom he had displaced. But the verdict of Italian *Risorgimento* historiography is that in the long run he did nothing but good for Italy. It praised Napoleon for having reduced the political divi-sions of the country, for constructing roads and bridges, thus facilitating communication, and for being the first to propose a united Italy. Dictating his memoirs on St Helena, Napoleon himself maintained:

[10] Harro Segeberg, 'Germany', in Dann and Dinwiddy (eds), *Nationalism*, pp. 137–56; Jörg Echternkamp, *Der Aufstieg des deutschen Nationalismus (1770–1840)* (Frankfurt am Main, 1998); Otto Dann et al. (eds), *Patriotismus und Nationsbildung am Ende des Heiligen Römischen Reiches* (Cologne, 2003).

[11] Fritz Valjavec, *Die Entstehung der politischen Strömungen in Deutschland 1770–1815* (Munich, 1951; reprint Düsseldorf, 1978), p. 329.

Italy, isolated within her natural frontiers, separated by the sea and by very high mountains from the rest of Europe, seems to be called to be a great and powerful nation ... The unity of customs, of language, of literature in some future more or less distant—ought to unite all its inhabitants under one sole government ... It is necessary to the happiness of Europe that Italy should form one sole State which will maintain the equilibrium on the Continent between France and Austria, and on the sea between France and England.[12]

How far Napoleon did, in fact, contribute to the unification of Italy and help to create the nation-state of 1861 remained a matter of controversy, particularly among the leaders of the Italian national movement. That he did prepare the ground for the *Risorgimento*, consciously or unintentionally, was recognised by Italian patriots, foremost among them Giuseppe Mazzini. However, in the last resort, it was Napoleon's occupation of Italy, not the very man himself or his message, that ignited the national movement, as Mazzini put it, 'the burst of fraternisation ... especially in the period 1805–13'. For Mazzini, in those crucial years, 'the feeling of nationality specially incorporated in our brave army elevated our souls, picturing in the distance the oneness of Italy, the object of all our efforts'.[13] The British historian Sir John Marriott was more emphatic and outspoken when he wrote more than eighty years ago: 'The fact is not, indeed, open to question; the name of Napoleon the First must be inscribed upon the roll of the makers of modern Italy.'[14] Yet Marriott's modern fellow historian Adrian Lyttelton is more cautious. 'The Napoleonic regime', he wrote a few years ago, 'may have actually encouraged the growth of a feeling of Italian national identity.'[15]

We now come to my second category. This comprises cases in which the beginnings of a thinking in terms of the nation and the rise of a national movement were not directed against Napoleon and French occupation, but went along with Napoleon's support—real or imagined. The Poles and the South Slavs, the Slovenes and Croats in particular, are good examples. To the Poles and, to a much lesser extent, the South Slavs, who, as non-dominant ethnic groups, felt trapped in multi-ethnic empires, Napoleon appeared as a saviour. For them he was simply the liberator, the executor of the French Revolution and its glorious principles, the only

[12] Quoted in J. A. R. Marriott, 'Napoleon and Nation-making', *The Nineteenth Century and After*, 89 (1921), 854
[13] Quoted ibid., 855.
[14] Ibid.
[15] Adrian Lyttelton, 'The National Question in Italy', in Mikuláš Teich and Roy Porter (eds), *The National Question in Europe in Historical Context* (Cambridge, 1993), p. 72.

man who was able to crush the regimes under which they had to live and to suffer. On him they focused their hopes and aspirations for the renewal of their nations and the rebirth of their erstwhile independent states, for a chance to take, at last, more control of their own lives.

In the case of the Poles these hopes seemed to be well founded. Revolutionary and Napoleonic France had fought the three eastern powers which had partitioned Poland among themselves. When, in 1807, Napoleon established the Duchy of Warsaw, strategic considerations in a wider European frame might have been foremost in his mind. The Poles, however, saw Napoleon's initiative as a first step towards the restitution of an independent Polish state. It was no wonder, therefore, that they glorified Napoleon as an ally, as the liberator of their country, and did everything to support him and to profit from his victories over Prussia, Austria, and Russia. Polish legions under the command of General Jan Henryk Dąbrowski accompanied Napoleon in Italy, and when the French Emperor invaded Russia in 1812 the Polish contingent made up more than a fifth of the *Grande Armée* (100,000–120,000 men). Their marching song, 'Poland will not be lost as long as we live', written by Józef Wybicki while in Italy in 1797, was later to become the unofficial and, then, in 1926, the official Polish national anthem. Its second, rather incoherent verse refers explicitly to Napoleon: 'We will cross the Vistula and Warta Rivers,/ we will be Poles,/ Bonaparte showed us how to win.'[16] But, alas, eventually all their hopes were dashed and the Poles did not win.

Some South Slavs shared the Polish national aspirations and, ultimately, also their disillusionment with Napoleon. Opposition to Austrian rule and Napoleon's creation of the Illyrian Provinces in 1809 seemed to indicate that a South Slav state was on the agenda. But there is, in fact, no convincing proof suggesting that Napoleon deliberately played the national card in this part of Europe. His alleged sympathies for the national cause and plans to establish a precursor state to twentieth-century Yugoslavia are basically products of the well known myth-making industry fuelled by later generations of historians and politicians. A brochure, published in Ljubljana in 1929 and entitled 'Napoleon in Illyria', illustrates this. There we read:

> The national interests of the Slovenes were in wonderful unison with the intentions which Napoleon had towards Illyria . . . He could transform the Slav areas into a barrier against German Vienna. The fostering of Slav nationality could have won him the sympathies of all the other South Slavs . . . The French were

---

[16] Printed in *National Anthems from Around the World* (Milwaukee, WI, 1995), p. 132.

> not concerned with suppressing our nationality, but they wished to stir in us a
> consciousness of our identity.[17]

In this the French obviously succeeded. The British historian R. W.
Seton-Watson was therefore right to say: 'In Croatia the real awakening
of national sentiment dates from the Napoleonic era.'[18] Napoleon's political priority, however, was to win 'the sympathies of all the other South
Slavs' and to include them in his European empire. This, by the way, did
not deter the Viennese authorities from using the administrative term
'Illyria' when the South Slav territories reverted to the Austrian Empire
after Napoleon's downfall, and the Emperor added the 'Kingdom of
Illyria' to all his other realms.[19]

There can be little doubt that Ireland also belongs to this second category of my classification. It is undeniable that the French Revolution
had an immediate and electrifying effect on the Irish—in the south as
well as in the north of the island. The Revolution triggered, first of all,
the founding of the United Irishmen in 1791. Marianne Elliott has
analysed developments up to 1798 in great detail in her book, *Partners in
Revolution*.[20] It seems that, after the failed uprising of 1798, the close
intellectual (and political) ties between Ireland and France, the 'external
mentor' (M. Elliott) of Catholic Ireland, were broken, and Napoleon
remained, after all, a somewhat shadowy figure for the Irish. There is
some literary evidence from Ireland, dated around 1809, which sees
Napoleon as the distant redeemer of the Irish. A poet from Co. Meath
wrote:

> Still, the leader will come from France without delay
> And he'll take the English down a peg or two—that's Bony.

In a broadsheet ballad we read:

> As Gráinne was wandering along the sea shore,
> For seventy weary long years and more,
> She saw Bonaparte coming far-off at sea,

---

[17] Anon., *Napoleon in Ilirija* (Ljubljana, 1929), pp. 23 and 26.
[18] R. W. Seton-Watson, *The Southern Slav Question and the Habsburg Monarchy* (London, 1911;
reprint New York, 1969), p. 26.
[19] See Daniel Baric, 'Der Illyrismus: Geschichte und Funktion eines übernationalen Begriffs im
Kroatien der ersten Hälfte des 19. Jahrhunderts und sein Nachklang', in Jacques Le Rider *et al.*
(eds), *Transnationale Gedächtnisorte in Zentraleuropa* (Innsbruck, 2002), pp. 125–40.
[20] Marianne Elliott, *Partners in Revolution: The United Irishmen and France* (New Haven, CT,
1982).

Saying row away, my boys, we'll clear the way
So pleasantly.[21]

But, taken at random, neither Edmund Curtis in his *History of Ireland*, published as early as 1936, nor Robert Kee in his massive *The Green Flag*, nor Roy Foster in his *Illustrated History of Ireland* of 1989, include Bonaparte in the indexes of their respective works.[22] The same applies to many modern authors writing on Irish history.

The situation in neighbouring Britain was, of course, totally different. This brings me to my third category of responses to Napoleon's towering presence in Europe at the beginning of the nineteenth century. The third category comprises countries that fought Napoleon's political ambitions, erected barriers against his territorial expansionism, and thereby—a welcome side-effect of all these efforts—pushed forward their own nation-building and the fostering of a national consciousness in the interests of political progress and modernity. The fostering of a national consciousness certainly happened in Britain with much unplanned success. The prevailing mood in Whitehall seems to have been that national feeling among the population of the kingdom was something to be encouraged wholeheartedly rather than opposed because it could reinforce the established order at home.

In her admirable analysis of the contemporary press, images, caricatures, and all forms of monarchical cult revolving around George III, Linda Colley traces manifestations of the terms 'Great Britain', 'British', and 'Britishness' in the eighteenth and early nineteenth centuries. Not surprisingly, she points to the artificial character of the concept of the 'British' nation.[23] During the prolonged conflict with revolutionary France and Napoleon, the imagined 'British' nation easily incorporated older loyalties and created a new and effective solidarity above them. In other words, there was clearly a progressive shift of emphasis away from English, Scottish, and Welsh and towards 'British' to describe the King's subjects and their pre-eminent political loyalty. George III himself 'gloried in the name of Britain'.[24]

[21] Gearóid Ó Tuathaigh, *Ireland before the Famine 1798–1848* (Dublin, 1972), pp. 66–7.
[22] Edmund Curtis, *A History of Ireland* (London, 1936; reprint 1965); Robert Kee, *The Green Flag: A History of Irish Nationalism* (London, 1972); R. F. Foster (ed.), *The Oxford Illustrated History of Ireland* (Oxford, 1989).
[23] Linda Colley, *Britons: Forging the Nation 1707–1837* (New Haven, CT, 1992).
[24] L. B. Namier, *The Structure of Politics at the Accession of George III*, 2 vols (London, 1929), vol. 1, p. 19.

According to Linda Colley it was the real or assumed threat of a Napoleonic invasion, in particular, which helped to construct a 'British' consciousness and a new 'British' identity comprising the English, Scots, and Welsh. 'It was training in arms under the auspices of the state', says Colley,

> that was the most common collective working-class experience in the late eighteenth and early nineteenth centuries, not labour in a factory, or membership of a radical political organisation or an illegal trade union. Here, as in Continental Europe, the pressures of war, rather than the experience of work or the example of political revolution, may have had the most obvious potential to change lives, ideas and expectations.[25]

The battle of Trafalgar in 1805 and the victory at Waterloo ten years later were decisive events in this lengthy, but rapidly accelerating process of building the new frame of mind, the new political orientation: the 'British' nation.

A footnote: the enormous impact that Napoleon had on the national consciousness of the King's subjects shaped the British capital itself and made it an enduring site of commemoration of this heroic epoch. In the years after Napoleon's defeat eleven places, roads, streets, and squares in London were named after Trafalgar, fourteen after Waterloo, twenty-nine after Lord Nelson, and thirty-eight after the Duke of Wellington.[26] Today's *London A–Z* reveals that two insignificant roads in the capital are named after Napoleon, but we can be pretty sure that they are named after the emperor Napoleon III: one road in Hackney, the other in Twickenham. Waterloo Bridge, which had been under construction as Strand Bridge since 1815, was named and opened in 1817; Trafalgar Square was laid out in 1829–41.[27]

There is convincing evidence that the British experience of nation-building triggered by revolutionary France and Napoleon's aggressive expansionism was shared, to some extent, by Russia. However, it is not always clear (in this and other cases) what the facts are and what is the

---

[25] Colley, *Britons*, p. 312. See also eadem, 'The Apotheosis of George III: Loyalty, Royalty and the British Nation, 1760–1820', *Past and Present*, 102 (1984), 94–129; Gerald Newman, *The Rise of English Nationalism: A Cultural History 1740–1830* (London, 1987). On the role of the arts in creating a British identity, see Holger Hoock, *The King's Artists: The Royal Academy of Arts and the Politics of British Culture 1760–1840* (Oxford, 2003).

[26] Dana Arnold, 'London Bridge and Its Symbolic Identity in the Regency Metropolis: The Dialectics of Civic and National Pride', in eadem (ed.), *The Metropolis and Its Image: Constructing Identities for London, c. 1750–1950* (Oxford, 1999), pp. 83–5.

[27] Rodney Mace, *Trafalgar Square: Emblem of Empire* (London, 1976).

result of later myth-making. The Russian historian Nikolai Karamsin (1766–1826), for example, published twelve volumes on Russian history between 1816 and 1829 to popularise his view of the 'patriotic war' of 1812 against Napoleon's invasion. The war was allegedly supported by the entire Russian population. In later years this view was hardly ever called into question by Russian historians.[28]

For Austria, on the other hand, the war against the usurper Napoleon could hardly be interpreted as a rising and strengthening of the 'nation'. There was no Austrian nation. Nevertheless, Archduke Charles, the Emperor's brother, paid tribute to the *Zeitgeist* and circumvented the problem by addressing the dominant ethnic group in the multi-ethnic monarchy. The underlying purpose of his appeal of April 1809, 'To the German nation', was, first, to stimulate general resistance to Napoleon and, second, to strengthen the traditional, charismatic rule of the Habsburg dynasty. Monarchy and national movement (the latter obviously restricted to the German-speaking Austrians in those years) were to form an alliance in the fight against Napoleon—with little success, as soon became apparent. When in 1860 a monument was unveiled on Vienna's *Heldenplatz* to commemorate Archduke Charles's victory at Aspern in 1809, its agitated style recalled a short-lived episode from the 'people's' war of liberation which by then had entered popular folklore. The monument celebrates Archduke Charles's bravery and military genius during the battle at Aspern. At a decisive moment in the fighting, the Archduke seized the flag of the *Zach* regiment, thus refuelling the fighting spirit of his troops, and led them to victory. The monument is a mixture between the traditional equestrian statue, almost a copy of Peter the Great's statue in St Petersburg (erected in 1782), and the grand gesture characteristic of so many national manifestations of the time, astonishingly reminiscent of Jacques-Louis David's great painting *Napoleon Crossing the Great St Bernard*. Significantly, it glorifies the aristocratic hero, not the people or the soldiers led into battle by Archduke Charles.

I shall conclude my broad survey of Napoleon's impact on the development of the national idea in Europe with a slight change of perspective. What do we know, we should ask, about Napoleon's vision of the European order in the nineteenth century? About fifteen years ago Stuart Woolf wrote *Napoleon's Integration of Europe*,[29] offering a then fashionable view which interpreted the short-lived Napoleonic empire as an early

---

[28] See Eugen Lemberg, *Nationalismus*, 2 vols, 2nd edn (Reinbek, 1967), vol. 1, pp. 230–1.
[29] Stuart Woolf, *Napoleon's Integration of Europe* (London, 1991).

manifestation of a united Europe, peaceful and cooperative—the vision
of a people living in a war-torn continent. What order did Napoleon have
in mind in a long-term perspective? What would a 'united Europe' have
meant in political terms if he had been able to shape it? Hardly a loosely
knit federation of modern and equal nation-states, a liberal *Europe des
patries*. More likely a string of French satellite states, to varying degrees
dependent on Napoleon's grace and favour, the much dreaded universal
monarchy, residing in and ruling over Europe from Paris.

All this again raises the question as to how Napoleon handled the new
and explosive concept of the nation and its role in the shaping of post-
revolutionary Europe. It has often been said that Napoleon, much to his
disadvantage, missed the chance to reconstruct Europe and put it on a
progressive political basis by resolutely exploiting the national idea. This
seems still to be true today. There is evidence that, occasionally, he played
with the national concept, flirting with it when he deemed it helpful in the
pursuit of his political and military strategies. After his victory at
Wagram, for instance, in May 1809, he appealed to the Hungarians and
promised them freedom from Austrian domination—evoking little
response in the Hungarian lands because his intentions were too obvious
and national feeling among the Hungarians was probably still in its
infancy.

In short, Napoleon never seriously or systematically took the emerging national aspirations into consideration as the basis for a new and stable political order in Europe: a community of free and equal nations,
perhaps under French spiritual and political leadership, but definitely not
under French tutelage. Maurice Hutt, in his biography of Napoleon, has
observed that whenever Napoleon talked about the 'sovereign people',
'national self-determination fell far short of the right to repudiate French
suzerainty'.[30] Not unlike his contemporaries, the statesmen at the
Congress of Vienna in 1814–15, Napoleon underestimated (or feared) the
forces which could emanate from the nation once it had been 'awakened'
and stirred into action.

Ultimately, therefore, national aspirations turned against Napoleon
and his rule over Europe, and helped substantially to bring him down,
instead of lending him support in consolidating his overstretched empire.
Only after Napoleon had definitely lost his game does he seem to have
shown a deeper interest in the national idea and its enormous political

---

[30] Maurice Hutt, *Napoleon* (Oxford, 1965), p. 59.

potential in the post-revolutionary world. From his exile on St Helena he let it be known that his *Grand Empire*, like the revolution of 1789, had had one purpose only: the liberation of the peoples and the creation of a Europe of free, equal, and cooperating nations. It was only because of a series of unhappy mistakes and misjudgements, according to the deposed and exiled Emperor, now mournfully reflecting on his political career, that this message had not reached the European nations. However, this was said after the Congress of Vienna had dashed the political dreams of the emerging national movements. And it was said at a location that was far removed from Europe, lost somewhere in the vast expanses of the South Atlantic. But, then, hardly anyone bothered to listen.

Cosmopolitanism, Patriotism, Nationalism

SIEGFRIED WEICHLEIN

MODERN GERMAN MASTER-NARRATIVES OF HISTORIOGRAPHY love biblical language. Hans-Ulrich Wehler, Heinrich A. Winkler, and Thomas Nipperdey all start with a secular version of the first line of the gospel of St John:[1] 'In the beginning was no revolution' (Wehler); 'In the beginning was the Reich'; and, with a certain twist, 'At the beginning was Napoleon'.[2] The ironic twist is that the left liberal historians Wehler and Winkler use more biblical language than Nipperdey. Like St John they tell a story from its very principle: 'in principio' (John 1:1 Vulgata) should not be understood as 'in initio', the chronological beginning. Nipperdey, by contrast, seems to read 'in initio'. The beginning, for him, is a point in time, whereas Wehler and Winkler argue from a systematic standpoint. But the beginning of what? All three authors are interested in modern German national history, its origins, highlights, and its catastrophic climax. All three combine biblical language with national historiography.

With the French Revolution the 'nation' entered a new phase as a model for political order that replaced corporate societies and triggered a large-scale process of emancipation and modernisation in European societies. To be sure, the nation had already figured prominently in early modern German history. The humanist Ulrich von Hutten and others used the term 'nation' to convey the differences between various central European countries. Despite its growing importance, the nation remained a cultural concept. It was affiliated with cultural stereotypes and was used as a designation of origin, mostly for students at foreign universities. The

---

[1] John 1:1 is itself a variation on the first line of the Bible, Genesis 1:1.
[2] Hans-Ulrich Wehler, *Deutsche Gesellschaftsgeschichte*, 4 vols, 2nd edn (Munich, 1989), vol. 1, p. 35; Heinrich A. Winkler, *Der lange Weg nach Westen: Deutsche Geschichte*, 2 vols (Munich, 2000), vol. 1, p. 5; Thomas Nipperdey, *Deutsche Geschichte 1800–1866: Bürgerwelt und starker Staat*, 6th edn (Munich, 1993), p. 11. In this text 'Reich' refers to a specific set of practices and institutions, identified with the 'Holy Roman Empire of the German Nation'.

Proceedings of the British Academy, **134**, 77–99. © The British Academy 2006.

concept of the 'nation' was rarely used for self-expression, and never to describe the political order. Until the eighteenth century the political order in central Europe was organised along other lines, such as the state, the Reich, the monarchy, or the republic.[3]

That changed dramatically between the Seven Years War and around 1800. Despite its thorough universalism, the German Enlightenment combined universalism with patriotism, a rather unlikely combination in the twentieth century. For most educated authors in the age of Enlightenment, cosmopolitanism and patriotism were not opposites, but complementary. How, then, did contemporaries in the late eighteenth century conceptualise cosmopolitanism, patriotism, and nationalism, and relate them? How did they explain the complicity of cosmopolitanism and patriotism?

This essay will outline different answers to these questions relating to the period between the Seven Years War and around 1800. The arguments for a collectively shared identity were divided not between cosmopolitanism and patriotism, but rather between different modes of argument and between the different political levels with which patriotic loyalty could be associated. Patriotism could be projected on to different political levels: the Reich, the states, and the local community. Cosmopolitanism and patriotism provided the rhetoric for the same social groups. They shared a civic moral code. The German debate on patriotism in the Old Reich centred around two concepts: first, the relatively modern and future-orientated doctrine of natural law and, second, a more historical and cultural approach positing a unity in the past based on imperial corporate institutions. Although differing in their approach, the two arguments had much in common. Patriotism was a way of enhancing the social role of the rising German educated bourgeoisie. Communications networks played a crucial role in the enhancement of social self-esteem and the dissemination of a civic moral code. Patriotic language articulated the enlightened concept of autonomy in the German political context. The French Revolution incriminated the combination of patriotism and cosmopolitanism, since patriotic loyalty was now directed to a

---

[3] Wolfgang Hardtwig, 'Ulrich von Hutten: Zum Verhältnis von Individuum, Stand und Nation in der Reformationszeit', in idem, *Nationalismus und Bürgerkultur in Deutschland 1500–1914: Ausgewählte Aufsätze* (Göttingen, 1994), pp. 15–33; idem, 'Vom Elitebewußtsein zur Massenbewegung: Frühformen des Nationalismus in Deutschland 1500–1840', in ibid., pp. 34–54; Herfried Münkler, Hans Grünberger, and Kathrin Meyer (eds), *Nationenbildung: Die Nationalisierung Europas im Diskurs humanistischer Intellektueller. Italien und Deutschland* (Berlin, 1998).

morally aggrandised state apparatus and its constitution. None the less, moral universalism was a key factor in nineteenth-century nationalism.

Enlightened Patriotism

A myriad of tiny states in the Old Reich made patriotism and cosmopolitanism attractive to the rising educated bourgeoisie. Both concepts offered external points of reference and emphasised anti-absolutist policies. It was not only the French Enlightenment that served the anti-absolutist needs of the rising middle classes, but also patriotism. Patriotism became part of the enlightened discourse and sounded progressive. After the Seven Years War, an enlightened civic patriotism was *de rigueur* for the upper bourgeoisie.[4] Patriotism expanded the political imagination beyond the scope of small and medium-sized German states. It opened new dimensions of political legitimation and argument, thereby ideologically relieving the German bourgeoisie from the pressure of absolutist monarchism. Patriotism also incorporated a civic value system and underpinned the social role and self-esteem of the rising bourgeoisie. This civic patriotism centred around a vision of enlightened legislation that went along with a relatively modern moral code.

The nation was seen as a unit in which the standards of enlightened thought had been met. These standards encompassed progress, reform, mutual recognition, human rights, and the individual rights of every citizen.[5] These standards went against absolutism, but not against forms of enlightened monarchical government; rather they reinforced 'reform monarchism', in which the enlightened sovereign was seen as the principal agent of reform. This civic patriotism had a strong anti-absolutist and anti-aristocratic touch. Citizens gained merit by serving the common weal. The absolutist state dominated by the aristocracy denied non-nobles this kind of service. Not only was this contrary to the concept of citizenship, but it also damaged the state itself. For Thomas Abbt, a

---

[4] For enlightened patriotism, see Matthew Levinger, *Enlightened Nationalism: The Transformation of Prussian Political Culture, 1806–1848* (Oxford, 2000); idem, 'The Prussian Reform Movement and the Rise of Enlightened Nationalism', in Philip G. Dwyer (ed.), *The Rise of Prussia, 1700–1830* (Harlow, 2000), pp. 259–77.

[5] See Rudolf Vierhaus, '"Patriotismus"—Begriff und Realität einer moralisch-politischen Haltung', in idem (ed.), *Deutsche patriotische und gemeinnützige Gesellschaften* (Munich, 1980), pp. 9–29, at pp. 21ff.

modern citizenry and service for the fatherland became indistinguishable. Both were directed against the absolutist state.[6]

This kind of civic patriotism was not defined by birthplace. Its strong rationalism allowed patriotism to flourish wherever the individual saw fit. The influence of the rational doctrine of natural law and of the Enlightenment in general on the concept of the fatherland can be seen in Abbt's patriotic battle-cry of 1761: 'On Dying for the Fatherland'. He wrote this pamphlet in Frankfurt (Oder), a few miles from Kunersdorf, where two years previously Prussia had suffered a crushing defeat by the Russian army and was on the verge of extinction. Thomas Abbt, a lawyer and native of the southern imperial city of Ulm, opted for Prussia as his fatherland. The fatherland was for him not a question of birthplace, but rather the result of a decision made by a free citizen. 'If by accident of birth or of my own free will I am united with a state to whose healing laws I submit, laws that do not deprive me of any more of my freedom than is necessary for the good of the state as a whole, then I will call that state my fatherland.'[7] For Abbt, Prussia, the kingdom of Frederick II, was the most favourable to free citizens; it provided freedom and had an enlightened king, setting it apart from the narrow-mindedness of the imperial cities in southern Germany and from absolutist rule in France. His mode of argument was based on universalist principles, not on historical institutions. Abbt and other enlightened patriots were lawyers. They favoured a rational collective identity based on equal treatment of every individual. Civic egalitarianism was the cornerstone of this kind of patriotism, which was directed towards the state.[8]

Prussia, not Austria or France, became the homeland of the modern reformers. Its monarchy and legislation were widely praised for having realised the principles of natural law jurisprudence and good government. Abbt and others saw unity as something in the future. Patriotic love for the fatherland did not only motivate people to die for their fatherland. It was also a perfect way to overcome one's own death. To die for the fatherland would eternalise the individual in collective memory. As the motto for his book Abbt chose a quotation from the British statesman

---

[6] See Thomas Abbt, *Vom Verdienst* (Goslar, 1766; reprint Königstein, 1978); also Johann Georg Heinrich Feder, *Untersuchungen über den menschlichen Willen* (Lemgo, 1782).

[7] See Thomas Abbt, 'Vom Tode für das Vaterland (1761)', in Johannes Kunisch (ed.), *Aufklärung und Kriegserfahrung: Klassische Zeitzeugen zum Siebenjährigen Krieg* (Frankfurt am Main, 1996), pp. 589–650, at pp. 600f.

[8] For the enlightened rational and state-centred approach to patriotism, see Eugen Lemberg, *Nationalismus*, 2 vols (Reinbek, 1964), vol. 1, pp. 86–102.

and essayist Joseph Addison: 'What pity is it that we can die but once to serve our country.'[9] Dying for the fatherland was portrayed as a choice for progress. To die for Prussia would secure eternal remembrance for the individual.

Several things follow from this point. First, Abbt's construction of eternal memory and individual death for the fatherland reflected the intimate relationship between religion, pietism, and nationalism in the eighteenth century.[10] Second, Abbt interpreted personal loyalty as subjective, not as objective. Although objectively born in Ulm, Abbt owed his patriotic loyalty not to his birthplace, but to a modern enlightened state. He loosened the ties between birthplace and patriotism. Abbt's patriotism was not an expression of regionalism. Nevertheless, he did not put forward an individual argument, but a structural one. The state became the object of loyalty. 'Dying for the fatherland' was to die for a unit that deserved his loyalty in principle. Abbt defended state patriotism, not so much national patriotism. A decade after Abbt wrote his pamphlet, Prussia took part in the partitions of Poland, depriving the Poles of their state and forcing many to submit to Prussian rule. The Prussian idea of the state was at the centre of a supranational loyalty that was not limited to a specific cultural, ethnic, or linguistic group. It informed the attitude of the Prussian monarchy towards its subjects throughout the nineteenth century. King Frederick William III began his proclamation 'To my people' on 17 March 1813 as follows:

> Brandenburgers, Prussians, Silesians, Pomeranians, Lithuanians! You know what you have suffered for the past ten years; you know what your miserable fate will be, if we do not end the struggle that is now beginning with honour. Remember the time of antiquity, the great *Kurfürsten*, the great Frederick.[11]

For Thomas Abbt state patriotism was a feature not only of the Prussian monarchy, but of monarchies in general. Love of the fatherland

---

[9] See Abbt, 'Vom Tode für das Vaterland', p. 589 (Addison quotation); Christoph Prignitz, *Vaterlandsliebe und Freiheit: Deutscher Patriotismus von 1750 bis 1850* (Wiesbaden, 1981), pp. 7–38.

[10] For the impact of pietism on patriotism and nationalism, see Gerhard Kaiser, *Pietismus und Patriotismus im literarischen Deutschland: Ein Beitrag zum Problem der Säkularisation*, 2nd edn (Frankfurt am Main, 1973).

[11] Proclamation 'To my people', quoted in Levinger, *Enlightened Nationalism*, p. 64. For the tradition of Prussian state patriotism, see Ulrich Scheuner, 'Der Staatsgedanke Preußens (1965)', in Otto Büsch and Wolfgang Neugebauer (eds), *Moderne preußische Geschichte 1648–1947: Eine Anthologie*, 3 vols (Berlin, 1981), vol. 1, pp. 26–73; Ernst Rudolf Huber, 'Die friderizianische Staatsidee und das Vaterland', in idem, *Nationalstaat und Verfassungsstaat: Studien zur Geschichte der modernen Staatsidee* (Stuttgart, 1965), pp. 30–47.

characterised all monarchies. He linked patriotism to monarchies and broke with a long tradition in political theory that saw patriotism thriving only in republics. For Abbt's opponent, Johann Georg Zimmermann, patriotism required citizens, and citizens could be found only in republics.[12] For an enlightened state patriot like Abbt the monarch and the fatherland were mutually inclusive. This personalised the fatherland and depersonalised the monarch. People should honour the king in the fatherland and the fatherland in the king. The two were brought together by the rule of law.[13]

State patriotism was not restricted to Prussia. The Vienna professor of *Policeywissenschaft* (the science of government), Joseph von Sonnenfels, put forward the same argument for Austria. He came from a cameralistic tradition, conceptualising politics in purely secular and pragmatic terms. The welfare of its citizens was the state's principal political aim. Moral reform and moral progress were at the heart of his patriotism. Both could be achieved by enlightened state legislation. The people in turn owed loyalty to the state. Sonnenfels, like Abbt, equated fatherland, state, and legislation. For him the fatherland was:

– the country in which one had taken up permanent residence,
– the laws which the inhabitants of this country obey,
– the form of government which the laws prescribe,
– the other people who live in this country,
– the other people who enjoy the same rights.[14]

Nevertheless, the Habsburg dynasty and the Austrian government failed to foster state patriotism within its highly diverse population. People felt they were German, Czech, Polish, Hungarian, Croatian, etc., but not Austrian. Austrian state patriotism could be found in the upper echelons of the military, the bureaucracy, and the Catholic hierarchy. Its social reach was restricted to Habsburg state machinery and the dynasty.

---

[12] See Johann Georg Zimmermann, 'Von dem Nationalstolze' (2nd edn 1760; 1st edn 1758), in Fritz Brüggemann (ed.), *Der Siebenjährige Krieg im Spiegel der zeitgenössischen Literatur* (Darmstadt, 1966), pp. 9–94.

[13] See Abbt, 'Vom Tode für das Vaterland', p. 636.

[14] '— das Land, worin man seinen beständigen Sitz genommen,—die Gesetze, welchen die Bewohner des Landes gehorchen,—die darin festgesetzte Regierungsform,—die Mitbewohner dieses Landes,—die Mitgenossen derselben Rechte'. See Joseph von Sonnenfels, *Über die Liebe des Vaterlandes* (1771; reprint Königstein, 1979).

Historical Patriotism

Enlightened nationalism, with its focus on rational loyalty, legislation, and Prusso-centrism, had intellectual opponents. For Abbt's opponent, Friedrich Carl von Moser, the entire German people shared a common constitution, legal institutions, and an emperor who guaranteed freedom from absolutist rule. Imperial courts worked as a safeguard against absolutist rule. The problem was not how to get rid of these institutions, but rather how to revitalise them. For Moser these safeguards against absolutist rule had worked admirably in the past and deserved renewed attention. In his view, therefore, the national spirit lay in the past, not in the future. In his opening remarks on the German national spirit he linked national unity to the Reich and its institutions. Unity was preserved through the Reich, and unity secured freedom:

> We are one people, with one name and language, under one common head, under common laws that determine our constitution, rights and duties, committed to a common great interest in freedom, unified to pursue this purpose in a National Assembly that is more than one hundred years old, Europe's premier empire in terms of internal power and strength, whose royal crowns gleam on German heads.[15]

This ideal lay in the past. Unlike Samuel von Pufendorf, who interpreted the imperial constitution as a monster ('monstro simile'), Moser saw it as a mystery ('ein Räthsel politischer Verfassung'). Admittedly the history of the Reich was a list of failures. He suggested that it was

> the booty of the neighbours, the object of their scorn, distinguished in the history of the world, disunited among ourselves, powerless because of our divisions, strong enough to harm ourselves, unable to save ourselves, insensitive to the honour of our name, indifferent to the dignity of the law, jealous of our ruler, suspicious of each other, incoherent on principles, violent in their execution, a great but a despised people, one that is potentially happy, but in reality, pitiable.[16]

---

[15] 'Wir sind Ein Volk, von Einem Nahmen und Sprache, unter Einem gemeinsamen Oberhaupt, unter Einerley unsere Verfassung, Rechte und Pflichten bestimmenden Gesetzen, zu Einem gemeinschaftlichen grossen Interesse der Freyheit verbunden, auf Einer mehr als hundertjährigen Nationalversammlung zu diesem wichtigen Zweck vereinigt, an innerer Macht und Stärke das erste Reich in Europa, dessen Königscronen auf Deutschen Häuptern glänzen.' See Friedrich Carl von Moser, *Von dem deutschen Nationalgeist* (Frankfurt am Main, 1765), p. 5.
[16] 'ein Raub der Nachbarn, ein Gegenstand ihrer Spöttereyen, ausgezeichnet in der Geschichte der Welt, uneinig unter uns selbst, kraftlos durch unsere Trennungen, stark genug, uns selbst zu schaden, ohnmächtig, uns zu retten, unempfindlich gegen die Ehre unseres Namens, gleichgültig gegen die Würde der Gesetze, eifersüchtig gegen unser Oberhaupt, mißtrauisch untereinander, unzusammenhängend in Grundsätzen, gewaltthätig in deren Ausführung, ein grosses und

The miserable condition of his people was the result of a lack of insti-
tutional continuity. For the imperial lawyer Friedrich Carl von Moser,
institutions like the Imperial Chamber Court (*Reichskammergericht*) in
Wetzlar, the Court Tribunal (*Hofgericht*) in Vienna, and the Imperial Diet
(*Reichstag*) in Regensburg stood for freedom and justice. These institutions visibly represented the national unity of the German people. For
Moser the Seven Years War signified a dramatic decline in national identity. He deplored the rift in the imperial institutions caused by the
recently established kingdom of Prussia. Moser and the more conserva-
tively orientated writers of the late eighteenth century saw the structural
unity of the body politic as under attack from a new sort of despotism
whose strongholds lay particularly in Prussia. Military national law
(*militärisches Staatsrecht*) saw military society, not national society or the
imperial corporate institutions as the organising centre of state legislation. The bond between the Reich, the people, and legislation was thereby
cut. The nation was a 'community of justice'.[17] Under pressure from the
military, historical institutions such as the imperial courts had been abandoned. The absolutism of strong states such as the Hohenzollern monarchy in particular endangered the historical equilibrium of the Reich that
had always secured the common weal.[18] Only the reawakening of the
national spirit could bring about a change for the better. For Thomas
Abbt, as for Friedrich Carl von Moser, individuals did not constitute the
nation or the *patria*. Neither writer subscribed to the modern concept of
the representation of individual citizens, *repraesentatio singulariter*. Both
adhered to the tradition of *repraesentatio in toto*, either by the monarch
or by imperial institutions.[19]

Historical continuity and patriotic loyalty could be associated with
different political levels in the Old Reich: with the city, the state, and the
Reich. Justus Möser, a lawyer from the northern town of Osnabrück,

gleichwohl verachtetes, ein in der Möglichkeit glückliches, aber in der That bedauernswürdiges
Volk'. Moser, *Von dem deutschen Nationalgeist*, p. 5.
[17] See James Sheehan, *German History 1770–1866* (Oxford, 1989), p. 18.
[18] See Matthias Bohlender, 'Metamorphosen des Gemeinwohls: Von der Herrschaft guter
polizey zur Regierung durch Freiheit und Sicherheit', in Herfried Münkler and Harald Bluhm
(eds), *Gemeinwohl und Gemeinsinn: Historische Semantiken politischer Leitbegriffe* (Berlin, 2001),
pp. 247–74, at p. 258.
[19] See Eberhard Schmitt, 'Repraesentatio in toto und repraesentatio singulariter: Zur Frage
nach dem Zusammenbruch des französischen Ancien régime und der Durchsetzung moderner
parlamentarischer Theorie und Praxis im Jahr 1789', *Historische Zeitschrift*, 213 (1971), 529–76.

refused to restrict the concept of patriotism to the supra-state level.[20] Instead, he fervently argued for loyalty to his home town of Osnabrück. He even wrote a multi-volume history of Osnabrück.[21] Although often regarded as an adversary of the Enlightenment, Möser did not argue theologically. His political concepts were thoroughly secular, combining historical identity with modern loyalty towards legislation. He rejected the idea that reform would come from monarchist powers. Not a representative of anti-enlightened thought, Möser vehemently opposed rational universalism which, he believed, endangered liberty.[22] The reach of historical patriotism went beyond the supra-state and the state level. It was a socially attractive idea for local elites to foster local loyalty and thereby make it competitive with state or even imperial loyalty.

The difference beween enlightened and historical patriotism was not whether patriotism was rational or not. Indeed, patriotism was rational in both concepts. The difference lay in their notion of rationality. For historical patriotism, rationality meant continuity with the past, whereas for civic patriotism it was linked to natural law jurisprudence and universalism. Enlightened and historical patriotism did not argue for any kind of exclusiveness or for a hierarchical patriotism in which one *patria* ranked higher than another. Nevertheless the two concepts were profoundly different. In everyday life they were associated either with Prussia or with the Reich, either with the enlightened King Frederick II or with the Emperor in Vienna. This rift between the modern rational and the historical corporate concept of the nation divided the German bourgeoisie. Goethe's family in Frankfurt (Main) was one of those in which this antagonism divided family members. Young family members—the young Johann Wolfgang among them—thought *fritzisch* and were Prussia-orientated, whereas the older generation in the imperial city of Frankfurt were supporters of the old imperial institutions.[23]

---

[20] For Justus Möser, see Jonathan B. Knudsen, *Justus Möser and the German Enlightenment* (Cambridge, 1986).

[21] See Justus Möser, *Osnabrückische Geschichte* (1768), in *Sämtliche Werke*, ed. Akademie der Wissenschaften Göttingen, 12 vols (Oldenbourg, 1943), vol. 1.

[22] See Justus Möser, 'Der jetzige Hang zu allgemeinen Gesetzen und Verordnungen ist der gemeinen Freiheit gefährlich (1772)', in Eckart Pankoke (ed.), *Gesellschaftslehre* (Frankfurt am Main, 1991), pp. 39–44; William F. Sheldon, 'Patriotismus bei Justus Möser', in Rudolf Vierhaus (ed.), *Deutsche patriotische und gemeinnützige Gesellschaften* (Munich, 1980), pp. 31–49.

[23] See Johann Wolfgang Goethe, *Aus meinem Leben: Dichtung und Wahrheit. Erster Teil. Zweites Buch*, in idem, *Werke*, Weimarer Ausgabe (Munich, 1987), vol. 26, p. 71.

What Enlightened and Historical Patriotism had in Common

Despite their hostile rhetoric, the two positions had much in common which typified German political culture on the brink of the French Revolution. The most important common feature was first that they both engaged in a moral discourse on politics that was characteristic of the German educated bourgeoisie. Their patriotism often went along with the Prussian *raison d'état*. The idea of a *Nationalerziehung*, a moral education of the German people, was common among German intellectuals in the second half of the eighteenth century. Second, the social ideas of the emergent bourgeoisie resonated well with the demand for improvement and education. Patriots of all sorts—state patriots and imperial patriots for the Reich as well—demanded political engagement. To serve the state and the monarchy reinforced the civic self-esteem of the middle classes. The universalist concept of patriotism helped to advance civic society where the influence of the rising middle classes could be felt. Conversely, civic state patriotism and cosmopolitanism shared the sense of being bourgeois. They both appealed to civic selflessness and public service, as Rudolf Vierhaus has pointed out.[24]

Third, both concepts shared the view that reform was to be achieved from above, not below. Neither historical corporate patriotism nor the rational, state-centred version supported a real empowerment of the German bourgeoisie. Instead they buttressed its subservience to state authority. Intellectual patriotism did not demand participation in state affairs; rather, it legitimised bureaucratic demands on its citizens.[25] The primary aim of the patriotic citizen was not participation but freedom. 'Even in a state that is not in line with his ideas, the patriot behaves as if he were in his ideal fatherland.'[26] Patriotic loyalty, seen from this angle, meant especially a trust in the capacity of the state to guarantee freedom and individual property. This lack of participation explains the relatively small degree of politicisation among the broader German public. Without the demand for participation, the bourgeois patriot was a subject. German subjects did demand reform from their monarchs, but they

---

[24] See Vierhaus, 'Patriotismus', pp. 23f.

[25] Eckhart Hellmuth, *Naturrechtsphilosophie und bürokratischer Wertehorizont: Studien zur preußischen Geistes- und Sozialgeschichte des 18. Jahrhunderts* (Göttingen, 1985).

[26] 'Der Patriot betätigt sich auch in dem seiner Vorstellung konträren Staat so, als ob er in seinem Idealvaterland wäre.' Kaiser, *Pietismus und Patriotismus*, p. 226; Georg Schmidt, *Geschichte des Alten Reiches: Staat und Nation in der Frühen Neuzeit* (Munich, 1999), p. 311.

did not declare themselves to be the nation, as the French *Assemblée nationale* did in May 1789.

Patriotism calmed down the demand for political reform, regarding the monarchies as the principal agent of reform. The doctrine of natural law as taught by German cameralism and 'state sciences' (*Staatswissenschaften*) at the leading universities of the time, Göttingen and Halle, led thus to the further empowerment of the state, and not of the middle classes or the people in general. Moreover, the rationality of the state comprised the rationality of the monarch. Obedience to the state therefore meant loyalty to the monarch, although not on the basis of his 'divine right'. The monarch was no longer separate (*absolutus*) from society, society being the object of his reign. Rather, he encorporated the rational ideal of society. His obligation was to serve justice. But this did not entail any participation on the part of the people. Enlightened policies that deserved the loyalty of the state's citizens involved a host of other things: population policy, poor relief, the fight against idleness and vagrancy, the promotion of agriculture, trade, industry and mining, supervision of the banking and credit sectors, domestic and foreign trade, control of discipline, education, security, and protection against threats such as fire and water.[27] Hence the obedience of the citizens to bureaucratic demands was not a free decision, but an absolutely necessary consequence of the rational system of good government.

Patriotism, therefore, did not serve oppositional, critical, or even revolutionary purposes. It favoured a passive attitude towards the state above an active one. Participation meant being part of the state, being its object, not its subject. Natural law jurisprudence did not foster an active sense of citizenship. It required the loyalty of subjects, not of active citizens. An active citizenry developed neither from enlightened nor from historical patriotism, but from the market and early capitalism. German enlightened authors did not include individual freedom in the concept of the nation. The people proper did not constitute a relevant field of politics. Rather, it was a field for politics.[28] Participation was understood as a patriotic virtue. Citizens were to engage *for* the state, not *in* state affairs. In Germany, cosmopolitan patriotism of all sorts empowered the state and its bureaucracy through its moral code and rhetoric. It was reform

---

[27] See Ulrich Scheuner, 'Die Staatszwecke und die Entwicklung der Verwaltung im deutschen Staat des 18. Jahrhunderts', in Gerd Kleinheyer (ed.), *Beiträge zur Rechtsgeschichte*: *Gedächtnisschrift Hermann Conrad* (Paderborn, 1979), pp. 467–89, at p. 485.

[28] See Bohlender, 'Metamorphosen des Gemeinwohls', pp. 263 and 267.

orientated and had a conservative tendency to expect reform from the monarchies. Patriotism did not run against the state or the monarchies. Unlike the political function of the natural law doctrine in Western societies, eudaemonism and welfare patriotism served as powerful tools for securing state control over society in Germany, not as an opposition ideology for human rights and an active citizenry against state supervision.[29]

But this was not the whole story. Although cosmopolitan patriotism constructed a strong connection between state and society in Germany, this did not mean that the state possessed full sovereignty over society. On the contrary, sovereignty as one of the key concepts of politics was no longer reserved for the monarch as an individual. It was transferred to the state and was thereby transformed into state sovereignty, a process we can trace back to the seventeenth century. Indeed, it was not the sovereign power of the monarch that ruled over people, but rather the 'spirit' (*Geist*, *esprit*) as the totality of all relations within society. Montesquieu's *Esprit des lois* was widely read and commented on. It triggered a debate on patriotism in 1763. The question asked was: who could represent this totality, the monarch, a constitution, or a parliament? In late eighteenth-century German political culture, it was the monarch who represented this totality, but no longer necessarily so. Before he could govern, he himself had to obey the rules of this social totality. The result was a clear loss of sovereignty for the monarch as a person (*Entsouveränisierung politischer Macht*). He had lost his control over social communication in society, which had moved a step further towards autonomy.[30] 'Wenn Souverainetät höchste Gewaltübung ist, so gebührt sie weder dem Kaiser noch dem Reich, sondern dem Gesetz' (If sovereignty is the highest use of force, then it is the preserve neither of the Emperor nor the Reich, but of the law) was one of the arguments which the German *Fürstenbund* used against the Emperor in Vienna during the 1780s. People owed loyalty not so much to the monarch or the Reich as to the law.[31] A loss of sovereignty for the monarch as an individual meant a relative increase in importance for society. The abstract concept of political sovereignty corresponded to a more abstract understanding of society. In 1760 Johann Heinrich von Justi was aware of two 'oberste Grundgewalten' (highest

---

[29] See Ernst Troeltsch, 'Naturrecht und Humanität in der Weltpolitik', in idem, *Schriften zur Politik und Kulturphilosophie (1918–1923)*, ed. Gangolf Hübinger (Berlin, 2002), pp. 493–512.
[30] See Bohlender, 'Metamorphosen des Gemeinwohls', p. 256.
[31] See *Darstellung des Fürstenbundes* (Leipzig, 1787), pp. 102 and 110; Schmidt, *Geschichte des Alten Reiches*, p. 312.

fundamental powers): one was the 'tätige oberste Gewalt, welche durch die Grundverfassungen des Staats eingeführt ist' (active highest power, which is introduced by the fundamental constitutions of the state); the other was the 'Grundgewalt des gesamten Volkes, aus welcher jene entstehet' (the fundamental power of the whole people, which gives rise to the former).[32]

Communication, Patriotism, and Cosmopolitanism

How did society fit into this understanding of patriotism? The *Policeystaat* was enlightened and communication flourished. The general public of readers and writers was a force of its own. It became the subject of political and philosophical discourses. Johann Gottfried Herder was the theoretician of the public as a communicative network. By re-evaluating communication he integrated patriotism into a cosmopolitan worldview. Herder based his definition of nationhood and fatherland on communication and the public audience. He argued that the nation was a community of shared communication based on a common language. Language and communication could work as an integrative force, but communication was restricted to a certain linguistic group. While uniting a people, communication could also set a people apart from others. It could be denounced as a divisive rather than a unifying force. Herder did not subscribe to any kind of trans-linguistic universalism. The cosmopolitan Herder defended the socialising quality of specific languages. Linguistic prejudice thereby acquired a new meaning:

> If inclinations and circles of happiness touch upon each other in any two nations, it is called prejudice! Mob behaviour! Limited nationalism! Prejudice is good, in its time, for it makes people happy. It brings peoples together at their centre point, sets them more firmly on their stem, makes them more flourishing in their manner, more passionate and also happier in their inclinations and purposes. The most unknowing, prejudiced nation is, in this respect, often the first: the age of foreign wishful thinking and flights of fancy already indicates illness, flatulence, unhealthy bloating, premonition of death![33]

---

[32] Johann Heinrich Gottlob von Justi, *Natur und Wesen der Staaten als die Quelle aller Regierungswissenschaften und Gesezze* (1760) (Mittau, 1771; reprint Aalen, 1969), pp. 99f.; Hans Boldt, 'Souveränität', in Reinhart Koselleck, Otto Brunner, and Werner Conze (eds), *Geschichtliche Grundbegriffe: Historisches Lexikon zur politisch-sozialen Sprache in Deutschland*, 8 vols (Stuttgart, 1990), vol. 6, pp. 1–154, at p. 126.

[33] 'So jede zwo Nationen, deren Neigungen und Kreise der Glückseligkeit sich stoßen—man nennts Vorurteil! Pöbelei! eingeschränkten Nationalism! Das Vorurteil ist gut, zu seiner Zeit:

To our ears this itself sounds nationalist. How could Herder simultaneously defend national prejudice and subscribe to enlightened cosmopolitanism? Three different aspects explain this *coincidentia oppositorum*:

1. Herder was a pastor and his model for the socialising impact of communication was the Bible. In his answer to the question 'Do we still have the public of the [biblical] Israelites?' he had in mind the socialising quality of a divine revelation to all mankind:

    > The ties of tongue and ear create a public. . . . Anyone who was brought up in the same language, who learned to pour out his heart and soul in it belongs to the *people of this language*. . . . By means of language, a nation is brought up and educated, by means of language it learns to love order and honour, it becomes obedient, polite, sociable, famous, hard-working, and powerful. Anyone who despises the language of his nation dishonours its noblest public; he becomes the most dangerous murderer of its spirit, its internal and external fame, its inventions, its finer points of politeness and diligence.[34]

    Taking religious community-building through divine revelation as a model, he maintained the relevance of human communication *a fortiori*. If God unites a religious community through his word and divine revelation, then human communication is to follow this example and unite through communication. Language embodied more than just particular propositions; it communicated ideas and the 'soul' of a particular people.

2. His defence of the specific community reflected the intensification of social communication in Germany in the decades before the French Revolution, the founding of new universities, and the rise

---

denn es macht glücklich. Es drängt Völker zu ihrem Mittel-Punkte zusammen, macht sie fester auf ihrem Stamme, blühender in ihrer Art, brünstiger und also auch glückseliger in ihren Neigungen und Zwecken. Die unwissendste, vorurteilendste Nation ist in solchem Betracht oft die erste: das Zeitalter fremder Wunschwanderungen und ausländischer Hoffnungsfahrten ist schon Krankheit, Blähung, ungesunde Fülle, Ahnung des Todes!' Johann Gottfried Herder, *Auch eine Philosophie der Geschichte zur Bildung der Menschheit*, ed. Hans-Georg Gadamer (Frankfurt am Main, 1967), p. 46.

[34] 'Das Band der Zunge und des Ohrs knüpft ein Publikum. . . . Wer in derselben Sprache erzogen ward, wer sein Herz in sie schütten, seine Seele in ihr ausdrücken lernte, der gehört zum *Volk dieser Sprache.* . . . mittelst der Sprache wird eine Nation erzogen und gebildet, mittelst der Sprache wird sie Ordnung- und Ehrliebend, folgsam, gesittet, umgänglich, berühmt, fleißig und mächtig. Wer die Sprache seiner Nation verachtet, entehrt ihr edelstes Publikum; er wird ihres Geistes, ihres inneren und äußeren Ruhms, ihrer Erfindungen, ihrer feineren Sittlichkeit und Betriebsamkeit gefährlichster Mörder.' Johann Gottfried Herder, Briefe zur Beförderung der Humanität, Fünfte Sammlung, 57. Brief, in idem, *Werke in Zehn Bänden*, ed. Hans Dietrich Irmscher, 10 vols (Frankfurt am Main, 1991), vol. 7, pp. 304f.

of print capitalism that favoured stronger communicative bonds within a linguistic group. In the first half of the eighteenth century, only 10 per cent of all Germans read journals and pamphlets. By the end of the century this group had more than doubled in size. In 1800 the community of readers (and writers) comprised about 25 per cent of all Germans.[35] The rise of a general audience was triggered by the unprecedented growth in the publishing of books, journals, and newspapers. Around 1780, Prussia was said to be run by the king, Frederick II, and the publisher Friedrich Nicolai.[36] The rise of a reading audience and the growth of newspapers and a literate public was seen as a characteristic of the Enlightenment.

3. German patriotism shared the mutual inclusiveness of cosmopolitanism and patriotism with Montesquieu's *De l'esprit des lois* (1748). Unlike others, Montesquieu linked the national character not only to climate and geography, but also to politics and the constitutional development of a people. For him a nation did not arise out of the unambiguous nature of its constitutional system (monarchy, aristocracy, democracy). Its constitution resulted from natural preconditions, such as climate and geography on the one hand, and historical characteristics, such as religion, dress, conditions of labour, property, and legislation on the other. Montesquieu's credo was that if a people was unique, it would develop its proper political constitution.[37]

For more than a century the German elite had looked westwards. The German aristocracy had imitated French culture. Montesquieu, a French enlightened *philosophe*, taught that Enlightenment in constitutional affairs meant having a specific congruence between cultural and political affairs. Seen from this perspective, Germans had been wrong all

[35] See Wehler, *Deutsche Gesellschaftsgeschichte*, vol. 1, p. 303.
[36] Horst Möller, *Aufklärung in Preußen: Der Verleger, Publizist und Geschichtsschreiber Friedrich Nicolai* (Berlin, 1974).
[37] See Charles de Secondat Baron de la Brède et de Montesquieu, *The Spirit of Laws*, with D'Alembert's analysis of the work, translated from the French by Thomas Nugent (Littleton, CO, 1991); Voltaire, *Essai sur les mœurs et l'esprit des nations et sur les principaux faits de l'histoire depuis Charlemagne jusqu'à Louis XIII* (1756) (Paris, 1963); Rudolf Vierhaus, 'Montesquieu in Deutschland: Zur Geschichte seiner Wirkung als politischer Schriftsteller im 18. Jahrhundert', in *Collegium Philosophicum: Studien. Essays in Honour of Joachim Ritter* (Basle, 1965), pp. 403–37; Conrad Wiedemann, 'Zwischen Nationalgeist und Kosmopolitismus: Über die Schwierigkeiten der deutschen Klassiker, einen Nationalhelden zu finden', *Aufklärung*, 4 (1989), 75–101, at 87ff.

along when they had adopted French culture and its absolutist political system. The French *esprit des lois* could not be the German one. True Enlightenment required not the imitation, but rather the emulation of the French path to national unity and identity. German thinkers learned from Montesquieu that German identity was not the same as French identity. What Germans had to learn from the French was to be autonomous and to have a specific identity.

Whereas 'prejudice' was traditionally seen as the opposite of 'autonomy', a new understanding of 'prejudice' was now coming about. Prejudice came to be seen as complementary to autonomy, and not as contradictory to it. Autonomy was achieved by a positive attitude towards particular aspects that set a people apart from others: history, culture, religion, climate, and geography. For Herder, nations were therefore 'inexpressible'. Their cultural autonomy justified the patriotic claim that they could not be imitated. They had a soul of their own and were inexplicably different. Herder became the prophet of cultural particularity. To the present day he is still the favourite national theoretician in the 'small' eastern European nations such as the Czech and Baltic nations. A native of the Baltic himself, Herder did not disparage the neighbouring Slavic culture, but praised it as a distinctive culture of its own. The defender of Prussian legislation Thomas Abbt and the philosopher Georg Friedrich Meier from Halle shared his positive attitude towards prejudice.[38] The same held true for the philosopher Johann Georg Hamann, whose defence of prejudice made him one of the founders of modern linguistics.[39] Hamann taught that autonomy and identity could be achieved only through communication—individual as well as collective. Hamann famously coined the phrase: 'Speak, that I may see thee!'[40]

German reformers understood this cultural autonomy not as a necessary break with patriotic cosmopolitanism, but as a consequence of the enlightened principle of autonomy. Johann Joachim Winckelmann,

[38] See Georg Friedrich Meier, *Beyträge zu der Lehre von den Vorurtheilen des menschlichen Geschlechts* (Halle, 1766); Thomas Abbt, 'Über die Vorurtheile', in idem, *Vermischte Werke* (Stettin, 1780), vol. 4, pp. 135–88. This text was Abbt's answer to the literary competition on the prize question by the Patriotic Society in Basle in 1763: 'Finden sich dergleichen Vorurtheile, die Ehrerbietung verdienen, und die ein guter Bürger öffentlich anzugreifen sich ein Bedenken machen soll?'
[39] See Karl Menges, 'Vom Nationalgeist und seinen Keinem: Zur Vorurteilsapologetik bei Herder, Hamann und anderen "Patrioten"', in Helmut Scheuer (ed.), *Dichter und ihre Nation* (Frankfurt am Main, 1993), pp. 103–20, at pp. 109f.
[40] Johann Georg Hamann, 'Aesthetica in Nuce: A Rhapsody in Cabbalistic Prose (1762)', in M. Bernstein (ed.), *Classic and Romantic German Aesthetics* (Cambridge, 2003), pp. 1–20, at p. 4.

Friedrich Gottlieb Klopstock, Johann Gottfried Herder, and Justus Möser articulated their desire for a specific German identity as an expression of the general enlightened principle of autonomy.[41] Cultural self-determination was therefore a consequence of Enlightenment, and did not run contrary to it. Patriotic authors could point to Montesquieu himself for their patriotic inspiration. For Montesquieu, the spirit of liberty came out of the Teutonic forests.[42]

This general reappraisal of prejudice and cultural particularity must be qualified. Not every German intellectual cherished prejudice. Friedrich Schiller, for instance, saw himself as living in an age of the 'supremacy of prejudice' which was responsible for the rise of sinister and dark personalities—quite the contrary of Enlightenment![43] He was joined by the Gotha publisher Rudolf Zacharias Becker. Becker argued for a liberation from prejudice which endangered Enlightenment, just as Immanuel Kant did in his answer to the question 'What is Enlightenment?'[44]

Intentions are not identical with implications and certainly cannot be identified with their impact. What had been driven by the enlightened impulse for cultural autonomy soon turned into a drive for superiority. This shift is associated with the works of Friedrich Gottlieb Klopstock.[45] His drama *Arminius* inaugurated a tradition of anti-French and anti-Roman poetry which explicitly heralded German liberty and 'German virtues' against foreign cultural dominance. Klopstock became the 'poet of the fatherland'. Liberty had turned xenophobic.

Along with the re-evaluation of the concepts of *patria* and 'nation' a new understanding of history developed. In particular, the French tradition from Descartes to Voltaire saw history as unreliable for any operation intended to result in individual and collective reason and responsiblity. History could provide only probabilities, no certainties. 'Les vérités historiques ne sont que des probabilités.'[46] Contemporaries in the second half

[41] See Wiedemann, 'Zwischen Nationalgeist und Kosmopolitismus', p. 87.

[42] Montesquieu praises the British political system for its liberty. 'Si on veut lire l'admirable ouvrage de Tacite sur les mœurs des Germains, on verra que c'est d'eux que les Anglais ont tiré l'idée de leur gouvernement politique. Ce beau système a été trouvé dans les bois.' Charles Louis des Montesquieu, *De l'esprit des lois*, ed. Victor Goldschmid, 2 vols (Paris, 1979), vol. 1, p. 304.

[43] See Friedrich Schiller, *Briefe*, ed. Fritz Jonas (Stuttgart, 1893), vol. 3, p. 370.

[44] See Rudolf Zacharias Becker, *Versuch über die Aufklärung des Landmannes* (Dessau, 1785), pp. 5ff., 13ff., 17.

[45] See Harro Zimmermann, 'Vom Freiheitsdichter zum Nazi-Idol: Friedrich Gottlieb Klopstock unter den Deutschen', in Scheuer (ed.), *Dichter und ihre Nation*, pp. 68–87.

[46] Voltaire, *Œuvres complètes* (Paris, 1879), vol. 20, p. 560.

of the eigtheenth century increasingly disagreed and no longer saw history in terms of the polarity of 'absolutely sure versus likely', but as a contemporary narrative, a medium of communication. History was no longer dependent on the master narratives of the churches and the monarchies. It was a way of expressing cultural autonomy through the narration of a specific history. The longer a people was autonomous, the more it was connected with specific historical narratives.[47]

The French Revolution and German Nationalism

What impact did the French Revolution and the Napoleonic wars have on the relationship between the cultural nation and state patriotism? A realignment occurred under the impact of the French occupation and the military defeat of 1806. State authority now had to find new ways of countering French domination. Whereas state diplomacy had tried to use eighteenth-century negotiating mechanisms to contain military conflicts, public opinion now violently turned against the French occupation, although it had welcomed the Revolution in its early stages. Cultural patriotism thereby lost the cosmopolitan framework in which it had been embedded. The mobilisation efforts of the anti-Napoleonic wars loosened the ties between universal and patriotic commitment. The change from patriotism to nationalism went along with the transformation of the horizontal egalitarian universalism of the Old Reich into a vertical hierarchy of nations after 1800. Under the influence of twenty years of war, German nationalists now saw the German national character not as one among equals, but as higher than others.

The patriotism of the Old Reich had been futile in the anti-Napoleonic war of 1806. The year 1806 was considered Prussia's nineteenth-century *Urkatastrophe* (primal catastrophe). The commitment of enlightened and historical patriotism had not been honoured by the political authorities. Instead the philosophically buttressed state authority had been proven wrong on the battlefield. The result of enlightened patriotism and reform absolutism was defeat and occupation. The bureaucratic state had not delivered on its promise that had been embedded in natural law jurisprudence. After all, patriotism and nationalism were secular

---

[47] Reinhart Koselleck, 'Geschichte', in *Geschichtliche Grundbegriffe* (Stuttgart, 1979), vol. 2, pp. 647–58.

endeavours and went along with secular ethics. Patriotism demanded the fulfilment of its promises for its own legitimation, whereas religious ethics did not require innerworldly fulfilment to justify its demands on the faithful.[48] Patriotic commitment had to be met by success—otherwise it would sooner or later lose its legitimation.

Germany's political culture displayed three ways of reacting to the failure of the state to live up to its citizens' patriotic expectations: resignation, radicalisation, and spiritualisation.[49] Disappointment at Germany's political affairs made several authors sceptical about the prospects of a German patriotism. For the Leipzig scholar and writer Johann Adam Bergk, patriotism could develop only through a common cause that brought people together by its 'dignity, importance and magnitude'. In fact, he did not see such a common cause.[50] Instead a philosophical territory, namely, that of pure reason and justice, became his homeland. Resignation could also turn spiritual. Since no German state and very few common institutions existed in the Old Reich, the nation was more than ever to be found in the cultural area. The language constituted Germanness, argued the philosopher Johann Gottlieb Fichte in his *Addresses to the German Nation*. 'Wherever a separate language is found, there a separate nation exists.'[51] And he went so far as to argue that the German language made the Germans an *Urvolk* which had an obligation to teach others what a people should be like. Fichte called for a spiritual regeneration of the German people. That mixture of radicalisation and spiritualisation, as is all too well known, became the signature of early German nationalism after 1800. The radical nationalism of the anti-Napoleonic wars realigned society and the state. Where the political mechanisms of state politics did not deliver, highly moralised nationalism urged state officials (and the king!) to go to war. The next disappointment came when the civic engagement of the Wars of Liberation did not result

---

[48] Friedrich-Wilhelm Graf, 'Die Nation—von Gott "erfunden"? Kritische Randnotizen zum Theologiebedarf der historischen Nationalismusforschung', in Gerd Krumeich and Hartmut Lehmann (eds), *'Gott mit uns': Nation, Religion und Gewalt im 19. und frühen 20. Jahrhundert* (Göttingen, 2000), pp. 285–317.

[49] See Vierhaus, 'Patriotismus', p. 24.

[50] Johann Adam Bergk, *Untersuchungen aus dem Natur-, Staats- und Völkerrecht* (Kronberg im Taunus, 1975; reprint 1st edn 1796); Vierhaus, 'Patriotismus', pp. 24f.

[51] Johann Gottlieb Fichte, *Addresses to the German Nation* (Chicago, IL, 1922), p. 215. On Fichte's nationalism, see Margaret Canovan, *Nationhood and Political Theory* (Cheltenham, 1996), pp. 52ff.

in a constitution. That disappointment would later be essential for the next phase of nationalist radicalisation.[52]

Moral Universalism and Nationalism after 1800

The years around 1800 witnessed a shift from cosmopolitan patriotism to modern nationalism. The French Revolution was a turning point in the history of cosmopolitanism, patriotism, and nationalism. It produced new semantic dichotomies, reversed older ones, reconfigured them, and added new experiences. The war and the Terror of 1793–4 changed the relationship between nationalism and cosmopolitanism. The revolutionaries had seen themselves, first, as representatives of sovereignty in general and as the first self-determined nation in modern history. This was the *post factum* legitimation for the French troops robbing pieces of art from all over Europe and transferring them to Paris. These paintings and sculptures, it was argued, should belong to mankind as embodied by the French nation, and not by other states under absolutist rule. This hierarchy between France and the other states was common to the early revolutionaries. On 23 August 1789 Rabaut Saint-Etienne declared: 'French nation, you are not here to follow the example of others but to set an example of your own.'[53]

Second, the dichotomies of 'us' and 'them', of 'friend' and 'foe', had been propelled to omnipresence by the revolutionary war since 1792. The revolutionaries had welcomed writers and intellectuals from foreign countries and naturalised them. The former Rhenish baron Anarcharsis Cloots had been known in France as the 'orator of mankind', as a 'citoyen de l'humanité' and—as a prominent anticleric—'a personal enemy of God'.[54] Sympathisers of the revolution from abroad founded the Club of Foreign Patriots. In December 1791 Pierre Proli, a Belgian writer, issued the first pacifist newspaper, *Le Cosmopolite*. After France declared war on the central European monarchies on 20 April 1792, these foreigners soon became objects of suspicion. Their loyalty to the

---

[52] This was one of Ernst-Rudolf Huber's central observations in his *Deutsche Verfassungsgeschichte*. In his opinion Germany took the wrong turn in 1821 after all constitutional promises had been broken.

[53] Virginie Guiraudon, 'Cosmopolitism and National Priority: Attitudes Towards Foreigners in France between 1789 and 1794', *History of European Ideas*, 13 (1991), 591–604, at 594.

[54] Gilda Pasetzky, 'Ein revolutionärer Utopist: Bemerkungen zu Roland Mortiers Anarcharsis Cloots—Biographie', *Francia*, 24 (1997), 205ff.

Revolution was constantly under question. Cloots, who was fervently anticlerical, was accused of treason, jailed, and guillotined on 22 March 1794. Cosmopolitanism and xenophilia, prominent ideas at the beginning of the French Revolution, were proscribed. Frenchmen with ties to foreigners and foreign customs were refused certificates of good citizenship. Cosmopolitanism was now believed to hamper the war effort. Cosmopolitans were not considered citizens of a particular country unless they recognised a particular government. Under the pressure of war, the French government and its legislation were seen as expressions of the general will of the people.[55]

The combination of state-centred patriotism and moral universalism did not fade away with the French Revolution or the demise of the Old Reich.[56] The particular and the universal were not opposites at the same level, but complementary notions at different levels. Although the French Revolution represented a break in cosmopolitan patriotism, the combination of the two had considerable influence in nineteenth-century political culture in Germany and beyond. The Freemasons were a case in point. Their lodges were the classic institutions of moral universalism and nationalism in the nineteenth century and later. They favoured a combination of universalist moralism and national particularism, when nationalism had overcome its particularist opponents and encountered internationalism as its new enemy. Nationalists turned anti-international, but at the same time steadfastly clung to universalism. Before 1914 German lodges held that 'it is possible and indeed essential to be a world citizen without being international'.[57]

The nation-state itself was then endowed with a moral mission. According to Johann Caspar Bluntschli, one of the key figures in the nineteenth-century debate on nationalism, cultural nations stood for civilisation, for 'progress for individuals, who now obtain a share in a higher

---

[55] See Guiraudon, 'Cosmopolitism and National Priority', 591, 593, 595; article VI of the Declaration of the Rights of Man and of the Citizen of 26 August 1789 substantiated the distinction which the French Revolution drew between man and citizen.

[56] See Otto Kallscheuer and Claus Leggewie, 'Deutsche Kulturnation versus französische Staatsnation? Eine ideengeschichtliche Stichprobe', in Helmut Berding (ed.), *Nationales Bewußtsein und kollektive Identität: Studien zur Entwicklung des kollektiven Bewußtseins in der Neuzeit*, 3 vols (Frankfurt am Main, 1994), vol. 2, pp. 112–62, at p. 127. Montesquieu had a profound impact on Zimmermann and Abbt.

[57] *Hamburger Logenblatt*, 47 (1913/14), 50; quoted in Stefan-Ludwig Hoffmann, 'Nationalism and the Quest for Moral Universalism: German Freemasonry, 1860–1914', in Martin H. Geyer and Johannes Paulmann (eds), *The Mechanics of Internationalism: Culture, Society, and Politics from the 1840s to the First World War* (Oxford, 2001), pp. 259–84, at p. 280.

cultural life and [for] progress for mankind at large, whose destiny is not the preservation of all barbarism but rather civilisation'.[58] Thus nation and nationalism found a new mission: the culturally civilised nation was to civilise the uncivilised. Civilisation as the heir of eighteenth-century moral universalism became a national project. Particularism and universalism could reinforce and supplement each other. 'Universalism and particularism endorse each other's defect in order to conceal their own; they are intimately tied to each other in their accomplice.'[59] Although universalism and particularism constitute formal opposites, as essential elements of nationalism they are 'bound to affect the other from the inside'.[60] These universal missions of the European nation-states could not coexist peacefully. Emanuel Geibel's famous line of 1861, 'And the German character may heal the world one day', turned into a battle-cry during the Franco-Prussian war of 1870–1.[61] The moral argument made modern nation-states fight even harder and more brutally in the nineteenth century. German Freemasons were convinced that the war against France in 1870–1 was 'basically about safeguarding Western civilisation, the triumph of justice, education, and humanity'. Conversely, the French Freemasons believed 'that the function of France in the World was to develop the idea of human progress and that to love, to serve, and, if need be, to die for France was to love, to serve, and to die for humanity'.[62]

German historiography in particular embedded the ideas of cosmopolitanism and moral universalism into the nation-state. Liberal historians such as Friedrich Meinecke saw the specific nation-state not as opposed to the cosmopolitanism of the eighteenth century, but rather as incorporating universalism.[63] After 1800, the universalist background of pre-revolutionary patriotism was invested in a civilising mission and in history. Time immemorial became the field in which nations unfolded and

---

[58] Johann Caspar Bluntschli, 'Nation und Volk, Nationbalitätsprinzip', in idem and Karl Brater (eds), *Deutsches Staatswörterbuch* (Stuttgart, 1862), vol. 7, pp. 152–60, at p. 156; Hoffmann, 'Nationalism and the Quest for Moral Universalism', p. 261.
[59] N. Sakai, 'Modernity and Its Critique: The Problem of Universalism and Particularism', *South Atlantic Quarterly*, 87 (1988), 475ff., at 487.
[60] Étienne Balibar, 'Racism as Universalism', in idem, *Masses, Classes, and Ideas* (London, 1994), pp. 191–204, at p. 198.
[61] Quoted in Hoffmann, 'Nationalism and the Quest for Moral Universalism', p. 261: 'Und es mag am deutschen Wesen einmal noch die Welt genesen.'
[62] *Die Bauhütte*, 14 (1871), 41; Hoffmann, 'Nationalism and the Quest for Moral Universalism', pp. 274, 276.
[63] Friedrich Meinecke, *Weltbürgertum und Nationalstaat: Studien zur Genesis des deutschen Nationalstaates* (Munich, 1907).

were constituted. National identities were now seen as historically embedded. They could be universalised on the time scale. Ernest Renan reminds us that 'historical error is a crucial factor in the creation of a nation'.[64] To activate the nation retrospectively was the job of historians. The underlying themes of most German master-narratives were the nation and the nation-state. Historians tended to be more national than their subject.

[64] Ernest Renan, 'What is a Nation?', in Homi Bhabha (ed.), *Nation and Narration* (London, 1990), pp. 8–22, at p. 11.

Art in a Cool Climate: The Cultural Policy of the British State in European Context, *c.* 1780 to *c.* 1850*

PETER MANDLER

CAN WE SPEAK OF A 'CULTURAL POLICY' of the 'State' in this period without falling into anachronism? Certainly we can recognise across Europe in the eighteenth century a growing concern for the significance of the 'fine arts': socially, as conducing to the development of psychological traits (such as 'sympathy', 'politeness', or 'refinement') crucial to the smooth functioning of complex, sometimes very crowded and mobile societies; economically, as developing the appetite for and improving the quality of manufactures; and politically, as one key expression of a distinctive 'national character', which might help bind peoples to the emerging nation-states. Between them these concerns extended substantially the range of persons deemed to be capable of benefiting from exposure to fine art and so, gently and patchily, the fine arts became a part—admittedly, a small part—of the traditional police functions of government in late eighteenth-century Europe.

Thus 'cultural policy'; 'the State' may actually be a more problematic term. Patronage of the fine arts had been a traditional (self-selected) responsibility of individual nobles and princes, and, although sovereign nobles and princes were taking on in this period more explicit responsibilities for police and for more of their people, it is often difficult to distinguish between their activities as individual patrons, their activities as

* I have benefited greatly from the expertise and disputations of Jonathan Conlin, Holger Hoock, and Emma Winter, well beyond what I can suggest in the notes. I am also grateful to Deborah Cohen, Christof Mauch, and the other participants in the colloquium on 'Art and society in Europe in the long nineteenth century: connections and comparisons' at the German Historical Institute, Washington, December 2002, as well as to Tim Blanning, Hagen Schulze, and the audience at the British Academy–German Historical Institute conference in London in September 2003.

courtly patrons, and their activities as States. Royal palaces, for example, were built to accommodate both the comforts of the monarch and the public or governing functions of the monarchy, and their embellishments aimed simultaneously to please the monarch, to glorify his name and taste, to demonstrate his patronage of the arts, and in many cases to instruct and edify large sections of his people. As courts grew and their functions diversified, a wider range of courtly cultural institutions became available to play these multiple overlapping functions. The opera house which Frederick the Great opened in 1742 as a courtly institution had, by 1789 under the rather different regime of Frederick William II, become accessible to people who purchased their tickets on the open market. Even so, it was not yet a 'national' institution, more a courtly institution with collateral benefits to a wider public.[1] These distinctions were fuzzier still at a local level, where cultural institutions sponsored by elite groups were open to commercialisation and other kinds of public infiltration and as a result had a very ambiguously 'civic' character—for example, in the British context, the assembly rooms, pleasure-grounds, racecourses, and other institutions of the so-called 'Urban Renaissance' of the early eighteenth century.[2]

Then there is the thorny question of the churches. They had long had public cultural functions, which in the eighteenth century could now threaten to slip out of the control of the ecclesiastical authorities or lose their religious character altogether. The great organ debates that raged in Britain and in the German states showed how sensitive a topic this could be. In Britain, the Handel Commemoration Concerts held in Westminster Abbey in May 1784 drew massive crowds and established a tradition of grand-scale public performances of the *Messiah* that soon migrated into secular halls, but they drew, too, anxious comment from evangelicals, worried that the churches were turning into the cultural arm of the State. As William Cowper wrote in *The Task*, 'Man praises man. Desert in arts or arms/ Wins public honour; and ten thousand sit/ Patiently present at a sacred song,/ Commemoration-mad; content to hear/ (O wonderful effect of music's power!)/ Messiah's eulogy, for Handel's sake.' It is difficult,

---

[1] James J. Sheehan, *Museums in the German Art World: From the End of the Old Regime to the Rise of Modernism* (Oxford, 2000), pp. 14–41; Thomas DaCosta Kaufmann, *Court, Cloister and City: The Art and Culture of Central Europe 1450–1800* (London, 1995), pp. 395–416, 442–9.
[2] Peter Borsay, *The English Urban Renaissance: Culture and Society in the Provincial Town, 1660–1770* (Oxford, 1989).

then, to keep clear the cultural policy of the State from much older religious policies of the Church.[3]

Holding these difficulties in mind, this essay seeks to pin down what was distinctive about the British State and its cultural policies in the period during and after the Napoleonic Wars. Briefly, the argument will be that both the British State and its posture towards culture carried certain features that put them in the Western European mainstream towards the end of the eighteenth century, and certain features that distinguished them, notably a reticence about the court's role that derived from parliamentary government, and a reticence about State promotion of the arts that stemmed both from that unusual constitutional arrangement and from deeper national–Protestant reservations about art. These latter divergences were widened by the divergent impacts and aftermaths of the great European war of 1794–1814 and, although some reconvergence was experienced during the 1830s and 1840s when Britain and the rest of Western Europe shared a common 'nationalising' impulse, divergence was again more pronounced after 1848. The story resembles a ballet between British and European (principally French and German) cultural policies which combines *pas de deux* and solo elements in different measure, following a distinct chronological pattern.

I

First, to state the obvious: eighteenth-century Britain lacked a court that could or would lead in the nation's or even the capital's cultural life. No Versailles or Potsdam was built in or around London, and, after the Palace of Whitehall burnt down in 1698, successive British monarchs huddled in fragments until George III acquired a townhouse in 1762. It did not become anything like a palace until his ambitious son inherited in 1820. While George III opened portions of Windsor, Hampton Court, and Greenwich to public view, showing that the taste for monarchical display was not entirely lacking, none of these was intended to or ever did serve as an extra-metropolitan centre sufficient to attract a court. As John Brewer has argued, 'the British monarchy's inability or unwillingness to use the arts effectively to create a special sense of kingship' stemmed from a compound of personal indifference, parliamentary constraints, and,

---

[3] William Weber, *The Rise of Musical Classics in Eighteenth-century England* (Oxford, 1992), pp. 234–7.

most importantly, the existence of a lively commercial sphere for the arts which threatened humiliatingly to rival or invade royal displays.[4] The Hanoverian monarchs were simply not as free to impose themselves upon the public sphere as were their Bourbon, Hohenzollern, Wettin, or Wittelsbach contemporaries.

Even George III, undoubtedly the Hanoverian with the strongest sense of the public responsibilities of the monarch, made an indifferent patron of the arts. While he commissioned Benjamin West to glorify his kingship with a series of canvasses for the renovated apartments at Windsor, Windsor was not much of a public showcase, and by removing the much loved Raphael Cartoons to Windsor from Hampton Court, which could have been such a showcase, George in fact contributed to the reprivatisation of the one part of the royal collection that had gained some public reputation. He added little to the royal collections.[5] His court orchestras were small and essentially private adjuncts to the Chapel Royal, and they did not spawn public subscription concerts. Public concerts grew out of commercial subscription series, to which George lent his cachet but not his leadership (nor much of his cash).[6]

The monarchy's semi-detached relationship to the arts testifies not to the philistinism of the Hanoverians—they were not conspicuously more philistine than their German cousins in Munich or Dresden or Berlin— but rather to the different norms prevailing in Britain as to the appropriate roles of court, Parliament, and commerce. Another musical illustration might bring out this point more clearly. Many continental monarchs opened their own opera houses in the eighteenth century; by the end of the century the Austrian and French monarchs had three houses each. As their number proliferated and their operations grew more complex, the royal nature of these houses became diluted, but they retained (and retain today) first a royal and then a national status which a more purely commercial operation would not. Britain followed this model, though only roughly, through the middle of the eighteenth century. The King's Theatre, Haymarket, was not a result of the personal

---

[4] John Brewer, *The Pleasures of the Imagination: English Culture in the Eighteenth Century* (Chicago, IL, 1997), ch. 1, quote at p. 25.

[5] Jonathan Conlin, 'The Origins and History of the National Gallery, 1753–1860', Ph.D. dissertation (University of Cambridge, 2002), 40–2. George III's single major acquisition, the Venetian collection of Joseph Smith, was hung in private galleries in Buckingham Palace: Brewer, *Pleasures of the Imagination*, p. 219.

[6] Simon McVeigh, *Concert Life in London from Mozart to Haydn* (Cambridge, 1993), pp. 5–7, 29, 44–50.

initiative of the King as were the continental houses, but, as William Weber says, 'even though the English crown kept a much greater distance from it than monarchs on the Continent, the King's Theatre came to function on a stable basis only when George I supported it in 1720'.[7] By George III's time, however, the King's Theatre was sufficiently commercial no longer to require that patronage. By the 1780s, there were four houses offering opera in London—the King's, Covent Garden, Drury Lane, and the Little Theatre, Haymarket—none of them identified clearly with the Crown, but each had a specific social and political character. The King bestowed command performances on three of them, according to his political preferences, a *lagniappe* appreciated but not required by the principals. When the King's Theatre burned down in 1789, a lively dispute ensued over the disposition of its royal patent, between the current owner and a rival syndicate. In theory it was the King's right to grant the patent to whomever he wished; in practice it was a matter for legal arbitration. Lord Chancellor Thurlow in fact made the decision, to leave the patent in the current owner's hands, entirely on the basis of commercial law. A system of royal patents had, in short, become hardly more than a municipal licensing scheme.[8]

George III *was* personally responsible for one major cultural institution, the Royal Academy of Arts. Holger Hoock has made a strong case for seeing the Royal Academy as a 'national institution' through which the monarchy associated itself with the public sphere and with the national good very much along the lines of the Prussian or Bourbon monarchies. While Britain did not worry that it was a 'backward' nation requiring royal leadership, it did accept that its artistic traditions had been held back by the disruptions of the Civil War and by some national indisposition since then to indulge in artistic experimentation, which might be useful in promoting 'virtue and refinement' and national glory, and to which a royal initiative might usefully contribute.[9] Three qualifications to this argument will take us into the Napoleonic period proper.

First, George III's sponsorship of the Royal Academy was more daring than his ventures into the music business, but it encountered some of

---

[7] Weber, *Rise of Musical Classics*, p. 234.

[8] Jane Girdham, *English Opera in Late Eighteenth-century London* (Oxford, 1997), p. 39; Curtis Price, Judith Milhous, and Robert D. Hume, *Italian Opera in Late Eighteenth-century London, vol. 1: The King's Theatre, Haymarket, 1778–1791* (Oxford, 1995), pp. 547–8.

[9] Holger Hoock, *The King's Artists: The Royal Academy of Arts and the Politics of British Culture 1760–1840* (Oxford, 2003).

the same hazards: that is, it could bring him into conflict with both commercial or professional interests and with Parliament. Even when George
III was on the best of terms with his Parliament, it proved difficult to
extract funds to house and support the Academy; the King had to contribute from his own pocket to get it comfortably ensconced in Somerset
House, and the Academy still had to commercialise its exhibitions in
order to survive. Then the commercial success of its exhibitions per-
versely raised the question of what exactly the Academy was providing
that the market could not provide on its own, reflecting wider doubts
about the purposes and value of royal patronage.

Parliament might, of course, have substituted its own patronage for
that of the Crown. When George II had characteristically declined Sir
Hans Sloane's 1753 bequest of his diverse collections, Parliament had
agreed to purchase them 'for the use and benefit of the publick, who may
have free Access to view and peruse the same'. Installed in a deserted aristocratic residence in Bloomsbury, under a board of private trustees, the
British Museum had some claim to being the first genuinely public
museum in the world. Admission was not charged, and the Museum
could therefore claim — as the Academy and the market could not — that
it was performing an irreplaceable national service to, at least virtually,
the whole of the people.[10] Functionally, it was taking the place of the
Hanoverian monarchs' failure to display royal collections in an urban setting, as the Bourbons did at the Luxembourg from 1750, as Frederick II
of Hesse-Kassel did at the Museum Fridericanium from 1769, as
Frederick Augustus III of Saxony did with his 'museum for public use' at
the Zwinger from the 1770s, and as Joseph II of Austria did at the
Belvedere from the early 1790s.[11]

However, as Jonathan Conlin has pointed out, the most consistent
advocate of a parliamentary arts policy to rival the great royal patronages
of the Continent was John Wilkes, George III's radical adversary; few
MPs shared either Wilkes's animus against the Crown or his quasi-
populist motives for the promotion of the arts. Wilkes's campaign in 1777
to persuade Parliament to purchase the rich art collections of Sir Robert
Walpole proved a humiliating failure, and they went instead to Catherine

---

[10] Anne Goldgar, 'The British Museum and the Virtual Representation of Culture in the
Eighteenth Century', *Albion*, 32 (2000), 195–231.
[11] Andrew McClellan, *Inventing the Louvre: Art, Politics, and the Origins of the Modern Museum
in Eighteenth-century Paris* (Cambridge, 1994), pp. 13–25; Kaufmann, *Court, Cloister and City*,
pp. 444–5; Sheehan, *Museums in the German Art World*, pp. 21–41.

the Great.[12] Apart from the £30,000 to establish the British Museum, Parliament was slow and mean when it came to funding artistic projects in the late eighteenth century. Even the placing of the British Museum at arm's length under a board of private trustees might be seen as an explicit statement that museum-making was not one of the core activities of government.

So a royal policy for the arts faced formidable opposition from Parliament, which could not itself decide whether it wished for a royal policy, a parliamentary policy, or no policy at all. This brings me to the second difficulty of establishing a royal arts policy, which was not only Parliament's but also public opinion's doubts as to whether an arts policy was necessary at all. The longstanding view (held by the English but also by others, like Montesquieu) that the English were fundamentally practical, hardheaded, and materialistic, uninterested in fripperies such as art and music, was intensifying towards the end of the eighteenth century, on both socio-political and religious grounds.[13] Socially and politically, the period saw a growing Protestant, nationalist protest against a cosmopolitan and aristocratic culture, typified by 'grand manner' art collections, French fashions, and Italian opera. This could take the form of the promotion of an 'English' school of the arts, or the promotion of English arts (such as poetry and literature) against non-English arts (such as painting and music), or a campaign against the arts in general.[14] Religious objections were more likely to take the last, purely negative form. The rising tide of evangelicalism sought not only to separate art and religion, as in William Cowper's protest against the contamination of Westminster Abbey with Handel, but to damn the arts altogether as the impious rival of religion. Among the long-term consequences in the nineteenth century were the closure of museums and the banning of public performances on Sundays, the channelling of leisure-hour energies into physical exercise

---

[12] Jonathan G. W. Conlin, 'High Art and Low Politics: A New Perspective on John Wilkes', *Huntington Library Quarterly*, 64 (2001), 357–81; Andrew Moore (ed.), *Houghton Hall: The Prime Minister, the Empress, and the Heritage* (London, 1996).

[13] Charles Louis de Secondat, Baron de Montesquieu, *The Spirit of the Laws* (1748), ed. David Wallace Carrithers (Berkeley, CA, 1977), pp. 243–7; Paul Langford, *Englishness Identified: Manners and Character 1650–1850* (Oxford, 2000), pp. 75–81

[14] Gerald Newman, *The Rise of English Nationalism: A Cultural History, 1740–1830* (New York, 1987); cf. Linda Colley, *Britons: Forging the Nation 1707–1837* (New Haven, CT, and London, 1992), ch. 5, on the extent to which George III was able to co-opt these 'nationalist' tendencies; and, on the continuing appeal of French culture to the English elite, Robin Eagles, 'Beguiled by France? The English Aristocracy, 1748–1848', in Laurence Brockliss and David Eastwood (eds), *A Union of Multiple Identities: The British Isles c. 1750—c. 1850* (Manchester, 1997), pp. 60–77.

and the study of sacred literature (the YMCA movement in Britain, for example, excluding music and art entirely, where other countries were more lenient), and, more diffusely, giving literature the decisive edge over the performing and decorative arts even among the less devout.

The Scottish Enlightenment accommodated these views in arguing that a civilised society was best achieved not through the practice of the fine arts, as many of their continental contemporaries were urging, but through the socialising and polishing effects of commerce, which those same contemporaries worried had the reverse effect. In other words, they gave to commerce the role, as James Sheehan has put it, of 'advancing the culture of the mental powers in the interests of social communication' that Kant gave to aesthetics.[15] When Adam Smith raised concerns about the demoralising effects of the division of labour, it was not materialism that concerned him, but liberty.[16] The high value placed upon liberty meant that those Enlightenment thinkers in Britain who did recognise the civilising effects of the arts felt that these beneficial effects could be fully registered only in the voluntary, wholehearted embrace of the free-born citizen, not through the tuition of a royal or governmental overlord. As John Brewer and Tim Blanning have pointed out, the flourishing market for cultural products of all kinds in eighteenth-century London made it difficult to justify compensatory acts of patronage by the court.[17] It was almost certainly the case that more sculptures and pictures were viewed and bought, more concerts heard (though probably not more opera or ballet attended), and more public buildings entered by more people in Britain than anywhere else in the world.

And these obstacles to a State arts policy became more formidable still because of the long-term changes that the Napoleonic Wars wrought on the structure and ethos of the British State.

---

[15] Sheehan, *Museums in the German Art World*, pp. 8–9.

[16] In this Smith was closer to Montesquieu and his French successors, who were also most concerned about public spirit, than to German philosophers for whom the aesthetic capacities of the individual were more central. See, on Smith, the useful discussion in Donald Winch, *Riches and Poverty: An Intellectual History of Political Economy in Britain, 1750–1834* (Cambridge, 1996), pp. 119–23; and, on the French debate, Roberto Romani, *National Character and Public Spirit in Britain and France, 1750–1914* (Cambridge, 2002), ch. 1.

[17] In addition to Brewer, *Pleasures of the Imagination*, see T. C. W. Blanning, *The Culture of Power and the Power of Culture* (Oxford, 2002), ch. 7.

II

Another of John Brewer's seminal contributions to our understanding of eighteenth-century Britain has been, of course, his demonstration of the strength and size of the 'fiscal–military' State even before the Napoleonic Wars.[18] Despite—or indeed because of—their attachment to liberty, the British allowed their State to outgrow all others over the course of the century, and then after Brewer's period grossly so; by 1815 State expenditure was perhaps absorbing a quarter of GNP.[19] What made this possible was that, first, the fiscal–military State was primarily aimed not at Britons but at coercing, exploiting, or defending against foreigners, and, second, that it was driven not by the Crown but by Parliament. Thus it proved to be a self-dismantling State, which, once it had achieved its stated purposes—establishing British commercial mastery and defending against real external threats—unravelled with astonishing speed. In fact, what we can now see as a considerable *over*-reaction to the fiscal–military State set in after 1815, as a revulsion against high levels of taxation, State expenditure, and State employment swept through politics and society. This revulsion was further fuelled by the mounting tide of evangelical fervour which held all attempts to legislate for God's providence as impious, and reinstated in more intense form traditional English prejudices on the side of self-government, self-discipline, and self-help.[20]

Historians have been at pains to point out the limits to this retraction of State power; clearly it was neither possible nor desirable to run an advanced society and economy without considerable public inputs from taxation, legislation, and bureaucracy.[21] Still, the contrasts with developing continental States are striking. Britain's was the only major European State, apart from Austria–Hungary, to contract its absolute levels of expenditure in the half century after 1815. While in Britain expenditures in 1851 were still below the wartime peak—even below the 1821 levels of

---

[18] John Brewer, *The Sinews of Power: War, Money and the English State 1688–1783* (New York, 1989); Lawrence Stone (ed.), *An Imperial State at War: Britain from 1689 to 1815* (London and New York, 1994).

[19] Philip Harling, *The Modern British State: An Historical Introduction* (Cambridge, 2001), p. 42.

[20] Philip Harling and Peter Mandler, 'From "Fiscal–Military" to Laissez-Faire State, 1760–1850', *Journal of British Studies*, 32 (1993), 44–70; Philip Harling, *The Waning of 'Old Corruption': The Politics of Economical Reform in Britain, 1779–1846* (Oxford, 1996); Boyd Hilton, *The Age of Atonement: The Influence of Evangelicalism on Social and Economic Thought 1785–1865* (Oxford, 1988).

[21] See the various assessments in Peter Mandler (ed.), *Liberty and Authority in Victorian Britain* (Oxford, 2006).

immediate post-war deflation—expenditures in other European States had doubled or trebled over the same period. There were many reasons for these diverging experiences—low bases, territorial consolidation, the delayed impact of urbanisation, the delayed arrival of British-style constitutional mechanisms to enhance tax extraction, the need to promote industrialisation. For the moment, I will confine myself to reasons for State expansion specifically relating to cultural policy.

France's experience was just as distinctive as Britain's, though at the other end of the spectrum, for in France the advent of the Napoleonic State had undoubtedly ushered in a new era of State patronage of the arts which long outlasted Napoleon himself. From 1789 onwards, the revolutionaries were determined not to break up the arts institutions of the *ancien régime* but to reconstitute and fortify them as instruments of the constitutional or republican nation. The confiscation of Church property in 1789 was quickly followed by the appointment of a *Commission des monuments* in 1790, which drew up a utopian plan for eighty-three departmental repositories of church monuments, 'for it is clear how much public instruction will benefit from these *museums*'. This utopian plan was not realised but the central Parisian depot for confiscated monuments was opened to the public as the *Musée des Monuments Français*.[22] The nationalisation of the royal collections in August 1792 was also quickly followed by a plan to open a public museum, in this case reviving a specific notion of the *ancien régime* for a grand conversion of the Louvre to museal purposes. Swelled by other confiscated works of art and then engorged by Napoleon's rape of Europe, the Louvre remained the world's greatest collection of art and antiquities even after post-1815 restitutions, which left half of Napoleon's booty *in situ*. The sense that public displays of art both represented and glorified the nation was therefore not cast into doubt but rather greatly magnified in France after 1789. The words of the interior minister of October 1792 could have been echoed by any of his many successors: 'The museum must demonstrate the nation's great riches . . . France must extend its glory through the ages and to all peoples: the national museum will embrace knowledge in all its manifold beauty and will be the admiration of the universe. By embodying these grand ideas, worthy of a free people, the museum . . . will become among the most powerful illustrations of the French Republic.'[23] Or the monarchy or the empire, as the case may be. The national museum's example

---

[22] McClellan, *Inventing the Louvre*, pp. 92, 155–97.
[23] Ibid., pp. 91–2.

was certainly extended across the nation. The *envoi* system inaugurated in 1801 established a network of local museums (originally fifteen, growing to 275 by 1880) eligible to receive distributions of art from central government; when the booty dried up, a new supply was found in central government purchases of new French art. Nothing like this system appeared anywhere else in Europe.[24] The same spirit animated the preservation of antiquities. After centuries of fruitless papal edicts to protect antiquities and preserve archaeological sites in Rome, it was only under the Napoleonic occupation of 1809–14 that export of antiquities was controlled, albeit temporarily, and, more lastingly, the great classical buildings of Rome were excavated and preserved.[25] As for France's own antiquities, though the Bourbons out of family piety closed down the *Musée des Monuments Français*, Louis Philippe's regime reopened it in expanded form as the *Musée de Cluny* and established pioneering inspectorates and commissions for historical monuments and architecture, serving as a model for German developments in subsequent decades; the British did not follow suit until after 1900.[26]

France thus had an unusually well fleshed-out concept of *patrimoine* and why it was important to the nation, as well as at least the machinery of a central-government apparatus to protect it, by the middle of the nineteenth century.[27] No other European State had the same convulsive experience, or possibly the same *ancien régime* ambitions to imitate. Nevertheless, other European States were affected by the Napoleonic experience in parallel, if more dilute ways, and some had other powerful motives of their own to promote the arts to the nation by means of State initiative. The small States, especially, were affected by the Napoleonic experience in a direct, brutal sense; many drew the conclusion that they had to emulate it to survive in a new world of bureaucratic efficiency and national integration. The arts were not the principal beneficiary of this Napoleonic effect, but they were recognised as a convenient and relatively

---

[24] Daniel J. Sherman, *Worthy Monuments: Art Museums and the Politics of Culture in Nineteenth-century France* (Cambridge, MA, 1989).

[25] Ronald T. Ridley, *The Eagle and the Spade: Archaeology in Rome during the Napoleonic Era* (Cambridge, 1992).

[26] Stephen Bann, *The Clothing of Clio: A Study of the Representation of History in Nineteenth-century Britain and France* (Cambridge, 1984), pp. 79–88; G. Baldwin Brown, *The Care of Ancient Monuments* (Cambridge, 1905).

[27] André Chastel, 'La Notion de Patrimoine', in Pierre Nora (ed.), *Les Lieux de Mémoire*, 7 vols (Paris, 1984–92), vol. 3, pp. 405–50; and see also Edouard Pommier, 'Naissance des Musées de Province', ibid., p. 489.

cheap means by which a stronger sense of national purposefulness and patriotism could be projected onto the citizenry.

In Prussia, Hardenberg's new *Kultusministerium*, established in 1810, was the classic bureaucratic vehicle for projecting national purposefulness through the triple combination of religion, education, and the arts. Among its immediate material products in Berlin between 1815 and 1830 were Schinkel's war monument, the Neue Wache (1816–18), his Schauspielhaus (1818–21), and especially his Altes Museum (1823–30). Equally important, however, were its conceptual innovations, moving art firmly from the slightly effete realms of aristocratic cultivation and royal power into the centre of the State's programme of national integration. The claim that the arts had unusual capacities to bind together the classes in a morally uplifting way, and also to help develop the economy, could be used to justify expenditures on a newly lavish scale, particularly in times of political division when other, more pointed programmes of political or social reform were controversial.[28] Something of the same sort was attempted in Bavaria under Max Joseph and Ludwig I, in Baden and Württemberg, and in Denmark, which even at its lowest ebb during the Napoleonic Wars managed to sustain considerable national expenditures on its Academy of Arts. As the Academy's president, Prince Christian Frederick, put it in 1810, 'Now we are poor and destitute. If we also become stupid, we can stop being a nation.'[29] For the same reasons, the Danes were also pioneers in State inventorying and protection of historical monuments: their 1807 Royal Commission on Antiquities subsequently inspired Ludwig I of Hesse's general decree on preservation (1818), which was in turn imitated in Prussia, Baden, and Württemberg.[30]

In a thoughtful article, Celia Applegate has warned us not to overestimate such cultural projects of national integration, at a time when the national 'coding' of cultural artefacts was 'far from fixed or obvious' and especially 'when the passage from folk to national stereotypes

[28] Steven Moyano, 'Quality vs. History: Schinkel's Altes Museum and Prussian Arts Policy', *Art Bulletin*, 72 (1990), 585–608; Gottfried Riemann, 'Schinkel's Buildings and Plans for Berlin', in Michael Snodin (ed.), *Karl Friedrich Schinkel: A Universal Man* (New Haven, CT, and London, 1991), pp. 16–25.

[29] Marit Bakke, 'Government and the Arts in Denmark', in Milton C. Cummings, Jr, and Robert S. Katz (eds), *The Patron State: Government and the Arts in Europe, North America, and Japan* (New York, 1987), pp. 138–9.

[30] Baldwin Brown, *Care of Ancient Monuments*, pp. 101–22; Michael Hunter, 'The Preconditions of Preservation: A Historical Perspective', in David Lowenthal and Marcus Binney (eds), *Our Past Before Us: Why Do We Save It?* (London, 1981), pp. 24–8.

was underway but unstable and in flux, when German culture and German-ness were inventing themselves, consciously and not'. She advises us not to take too seriously the self-promoting language of the artists themselves, who were responding to a crisis of patronage. However, the artists she discusses—in this case, they were musicians— *were* tapping into an existing language linking nationality to the arts. 'Whoever occupies himself with philosophy and art belongs to his fatherland more intimately than others', as Wilhelm von Humboldt wrote to Goethe. And they *did* succeed in winning a substantial programme of Prussian State patronage for music to parallel that available to other fine arts.[31]

III

To what extent was Britain also affected by these European processes, by which the fine arts were yoked bureaucratically to education and religion in programmes of national integration? As I have already suggested, Britain was neither so concerned about national integration—its integrity was already well established, and not under immediate threat— nor so ready to make recourse to the State. It did not have a strong tra- dition of viewing the fine arts as a natural function of the State, nor did British culture give to the fine arts such a prominent role in the moral training of the individual. There was a powerful sense in Britain, unusual in early nineteenth-century Europe, that the character of the people was basically sound, that it did not require artificial develop- ment, and in any case that the best test of that character lay in its exposure to the providential or natural order of labour and capital.

If anything, the new pressures and anxieties of the post-Napoleonic era only reinforced these prejudices. The more intense commercialising and urbanising experiences of early nineteenth-century Britain led its elites to see the social divisions of their day in more straightforwardly material than moral or spiritual terms, and to apply more straightforwardly material

---

[31] Celia Applegate, 'How German Is It? Nationalism and the Idea of Serious Music in the Early Nineteenth Century', *Nineteenth-century Music*, 21 (1998), 274–96. In music, too, the French model was more robust and centralised—a free music school for the Parisian National Guard had been established as early as June 1792, and this quickly metamorphosed into a National Institute for Music (1793), later renamed the Conservatoire (1795).

solutions—to reform the poor laws and the currency, to repair the price
and wage mechanisms. The drift of evangelical religion in this period of
so-called 'Christian political economy' went in the same direction. This
did not mean that everyone was completely immune from the claims of
aesthetics. The *Pax Britannica* was celebrated in public rituals and monuments, though the modesty of Trafalgar Square (in its early nineteenth-
century state) and Calton Hill in Edinburgh (left unfinished, whether by
design or because the money ran out) next to the Bavarian Walhalla or
Schinkel's monumentalisation of Berlin ought to be noted.[32] Certainly
George IV had quasi-Ludovician delusions of grandeur and the work
that John Nash did for the Crown Estate in London between 1811 and
1830 provided one of those rare occasions when Britain astonished the
world by an act of State patronage of the arts. There were limits even to
this large-scale project, however. It was only loosely a State enterprise
and only roughly an artistic experiment; it was, as John Summerson put
it, 'not only a dream of antique architecture' but 'just as much a finance-
fantasia over risk and profit'.[33] Most of the building was commercial
and residential. A planned 'National Valhalla' for Regent's Park was
never built. In compensation, George IV got Parliament to authorise the
rebuilding of Buckingham House, though not yet on its current palatial
scale—that came a century later. 'I tell Nash ... at his peril ever to
advise me to build a Palace. I am too old to build a Palace', wrote the
King. 'I must have a pied-à-terre.'[34] All the same, Nash was cashiered for
extravagance by Parliament after the King's death in 1830, and the most
palatial elements of his scheme—the triumphal arches framing the
palace on the mall and park sides—were either moved (in the case of
the 'Marble Arch') or left unfinished (in the case of the 'Pimlico' arch at
Hyde Park Corner). Still, between them, Nash and George IV did their
best to bequeath to Europe a new idea of what Donald Olsen has called
'the city as a work of art'.[35]

Something more like true State patronage of the arts was involved in
two other post-war projects loosely connected to these royal metropolitan

---

[32] See also Nicholas Penny, '"Amor Publicus Posuit": Monuments for the People and of the
People', *Burlington Magazine*, 129 (1987), 793–800, on differences in *who* was being
commemorated.

[33] John Summerson, *Georgian London*, new edn (London, 1988), p. 171, adapting Rasmussen's
verdict on the Adelphi.

[34] John Summerson, *John Nash, Architect to King George IV*, 2nd edn (London, 1949), p. 234.

[35] Donald J. Olsen, *The City as a Work of Art: London–Paris–Vienna* (New Haven, CT, and
London, 1986).

improvements, plans for a National Gallery and a new British Museum. After 1815, with the Louvre looming uncomfortably and the Altes Museum in the works, Britain's lack of a National Gallery began to seem a source of 'national reproach'. As a result of the Napoleonic dislocations, a veritable avalanche of art was pouring into Britain, but all into private hands, and it was unclear that private enterprise alone would ever bring a sufficient portion of it into public view. George IV and other leading collectors organised the British Institution in 1805, a private body that aimed to put on public exhibitions in the West End. Commercial exhibitors such as the Boydell brothers were keen to fill the same gap. 'The encouragement of the arts', they wrote, 'must be placed on a *firmer* basis . . . that will not only support itself, but make a return to its patrons, for *this is a commercial country*.'[36] But with most Old Masters locked up in private collections a case could be made for market failure, and tentatively the Royal Academy began to make that case. 'In order to raise [the arts] to excellence . . . some enlarged and predominant direction of their powers to *public purposes* must be sought at the hands of the state', it argued in 1813. 'From the *state*, it must be repeated, from the state alone, it can be sought.'[37] Finally, in 1823, with finance available from the windfall repayment of an Austrian war loan, the government announced a package of grants which combined almost in Prussian style £300,000 for repairs to Windsor Castle, £500,000 for the building of new churches, and £57,000 to purchase the Pall Mall townhouse and art collection of J. J. Angerstein as a National Gallery. In language rather new to British ears, it was, said the government, 'consistent with the true dignity of a great nation, and with the liberal spirit of a free people, to give a munificent encouragement to the support and promotion of the Fine Arts'.[38]

At first, however, the National Gallery was not quite in the spirit of a great nation or of a free people. Its projectors had in mind not a substitute for the market in diffusing the fine arts among the people but an antidote to the market in shielding the finer qualities of the arts from the vulgar influences of commerce and democracy. For its first ten years, the gallery remained in Angerstein's house on Pall Mall, with restricted access, like the British Museum confided to the authority of a board of

---

[36] Conlin, 'Origins and History of the National Gallery', 60–2.
[37] Peter Funnell, 'William Hazlitt, Prince Hoare, and the Institutionalisation of the British Art World', in Brian Allen (ed.), *Towards a Modern Art World* (New Haven, CT, and London, 1995), p. 148.
[38] Conlin, 'Origins and History of the National Gallery', 19–23.

trustees without parliamentary oversight, and with no authorisation to extend its collections except at the private whim of ministers and trustees. At the same time, however, the British Museum did benefit from a burst of more generous patronage. Just as Parliament was shamed by continental comparisons into authorising a National Gallery, so it was shamed by the capture of the famed Aegina Marbles by Prince Ludwig of Bavaria into authorising a one-off expenditure of £35,000 on the Elgin Marbles in 1816. The demands of housing these marbles, and the royal library donated to the Museum on the death of George III, also drove Parliament into a considerable outlay on a new building in Bloomsbury, which Robert Smirke began to design in 1823.[39]

These grants to the National Gallery and the British Museum share a number of features. They were exceptional, one-time-only expenditures, aimed at exploiting the exceptional bounty of art unmoored in the wake of war. Parliament would not again authorise expenditure on this scale until the 1880s. Neither the parliamentary elite nor public opinion saw the patronage of the arts as one of government's core functions. At about the same time as the National Gallery grant of £57,000 for a house and thirty-eight paintings, the government turned down the offer of 3,000 paintings from the collection of Edward Solly, the leading British merchant in Berlin, which were purchased instead for £630,000 by the Prussian government to augment the royal collection for Schinkel's Altes Museum.[40] Unlike Britain's parliamentary government, the Prussian government had the will to buy art, the desire to transmute royal traditions of patronage into State patronage, and—crucially—the immunity from public scrutiny that made this transmutation possible. The National Gallery and the British Museum initiatives were modest not only in their scope, therefore, but in their stated rationales. They more resembled mid-eighteenth-century acts of royal patronage aimed at glorifying the Crown and cultivating the pleasures of gentlemen than French or German experiments in the State organisation of the public sphere. In certain respects, they represented an attempt by a section of the governing elite to shield the fine arts from a commercial public sphere which was seen as increasingly demanding and threatening. Public opinion, on the whole, preferred to leave the fine arts to the tender mercies of commerce.

---

[39] Nash's plan to link this new building to his West End development by means of a triumphal avenue was another of the schemes killed by Parliament later in the decade.

[40] Frank Herrmann, 'Peel and Solly: Two Nineteenth-century Art Collectors and their Sources of Supply', *Journal of the History of Collections*, 3 (1991), 94.

IV

To some extent these contrasts shrank in the decades after 1830. The rationales for State patronage familiar on the Continent became temporarily more palatable in Britain, as its social and political crises around 1830 signalled that the parliamentary elite's neglect of national integration had gone too far. Reliance upon the canons of political economy had either failed to elicit the desired degree of moral improvement and social cohesion or, arguably, had contributed to degeneration and disintegration. While Frenchified talk of national glory remained taboo, after 1830 there was a perceptible growth in British interest in Germanic formulae for religious, educational, and cultural programmes of popular uplift. This rhetoric recognised the importance of moral and spiritual progress, either independent of or possibly even at cross-purposes to material progress, and, to a more limited extent, recognised the value of elite, clerical, or State initiatives to cultivate that moral and spiritual development. In practical terms, it was applied more to the development of a State educational system, emphasising textual literacy compatible with Protestant traditions, than to innovations in the public patronage of the arts. As Jonathan Conlin has pointed out in a recent article, Gladstone in his *State in its Relations with the Church* (1838) proposed the National Gallery as a model for the State's responsibility for the spiritual well-being of its citizenry; but at that point such a proposition was widely viewed as a piece of outrageously crypto-Catholic Toryism, and the only programme of social reform with which Gladstone associated himself at the time to reach the statute books was the plan for State subsidy of religious schools.[41]

That said, the Whig governments in power for most of the 1830s and 1840s *were* more open to a range of arguments for State intervention on behalf of the people's moral, spiritual, and material well-being, and some of these arguments identified the arts as a likely arena for State action.[42] The most effective arguments were those which blended the material with the moral and spiritual, so that the most ambitious project of State patronage undertaken in this period emphasised the usefulness of art and design education to industry. A commonplace in German debates since

[41] Jonathan Conlin, 'Gladstone and Christian Art, 1832–1854', *Historical Journal*, 46 (2003), 341–74.
[42] Peter Mandler, *Aristocratic Government in the Age of Reform: Whigs and Liberals, 1830–1852* (Oxford, 1990), though strangely neglecting the arts and 'heritage'.

the 1790s, but only limply embraced by the Royal Academy in England, the harnessing of art and design to industry was now vigorously advocated in several parliamentary inquiries of the 1830s, leading to the foundation of the Central School of Design (later the Royal College of Art), a network of local schools and museums of art and design, and ultimately to the Great Exhibition of 1851 and the whole South Kensington complex. But this was only one of several distinct though intertwined lines of approach. The Select Committee on National Monuments and Works of Art (1841) struck themes that were much less utilitarian and much more hopeful about the morally and spiritually uplifting qualities of works of art, as well as the social benefits to be gained from cultivating public interest in the great national monuments such as cathedrals, castles, and palaces. As Emma Winter's work is now showing in great detail, most explicitly dependent upon German examples were the Select Committee on the Fine Arts (also 1841) and its successor Royal Commission, charged with overseeing the construction and decoration of the new Houses of Parliament. Not only did the Royal Commission adopt Pugin's and Barry's explicitly national Gothic–Elizabethan style for the exterior construction, but it also launched a very public (and very popular) competition to attract English painters to the fresco styles pioneered by Ludwig I in Bavaria and in the end commissioned a series of frescos depicting scenes of national glory cribbed directly from Ludwig's favourite Nazarene painters.[43]

All of these initiatives left their legacies, not least in bricks and mortar—the buildings in which the National Gallery and the British Museum still reside, the South Kensington complex, the Houses of Parliament, the local museums and art colleges around the country. But I want to close by suggesting that after the climax of these initiatives around 1848 the British approach to State patronage of the fine arts reverted to a condition more like that prevailing before 1830, and diverged once again from the approaches prevalent in France, Germany, and many other continental States. One context was a changed attitude to continental modes of governance after 1848. The sequence of revolutions in 1848 and authoritarianism thereafter refortified British determination

---

[43] Emma L. Winter, 'German Fresco Painting and the New Houses of Parliament at Westminster, 1834–51', *Historical Journal*, 47 (2004), 291–329. The bigger picture—ranging back to Anglo-German contacts in Italy after 1815, and taking in influences upon all of the major parliamentary inquiries of the 1830s and 1840s—is discussed in eadem, 'The Transformation of Taste in Germany and England, 1797–1858', Ph.D. dissertation (Cambridge, 2005).

to resist 'bureau and barrack' in all things.[44] This alone, as Matthew Arnold mourned, kicked out one of the slender props that supported State patronage of the arts in Britain. 'We have not the notion', he complained, 'so familiar on the Continent . . . of *the State*—the nation in its collective and corporate character, entrusted with stringent powers for the general advantage.'[45] Another context, to which Arnold was also sensitive, was a hardening of the heart against the specific aesthetic and spiritual qualities which the fine arts were traditionally held to foster. A renewed materialism, though couched (as Arnold complained) in religious language, did not exclude aesthetic concerns altogether, but decidedly subordinated them. Samuel Smiles's *Self-help* of 1859 praised Michelangelo, Titian, Cellini, Reynolds, and Wilkie as 'workers in art', but principally for their labour-inputs, the long years of work they put in, their care and diligence.[46]

In these altered contexts, the initiatives of the 1830s and 1840s did not flower in the way their projectors had intended. The National Gallery and British Museum came under the stricter financial and administrative control of Parliament. South Kensington leant to its science rather than its art side. Local authorities were very slow to take up their permissive powers to build museums: no rate-supported art gallery was founded until the Nottingham Castle Museum in 1876. Opera, theatre, dance, and music remained wholly outside the purview of the State. The Royal Academy of Music founded in 1823 was not a State institution, receiving no parliamentary funds and only a token 100 guineas from the King; it had virtually collapsed by 1867 and tried then to abandon its royal charter. This is not to say that the decades after 1850 saw a withering of cultural activity in Britain, only that such activity was floated by commercial and philanthropic rather than by State effort. Despite the lack of royal opera houses and full-time orchestras, there were probably more concerts performed before larger audiences in London than in any other city in Europe; despite the lack of local museums or lavishly funded royal academies, art clubs and exhibitions proliferated, and painters made fortunes. But the State had little to do with this. After Prince Albert's death, the court's contribution to the patronage of the fine arts was nearly nil. Members of

[44] Bernard Porter, '"Bureau and Barrack": Early Victorian Attitudes Towards the Continent', *Victorian Studies*, 27 (1983–4), 407–33.
[45] Matthew Arnold, *Culture and Anarchy and Other Writings*, ed. Stefan Collini (Cambridge, 1993), p. 83.
[46] Samuel Smiles, *Self-help*, 1866 edn (Oxford, 2002), ch. 6.

the traditional governing classes patronised the arts in their private capacity. Local elites, especially outside London, were much less interested in the arts than their equivalents in France or, especially, Germany. Britain had no *Bildungsbürgertum* to bring together local government and cultural patronage: it had too few universities, too few State clergy, its doctors and lawyers were concentrated in London and elsewhere subordinated to industrial and commercial groups. The liberal, commercial, nonconformist ethos that resulted was more likely to vest its local pride or identity in a gasworks or a tramway than in an art collection or orchestra.

To sum up: putting the British experience of State support for the arts into European context does not necessarily mean putting it in the European mainstream. Parliamentarism disrupted the ability of the Crown to play the role of patron. The commercial character of the public sphere ensured that the arts would be well represented on one level, but that level was not the level of the State, and aesthetes were divided as to whether this was a good or a bad thing. The Protestant and commercial character of the public sphere directed local and national elites' organised activity to other ends. And this divergence, temporarily narrowing at points along the way, probably widened over the whole period from the middle of the eighteenth to the middle of the nineteenth century. There were common experiences across Europe—professionalisation and institutionalisation, the growth of a middle-class public for the arts, the sacralisation of the arts—but there was no consensus either on the usefulness of the arts in expressing individual, social, and national development, or on the State's responsibility in this sphere.

The Invention of National Languages

OTTO DANN

WILHELM VON HUMBOLDT (1767–1835), Prussian envoy to the United Kingdom after the Congress of Vienna, lived privately in Paris from 1797 with the intention of witnessing at first hand the first modern republican nation in Europe. At the turn of the century, he travelled twice from Paris to Spain and discovered the Basque people there. Unexpectedly he immersed himself in studies of their language and in this way he became the linguist whom we remember today. Humboldt's study of Parisian society, on the other hand, faced no language difficulties. As an educated noble, he was well versed in French. It was a wholly new experience for the young Humboldt to find that there were still vernacular languages to be discovered and studied in Europe—not to be invented, but that is an issue we will discuss later.

Humboldt's travel account was published as *Untersuchungen über die Vaskische Sprache und Nation*.[1] In short, he hoped to approach the Basque nation by way of its language. This method—the study of an unknown people through their language—amounted to a new approach to an issue that had attained considerable significance among the European intelligentsia during the eighteenth century: an interest in knowing about other peoples, their manners and culture, and their 'national character'. A new development in their own social awareness was behind this outwardly directed interest of the intellectuals.

In the second half of the eighteenth century a qualified kind of ethno-genesis can be observed among the educated classes of the Western world. In the course of their social emancipation a new political identity emerged, one orientated towards the fatherland (*patria*), the state, and its population. This new ethnic consciousness bridged older identities such as estate, profession, or religion. It originated in connection with the great

---

[1] Wilhelm von Humboldt, *Werke in fuenf Baenden*, ed. Andreas Flitner and Klaus Giel (Stuttgart, 1979–86), vol. 5, pp. 113ff. and 430f.

Proceedings of the British Academy, **134**, 121–133. © The British Academy 2006.

eighteenth-century social movement of patriotism, which became more and more politicised. In this context, the modern, political concept of the nation was adopted by the educated classes. In the last third of the century, this concept became one of identity in the struggle against absolutism and, with the French Revolution, the leading political model for modern societies.

The civil nation also displayed new behaviour with regard to language: the use of mother tongue was celebrated and it was understood as a 'national language'. In this context, the great linguistic divergence that existed in societies at that time should be recalled. Since the seventeenth century, the language of conversation among nobles and the educated classes had been French, and academics had used Latin as a language of correspondence and publication since medieval times. This characteristic diglossia of the elites in the West had now lost its dominant social significance. The nation, which, according to the new concept, was to encompass all social classes, was also understood as a language community; the national population was seen as shaped by the national language, and no longer as divided into a multitude of class languages, dialects, and regional idioms. With respect to this issue Humboldt declared: 'Language always belongs to the whole nation because in it, the ways of thinking of people of all ages, both sexes, all classes, characters, and intellectual dispositions belonging to the same ethnic grouping—and by the transfer of words also to different nations—are mixed, purified, and reformed.'[2] His writings and letters convey the fascination that radiated at the time from the discovery of the connection between nation and language.

The philosophical discourse about the nature of language, which had existed since antiquity, intensified greatly during the eighteenth century. Locke and Berkeley in Britain and Condillac in France provided important stimuli in this respect. For our context, Johann Gottfried Herder is significant, since he was the first to take vernacular languages and popular poetry (*Volkspoesie*) seriously as expressions of the culture of illiterate peoples. His *Fragmentenschrift* of 1768 contains the earliest German usage of the term 'Nationalsprache' (national language) of which I am aware: 'Every nation has its own storehouse of thoughts that have become signs. This is its national language, . . . the treasury of thoughts of a whole people'.[3] The terms for 'people' and 'nation' were used as syn-

---

[2] Humboldt, *Werke*, vol. 3, p. 18; see Paul R. Sweet, *Wilhelm von Humboldt: A Biography*, 2 vols (Columbus, OH, 1978–80), vol. 1, pp. 218ff.

[3] Johann Gottfried Herder, *Werke in zehn Baenden* (Frankfurt am Main, 1985–2000), vol. 1, p. 553.

onyms, and this is where the problems of writing a history of the concept (*Begriffsgeschichte*) of 'national language' begin. To the best of my knowledge, no study of its genesis and development exists.

According to the Encyclopaedists, the age of the lexicographers began in the last third of the eighteenth century. They produced whole inventories of their languages: Noah Webster as a North American patriot and, in Germany, Johann Christoph Adelung followed by Jacob Grimm. Empirical–historical linguistics originated in parallel with this writing of dictionaries. In 1786, linguistics received a strong stimulus from the work of the Orientalist William Jones, who proved that Sanskrit is related to European languages and, moreover, is more complete in its linguistic structure than Greek or Latin. In addition to being reinforced by Jones's discovery, comparative linguistics assumed a global character. In Germany, Wilhelm von Humboldt was one its first and most important practitioners. After his political activities, he began to give lectures at the Prussian Academy. The first was entitled 'On the Comparative Study of Languages' (*Über das vergleichende Sprachstudium*),[4] and in it he presented an outline of his great linguistic project.

Around 1800, therefore, we see a great flowering of interest in languages. The elite classes of the modern nation had an elementary interest in communication, both among themselves and with those classes who had yet to be mobilised for the project of the nation. The huge expansion of the book and newspaper market resulted in the practice of a common language. And the emergent discipline of linguistics confirmed the close connection between the constitution of national languages and nation-formation.

These pivotal connections must be kept in mind as we now turn to the social and political dimensions of contemporary projects concerning national languages and juxtapose five different scenarios for the period around 1800. Finally we have to return to the general connections between nation and language.

First, however, it is necessary to be aware of the current situation with respect to national language, since our position is considerably different from that outlined above. In our linguistic behaviour, we on the Continent are on the way towards a new diglossia. English is considered indispensable as the language of European communication, while one's own mother

---

[4] Humboldt, *Werke*, vol. 3, pp. 1–25; see Hans Aarsleff, *From Locke to Saussure* (Minneapolis, MN, 1982).

tongue, the national language, is losing its monopoly in its own domain. Nationality is not as strongly bound up with the national language as it was even in the 1960s. We live, in a socio-linguistic sense, in a situation that is almost opposite to that obtaining around 1800!

The academic literature on national languages has been significantly shaped by this change. The writings of Hans Kohn, still unsurpassed in conveying the central data on the eighteenth-century situation, represent the tradition that language was central to the development and under-standing of nations.[5] In 1971 Joshua Fishman published a cautiously ana-lytical overview, based on the methodology of the sociology of language, of the connections between nationalism, national politics, and language that is still instructive today. He sees national languages in their primary, integrative function, and can thus also record and constructively discuss the many variations of modern language planning.[6] After John Armstrong's impressive studies of pre-national peoples, a new tendency gained acceptance at the end of the 1970s. Armstrong adopted Frederik Barth's exclusion thesis and characterised ethnicities in terms of their border experiences, myths, and symbols. He thus grants language only relative significance. It becomes the least important of his ethnic criteria, relevant mainly as a border guard of ethnicity.[7]

In 1983, three stimulating theses were put forward. First, there was Eric Hobsbawm's *The Invention of Tradition*. Although focusing particu-larly on the middle and end of the nineteenth century, at the end of the introduction Hobsbawm applies his argument generally to 'historical innovation [!], the nation', and claims that 'the national phenomenon can-not be adequately investigated without careful attention to the "invention of tradition"'.[8] Because of its title alone, Benedict Anderson's *Imagined Communities* had a strong impact on studies of nation and nationalism, especially in Germany. From an American, and especially South American, perspective, Anderson looks at national developments in nineteenth-century Europe and recognises that the question of the national language, which played practically no role in America, was at the centre of the dis-cussion there. Anderson thus understands European national movements

[5] See esp. Hans Kohn, *The Idea of Nationalism: A Study in Its Origins and Background* (New York, 1948 edn), pp. 6–8 and passim.

[6] Joshua A. Fishman, *Language and Nationalism: Two Interpretive Essays* (New York, 1972). See also idem (ed.), *Advances in Language Planning* (The Hague, 1974).

[7] John A. Armstrong, *Nations before Nationalism* (Chapel Hill, NC, 1982), pp. 7, 13, and 241–82.

[8] Eric J. Hobsbawm and T. Ranger (eds), *The Invention of Tradition* (London, 1984 edn), pp. 13f.

as essentially a 'lexicographic, philological revolution'.[9] And he formulates a unique thesis: the model of the modern national state was developed in America around 1800 and only imitated by the Europeans after 1830. Finally, in 1983 the anthropologist and cultural philosopher Ernest Gellner offered a special challenge to historical research on nationalism. Here, too, the question hinges on the social role played by languages. Gellner rightly observes that national languages were dependent on the modern state for their standardisation and expansion, which occurred through compulsory schooling and other means. Even if he gets lost in adventurous hypotheses about nations and nationalism, Gellner convincingly shows that our modern national languages come not at the beginning, but at the end, of linguistic developments.[10] As early as 1986, the Grand Old Man of today's research on nations, Anthony D. Smith, offered a significant but balanced answer to the many new theses on nationalism. He, too, sees ethnicities and nations no longer as primarily defined through language: 'Examples could be multiplied to show that language, long held to be the main, if not the sole, differentiating mark of ethnicity, is often irrelevant or divisive for the sense of ethnic community.'[11]

In his 1990 book *Nations and Nationalism*, Hobsbawm strikingly summarised the critical arguments on the historical role of national languages. 'National languages', he writes,

> are almost always semi-artificial constructs and occasionally, like modern Hebrew, virtually invented. They are the opposite of what nationalist mythology supposes them to be, namely the primordial foundations of national culture and the matrices of the national mind. They are usually attempts to devise a standardized idiom out of a multiplicity of actually spoken idioms, and the main problem in their construction being usually, which dialect to choose as the base of the standardized and homogenized language ... Thus in the era before general primary education there was and could be no spoken 'national' language.[12]

Finally, Hobsbawm asserts,

> the mystical identification of nationality with a sort of platonic idea of the language, existing behind and above all its variant and imperfect versions, is much more characteristic of the ideological construction of nationalist intellectuals,

[9] Benedict Anderson, *Imagined Communities: Reflections on the Origin and Spread of Nationalism* (London, 1986 edn), pp. 70–5, at pp. 41ff.

[10] Ernest Gellner, *Nations and Nationalism* (Oxford, 1983).

[11] Anthony D. Smith, *The Ethnic Origins of Nations* (Oxford, 1986), p. 27.

[12] Eric J. Hobsbawm, *Nations and Nationalism since 1780: Programme, Myth, Reality* (Cambridge, 1990), pp. 54, 52.

of whom Herder is the prophet, than of the actual grassroots users of the idiom. It is a literary and not an existential concept.[13]

None of the authors mentioned here truly investigates the developmental period of national languages, which, as such, are no more than about 200 years old. The reader gains the impression that these authors are arguing against a 'tradition' which they never specifically name or analyse; this also appears to be a case of the 'invention of tradition'. In the recent lit-erature of linguistics, the topic of national languages has been critically set aside. But recently keen attention has been paid to Humboldt and the thrilling discussion of language that occurred at his time.

Let us now direct the historical imagination to five different European regions. First we turn to *France*, which pioneered nation formation in Europe, and language politics appeared early here. As early as 1539 the French vernacular was declared the official royal language. This was fol-lowed by the foundation of the *Académie française*, which contributed greatly to the *bon usage* of the early standardised language. From 1789, the new French nation placed different emphases on the issue: in September 1791, the National Assembly created a *Comité de l'instruction publique*, and six months later Condorcet, as a member of the committee, presented a plan for universal schooling in French. After the creation of the first French republic, they intensified their efforts to unify language instruction. In 1794, Abbé Grégoire presented to the National Convention a *Rapport sur la nécessité et les moyens d'anéantir des patois et d'universaliser l'usage de la langue française*. He reported that more than 6 million citizens did not know the national language and that only 3 million at the most were capable of conversing in it. Thus, he concluded,

> On peut uniformer le langage d'une grande nation, de manière que tous les citoyens qui la compose, puissent sans obstacle se communiquer ses pensées. Cette entreprise, qui ne fut pleinement exécuté chez aucun peuple, est digne du peuple français, qui centralise toutes les branches de l'organisation sociale, et qui doit être jaloux de consacrer au plutôt, dans une République une et indivisible, l'usage unique et invariable de la langue de la liberté.[14]

The previous year, the Jacobin Republic had enacted a school law pre-scribing the teaching of the national language to all children. The repub-lican nation's political elite had recognised that the nation's future

[13] Hobsbawm, *Nations and Nationalism*, p. 57.
[14] René Balibar and Dominique Laporte, *Le Français national: Politique et pratique de la langue nationale sous la Révolution* (Paris, 1974), p. 200.

depended on communication and the participation of its citizens. The national language thus became a matter of prestige, and was enshrined in the leading slogan of the Revolution: 'la langue de la liberté'.

During the eighteenth century, the 'grand idea' of uniting all *Greeks* in their own state emerged among educated and wealthy Greeks living scattered throughout Europe. After 1789, the enlightened intelligentsia, such as the poet Rhigas, who used the existing written vernacular, quickly appealed to the example of the French Revolution. Other patriots, such as the doctor Korais, who devoted himself to the great national language project, preferred a return to classical Greek. He wrote:

> The only means which I found was the publication of the Greek authors with long introductions in vulgar Greek, which could be read not only by those who study the ancient language, but also by the people. But for such an enterprise a much greater knowledge of the Greek language was necessary; therefore I devoted myself entirely to acquiring it.[15]

Korais was convinced that 'the intellectuals of the nation are naturally the legislators of the language', and thus he took part in the controversial debate about the national language at the beginning of the nineteenth century. He became a productive language reformer, striving to mediate between the classical and the vernacular. Although groups within the Orthodox Church launched vicious polemics against him, he achieved his goal. Even if the debate on the national language continued long after the foundation of the state, Korais's contribution remains unforgotten. As in Norway, in Greece two national linguistic options long remained alive and, indeed, virulent.

In Britain, where the question of national language was never as explosive as on the continent, it is not easy to find a case applicable to our theme. Hans Kohn, however, writes of a kind of Welsh nationalism,[16] and, in fact, there was a special type of language movement in *Wales* during the eighteenth century. It emerged from a religious awakening, which was strongly shaped by missionary impulses among the common people. It first occurred within the Anglican Church, where the talented preacher Griffith Jones, encouraged by a noble, began in 1731 to enliven circulating charity schools by speaking to them in the Welsh vernacular. Through encounters with the Moravians (Herrnhuter) from Germany, this successful organised vernacular assembly movement continued in the second half of the century in the Sunday schools of the flourishing Methodist

---

[15] Quoted in Kohn, *Idea*, p. 540.
[16] Ibid., p. 462.

Church. In addition, vernacular poetry blossomed: for instance in the work of Goronwy Owen, the religious hymns of William Williams, and, finally, in the literary societies of educated Welsh circles in London, who were also active in historical and linguistic research. The industrialisation of southern Wales at the beginning of the nineteenth century and the social mobility it introduced brought this Welsh-language movement to an end. Modern in its organisation, it was ultimately produced by a traditional society that developed no further political ambitions.

In eighteenth-century *Bohemia*, Czech-speaking and German-speaking populations lived side by side, although after the catastrophe of 1620 Czech had declined into a purely oral language of the rural people. The *natio bohemica* of nobles, assembled in the parliament, conversed in Latin or German. Long developed as a written language (for example, the Bible was translated in 1549), Czech enjoyed new attention during the Enlightenment among individual nobles, priests, and intellectuals who spoke German colloquially, but nevertheless became actively engaged in the revival of Czech. The following should be mentioned: Count Franz Josef Kinsky, the Piarist Gelasius Dobner, Josef Jungmann who, in his lecture *Über die tschechische Sprache* (On the Czech language, 1803), made language the central criterion for the nation, and Josef Dobrowsky who, as linguist, was the founder of Slavic language studies. The establishment of German as a public language in the Josephine reforms (for example, replacing Latin in secondary schools) was often seen as a challenge. But we must also see that at the time the vernacular languages were in no way opposed, even in official circles. In 1775, a chair for the Czech language was established at the University of Vienna, and in 1792 at the University of Prague. The revival of the Czech language in a spirit of enlightened patriotism resulted in a new Czech self-confidence, and initiated the formation of a modern Czech nation. The vernacular became a national language. In the foreword to his German–Czech dictionary of 1834, Jungmann was thus able to write: 'A dictionary of the national language belongs among the first necessities of the educated individual.'[17]

The situation in *Germany* at the end of the Holy Roman Empire is complex, but of great interest for our topic. The poet Klopstock marks the beginning of an enormous upsurge in German literature in the middle of the eighteenth century; he demonstrated how much could be done

[17] Quoted in Derek Sayer, *The Coasts of Bohemia: A Czech History*, 2 vols (Princeton, NJ, 1998), p. 72.

poetically with the German language, and his head was filled with a hybrid and mythic idea of its history. In 1780, Frederick the Great criticised German literature and the German language—in French. Justus Möser, a patriot from Osnabrück, replied to this criticism with an essay *Über die deutsche Sprache und Literatur* (On the German language and literature). He showed that Germany did not have one national language, but rather a great variety of social languages: book language and popular language, poetic language and oratorical language, philosophical language, and so on. In addition, he wrote: 'The English language is the only vernacular language in Europe that is written down; a provincial dialect elevated to the throne, standing on its own ground ... All the rest are book languages, merely the conventional languages of the court or of scholarship.' Among such languages he included French and Old High German. Nevertheless, he continued, 'No language, perhaps, has changed to its advantage as much as ours ... Lessing was the first to nationalise provincial turns of phrase, where they served the purpose,' and he turned to Klopstock and Goethe.[18] In 1787 Herder elaborated the project of an *Institut für den Allgemeingeist Deutschlands* (Institute for the General Spirit of Germany). Its first section was to be dedicated to the 'Culture of Language', 'for it is a sign that we have a low opinion of ourselves so long as we are ashamed of our language both at home and towards other nations'. Countless efforts were made on behalf of the German language at that time because it was felt to be the most important tie between Germans in a situation of great political crisis, where the nation of the German princes was breaking apart and the citizen nation still lacked political concepts.

Ernst Moritz Arndt's poem, *Was ist des Deutschen Vaterland?*, which is often cited in our context as it points to the German-language community, should perhaps rather be understood as a patriotic representation of all German regions and not as a political programme. The philosopher Fichte's lecture about the German language as an 'Ur-Sprache' shows, however, in the context of the struggle against Napoleon, that intellectual chauvinism could be mixed with the myths circulating about the German language. At the Congress of Vienna, French was again the language of conversation and political negotiation, although the Bavarian delegation demanded that the languages of the five great powers should be used equally. In December 1816, the assembly of the German Federation

---

[18] Justus Möser, *Anwalt des Vaterlands*, ed. Friedemann Berger (Leipzig, 1978), pp. 414f.

resolved that, respecting 'its own dignity, the honour of the nation, and the high value of the German language', it was appropriate that its written correspondence should be conducted in German[19]—the earliest beginnings of language policy in a federal Germany. But there was still a long way to go to learn to distinguish between the German nation and the German-language community.

After looking through five historical contexts, we can summarise the situation at the turn of the nineteenth century. In France during the first Republic, the national language was the political project of a victorious modern nation. In Wales, by contrast, where traditional structures still dominated in the eighteenth century, an organised recovery of Celtic Welsh as a regional language took place accompanied by a religious revival. In Bohemia, the previously suppressed Czech vernacular enjoyed a renaissance as the result of the deliberate efforts of a group of language patriots supported by a wave of sympathy for folk culture among the Bohemian-German educated elite. Its rise had no national political ambitions or implications. The scattered communities of Greeks who, after the French Revolution, began to organise as a national movement, had to make a decision about their national language: should it be a standardisation of the vernacular or should it be a recreation of the classical literary language? The effectiveness of an individual language reformer was decisive in this situation. In Germany, beginning in the middle of the eighteenth century, the literary language became established as a vernacular in the context of a widespread cultural movement, pushing back the special languages of the nobility, the academics, the Jews, and of the various regions. It was understood as a national language, even though the national political situation in Central Europe was in profound upheaval.

In view of the divergent situations in which the first national languages were used in Europe, it is not easy to make general statements. In this context it may be useful to look at the historical emergence of the later national languages. All of these national languages arose out of vernacular languages, even if not directly or in a straight line. Being written down was an important stage along their developmental path. This entailed a process of objectification of the oral language, which in turn meant that it was standardised and used as a language of literature, trade, and politics. The transition from Latin to a written vernacular, which can gener-

---

[19] Quoted in Arno Borst, *Der Turmbau von Babel: Geschichte der Meinungen über Ursprung und Vielfalt der Sprachen und Völker*, 4 vols (Stuttgart, 1983), vol. 3.2, p. 1558.

ally be dated to the late Middle Ages, is considered as an important event in national histories and is often connected with the work of particular individuals. Two events played an important part in the further expansion of a written vernacular: their use in the translation of the Bible, and their use as a language of print. But we cannot speak of the emergence of a national language in the pre-modern and early-modern period. Even in the well known case of Italian, this did not happen until the nineteenth century. The concept of a national language did not appear before the middle of the eighteenth century. With respect to the 'national states' of the early-modern period, we must speak of a written culture of the state and its elites, and, where applicable, of the beginnings of a language policy which occurred with the establishment of official languages.

As we look forward, from 1800, into the nineteenth century, we quickly enter a period when national languages become a political issue. A national language belongs to the basic equipment of every national movement, and there are very few in Europe in which language issues played no part. Even the discovery—not invention!—of a national language could be a problem. In Greece it remained on the political agenda long after the foundation of the state. Belgium's history shows that two stages of language politics can be distinguished: first, the acceptance of a regional language as a language of schooling and an official language; and, second, the demand for its equal status as state language. Belgium also shows how difficult, but not impossible, it is to find a democratic arrangement in language conflicts. It is possible only after having passed through the era of nationalism.

The time around 1800 may be characterised with respect to the problem of national language as a period of transition. From the excitement over language at a moment of regional and religious awakening to the active language policies of a victorious nation-state, different forms and applications of national languages existed next to each other, and not every people had its 'national' language at that time. The issue of national language is first encountered in the texts of the mid-eighteenth century, in the milieu of contemporary patriotism. The use of this term means the attribution of a language to a people as a nation, even if the concept of nation might be applied to a variety of ethnicities. In the context of contemporary patriotism, however, it was clear that this attribution meant that this language was to become the language of all social classes, encompassing the entire nation. As the nation expanded, linguistic diversity needed to be overcome. Engagement in favour of the national language was a contribution to the formation of the nation, to be achieved through the integrative function of a common language. A special characteristic of this period is that the project of national languages was bound to a widespread interest in language among the contemporary educated classes, who likewise gave modern linguistics its initial impetus.

The concept of a national language, we can conclude, originated in the patriotism of the eighteenth century, and even today it has not lost its characteristics as a project. Its validity and meaning has always depended on the concept of nation and its political realisation. Pulling the above observations together, we arrive at two specific meanings of 'national language' around 1800. This notion signified either the language of a people or an ethnicity that was described as a nation or understood itself as a nation, or the language of a nation-state, which was politically legitimised to manage and supervise it.

The general question arises here as to what position the notion of national language has in our system of languages. It is reasonable and sufficient, in my estimation, to differentiate three types of languages: first, vernacular languages (*Volkssprachen*), that is, the spoken tongues of a social group or a language community; second, written languages (*Schriftsprachen*), that is, vernacular languages which are written down and thereby standardised and open to various applications, especially as literary languages (*Literatursprachen*); and, third, state or official languages (*Staatssprachen*), that is, written languages which are accepted and administered by state or public institutions as obligatory in the public arena. The term 'national language' cannot be unambiguously located within this typology, unless it is understood—as is commonly accepted today—in its third meaning of an official language belonging to a nation-state.

'The Invention of National Languages'—we return to the title of this essay. This is a challenge to engage with the thesis that Eric Hobsbawm put forward twenty years ago. His paradoxical formulation, 'invention of tradition', has given rise to countless applications. He himself had applied it to the issue of the nation, and this had a striking impact, especially in Germany, where since 1983 the national tradition has increasingly been felt to be a problem. Hobsbawm's formulation provided a means by which one could distance oneself from it. The translation into German of Benedict Anderson's title *Imagined Communities* as *Die Erfindung der Nation* (The Invention of the Nation) is one striking example of that effect.

The idea that national languages frequently originate in invention has often been repeated. What are the specific facts behind this suggestion?

The fact that brilliant individuals also played a part in the process of selection and standardisation of the vernaculars is familiar from the examples of Dante, or Martin Luther. Nevertheless, who would therefore maintain that Luther 'invented' the German national language? The example of Greek may be explicitly invoked here because of the role played by Korais. But who can say of any existing national language that it was invented? Each national language is based on a traditional vernacular or on a traditional written language. Thus it can be discovered, standardised, or reformed. Even national languages exist in a constant state of change, so long as they are living, practised languages. Is it possible to invent a language? That is an interesting topic on which Humboldt already had something to say.

The profound impact of Hobsbawm's thesis has also, in recent years, ensured some new scholarly attention being paid to this issue. A recent publication by Miroslav Hroch, in which he analyses the linguistic programme of nineteenth-century national movements, deserves mention.[20] But in the public and in the political domain, the issue of national language cannot yet be considered as resolved. Within the EU, every state is assured of respect for its language, and in 1992 all vernacular languages received a guarantee of survival. On the one hand, the currency is being unified, while, on the other, the individuality of national languages is being affirmed. We may soon see a variety of new political problems emerging from this situation—and we as scholars will be painfully unprepared to offer competent answers.

[20] Miroslav Hroch, *In the National Interest. Demands and Goals of European National Movements of the Nineteenth Century: A Comparative Perspective* (Prague, 2000), pp. 65–104.

The Debates about Universal History and National History, *c.* 1800: A Problem-oriented Historical Attempt*

HANS ERICH BÖDEKER

Jede Geschichte muß Weltgeschichte seyn, und nur in Beziehung auf die ganze
Geschichte ist historische Behandlung eines einzelnen Stoffs möglich.[†]

(Novalis)

I

FRIEDRICH RÜHS, recently appointed to the newly established University
of Berlin, opened the series of significant outlines of the principles of history of the nineteenth century in 1811 when he published one of the most
widely read, but now almost forgotten, textbooks of his time. He saw universal history, which unified all 'special histories' as the 'crown', 'in which
all strands of historical culture come together. The relation to universal
history gives the history of the individual and of the whole a new dignity.'
He continued, 'If a number of great men have declared themselves against
universal history, or others, with dignified mien, have rejected it, then
these judgements can only have come about through a misunderstanding,
or can relate only to the usual compendia which, under the name of universal history, contain . . . an aggregate of special histories' instead of a
'system', which, since August Ludwig Schlözer, had been the alternative.
Yet Rühs's conclusions agreed with those of the leading historians of the
early nineteenth century: universal history could 'always be described or

* Translated by Angela Davies, German Historical Institute London.
[†] All history must be world history, and the historical treatment of one particular type of
material is possibe only in relation to the whole of history.

presented only incompletely, but it is the ideal, the prototype of history, and in the head of anyone who studies it seriously and with success, individual pieces of knowledge must align in a universal historical way'.[1] Rühs outlined the problems in the complicated relationship between national history and universal history around 1800. Ultimately, it seemed to him, universal history was too complex for the inductive method used by historians; it resisted their attempts to resolve its contradictions. And at the same time, Rühs strongly retracted the claim of Enlightenment historians to have a total knowledge of history.

The change in theory from universal to national history, from the totality to the individual, which this addressed, was not only the result of methodological or intra-disciplinary consistency, but reflected nationalisation.[2] The background was provided by the particular historical experiences of the time around the turn of the century: the French Revolution and, even more, changes in the German states and the impact of Napoleonic rule. Leopold Ranke justifiably emphasised that historical studies had developed in opposition to the sole dominance of 'Napoleonic', but not of Enlightenment or revolutionary ideas.[3] The way

[1] 'Krone . . . worin alle Strahlen historischer Bildung zusammenfließen. Durch die universalhistorische Beziehung erhält die Geschichte des Einzelnen wie des Ganzen eine neue Würde.' 'Wenn einige große Männer sich gegen die Universalhistorie erklärt, oder andere sie vornehmer Miene verworfen haben, so können diese Urteile entweder nur aus Missverständnis entstanden sein, oder nur die gewöhnlichen Abrisse treffen, die unter den Namen von Universalgeschichte ein Aggregat von Spezialgeschichten . . . enthalten.' '. . . immer nur unvollkommen beschrieben oder dargestellt werden, aber sie ist das Ideal, der Urtypus der Geschichte, und in dem Kopf eines jeden, der sie mit Ernst und Erfolg studiert, müssen sich die einzelnen Kenntnisse universalhistorisch zusammenreihen.' See Friedrich Rühs, *Entwurf einer Propädeutik des historischen Studiums* (1811), ed. and with an introduction by Hans Schleier and Dirk Fleischer (Waltrop, 1997), pp. 11ff.; on the context, see esp. Ulrich Muhlack, 'Universal History and National History: Eighteenth- and Nineteenth-century German Historians and the Scholarly Community', in Benedikt Stuchtey and Peter Wende (eds), *British and German Historiography, 1750–1950: Traditions, Perceptions and Transfers* (Oxford, 2000), pp. 25–48 and the literature cited there, and 'Universalgeschichte in der Frühen Neuzeit: Ein Podium in Aachen', *Storia della Storiografia*, 39 (2001), 63–122.
[2] There is a rich literature on this topic. See esp. Hagen Schulze, *Der Weg zum Nationalstaat: Die deutsche Nationalbewegung vom 18. Jahrhundert bis zur Reichsgründung* (Munich, 1985); Otto Dann, *Nation und Nationalismus in Deutschland, 1770–1990* (Munich, 1993); Jörg Echternkamp, *Der Aufstieg des deutschen Nationalismus* (Frankfurt, 1998); and Dieter Langewiesche and Georg Schmidt (eds), *Föderative Nation: Deutschlandkonzept von der Reformation bis zum Ersten Weltkrieg* (Munich, 2000). There is a large specialist literature on historiography's contribution to the creation of the German nation. For the European context, see, among the most recent publications, Stefan Berger, Mark Donovan, and Kevin Passmore (eds), *Writing National History: Western Europe since 1800* (London, 1999).
[3] See Leopold von Ranke, *Sämmtliche Werke*, vol. 53/54, ed. Alfred Dove (Leipzig, 1840), p. 47.

in which these historical experiences were used, however, cannot be understood without looking at the special developments that took place in Germany before the French Revolution, not only in institutionalised historical research, but also in historical literature and philosophy. The philosophy of history gained in significance as a result of the French Revolution, which also produced the concept of a unified historical process.[4] This in turn provoked an increasing separation between academic history and philosophy. Academic history, in the form of the 'holy trinity of research, teaching, and writing', as Goethe mockingly called it,[5] now saw itself not only as an empirical discipline for specialists, but as an autonomous science of reality with its own theory and practice, and equal in status to philosophy and natural science.

The debates about the relationship between universal history and national history began during the heyday of Enlightenment history-writing. The switch from, in simplified terms, 'Enlightenment history' to 'historicism',[6] it seems, also took place in these debates, which were, for a time, its primary setting. The authors involved were historians, philologists, philosophers, theologians, and men of letters; the names ranged from Gatterer, Schlözer, and Herder to Kant, Humboldt, Ranke, and Droysen.

In order to explore the changing constellations in the relationship between universal history and national history around 1800, we must address six complexes of themes. First we will look at attempts to conceptualise universal history from the end of the eighteenth century, which was one of the most important fields of historical research during the late Enlightenment. That period saw the publication of many works on universal history which tried to present the history of mankind in its total chronological as well as global–spatial extent, and, finally, also in all its cultural diversity. Schlözer summed up this fundamental shift in the

---

[4] See esp. Reinhart Koselleck, 'Geschichte', in Otto Brunner, Werner Conze, and Reinhart Koselleck (eds), *Geschichtliche Grundbegriffe: Historisches Lexikon zur politischen Sprache in Deutschland* (Stuttgart, 1975), vol. 2, pp. 647–717, at p. 676.

[5] '... heiligen Dreieinigkeit von Forschung, Lehre und Darstellung'. Johann Wolfgang Goethe in conversation with the historian Luden, in Flodoard Freiherr von Biedermann (ed.), *Goethes Gespräche* (Leipzig, 1909), vol. 1, p. 433.

[6] For a brief overview, see Ernst Schulin, 'Die Epochenschwelle zwischen Aufklärung und Historismus', in Wolfgang Küttler, Jörn Rüsen, and Ernst Schulin (eds), *Geschichtsdiskurs, vol. 3: Die Epoche der Historisierung* (Frankfurt am Main), 1997, pp. 17–26; Horst Walter Blanke, *Historiographie als Historik* (Stuttgart, 1991); and, most recently, Ernst Wolfgang Becker, *Zeit der Revolution!—Revolution der Zeit? Zeiterfahrungen in Deutschland in der Ära der Revolutionen 1789–1848/9* (Göttingen, 1999).

historical thinking of the Enlightenment when he pointed out that the
universal history that he created was, 'in essence, a history of mankind, a
new type of history'.[7] The ambitious historical genre of universal history
was, as an academic discipline, cultivated chiefly in Göttingen. According
to the Enlightenment concept of the theory of history, universal history
was the epitome of history, thus going beyond the humanist tradition of
historia universalis in the direction of the modern concept of history as a
'collective singular'.[8] This gave rise to questions concerning the conceptualisation of the relationship between 'histories' and 'history', universal
history and specialised histories—in theoretical terms, between the particular and the general, the part and the whole.[9] Then we will look at how
'patriotic history' came about as a form of specialist history under the
specific conditions of the Holy Roman Empire and the particular
processes of nationalisation which emerged after the end of the eighteenth century. In order to understand the new, higher value already
placed on history from the late Enlightenment, we will have to explore the
epistemological changes which took place in dealing with history. In the
foreground here are the increased prestige of particularity, and insights
into the constructed nature of historical units and the development of the
modern concepts of science and art which it encouraged. The process,
addressed here, by which history became an academic discipline,[10] makes
it possible to understand why the historical discipline which was becoming established turned its back on universal history. Different and greater
methodological demands meant that world histories, universal histories,
and extended national histories could no longer be written without com-
plications. The growing concentration on the historical sources of one's
own nation and the ideological implications of national historiography

[7] '. . . im Grunde eine Geschichte der Menschheit, eine neue Art von Geschichte'. August
Ludwig Schlözer, *Vorstellung seiner Universal-Historie* (Göttingen, 1772; reprint Hagen, 1990),
p. 30; on Schlözer, see now Martin Peters, *Altes Reich und Europa: Der Historiker, Statistiker und
Publizist August Ludwig (v.) Schlözer (1735–1809)* (Münster, 2003).

[8] On this, see Koselleck, 'Geschichte', p. 677.

[9] Esp. stimulating is Peter H. Reill, 'Das Problem des Allgemeinen und des Besonderen im
geschichtlichen Denken und in den historiographischen Darstellungen des späten 18.
Jahrhunderts', in Karl Acham and Winfried Schulze (eds), *Teil und Ganzes: Zum Verhältnis von
Einzel- und Gesamtanalyse in Geschichts- und Sozialwissenschaften* (Munich, 1990), pp. 141–68;
and Otto Gerhard Oexle, '"Der Teil und das Ganze" als Problem geschichtswissenschaftlicher
Erkenntnis: Ein historisch-typologischer Versuch', in ibid., pp. 348–84.

[10] On this, see esp. Wolfgang Hardtwig, 'Die Verwissenschaftlichung der Geschichtsschreibung
zwischen Aufklärung und Historismus', in idem, *Geschichtskultur und Wissenschaft* (Munich,
1990), pp. 58–91.

meant that universal historiography took a back seat and its academic potential was doubted. Historiography turned to studies of detail. The ambivalent aspects of this distancing from universal history, which have not received much attention so far in the research, are the subject of the concluding section. Germany's incipient national historiography, too, could not manage without a universal historical perspective. In contrast to the existing research, this essay will examine the theoretical limits of this rejection. Even though a universal historical synthesis could not be achieved with the only historical methods considered legitimate, this perspective continued to be an indispensable premiss, in the logical or hermeneutical sense, for a knowledge of the particular. And German historians were fully aware of this.

This essay is based on the working hypothesis that the relationship between universal history and national history is to be explained as a change in the epistemological constellations of part and whole against the background of incipient nation-state-building. The discussion in this essay is restricted to the discourse of the theory of history. The linguistic–narrative aspect of historiography is deliberately excluded in this context.[11]

II

Since the middle of the eighteenth century, Enlightenment historians had been writing philosophically tinged universal histories in defiance of tradition. For Schlözer, who expressed the principles of Enlightenment universal history most concisely, 'to study world history means thinking connections between the main changes on the earth and within the human race in order to recognise how conditions today derive from both causes'.[12] Thus Schlözer identified the two criteria which distinguished the new universal history: spatially, it related to the whole globe, and

---

[11] For the results of this approach, see, in addition to Michael Gottlob, *Geschichtsschreibung von Johannes Müller und Friedrich Christoph Schlosser* (Berne, 1989), Daniel Fulda, *Wissenschaft aus Kunst: Die Entstehung der modernen deutschen Geschichtsschreibung, 1760–1860* (Berlin, 1996), and most recently Johannes Süssmann, *Geschichtsschreibung oder Roman? Zur Konstitutionslogik von Geschichtserzählungen zwischen Schiller und Ranke (1780–1824)* (Stuttgart, 2000).

[12] 'Weltgeschichte studieren heißt Hauptveränderungen der Erde und des Menschengeschlechts im Zusammenhang denken, um den heutigen Zustand aus beiden Gründen zu erkennen.' August Ludwig Schlözer, *Weltgeschichte nach ihren Hauptheilen im Auszug und Zusammenhang*, 2 parts (Göttingen, 1785/89), i, pt 1, p. 70; see also idem, *Vorstellung seiner Universal-Historie*, p. 4: 'Die

temporally, to the whole of the human race, whose interrelations were to be recognised and explained in relation to the present. Enlightenment universal history was the first to postulate the internal unity of world history—the unity of individual histories, not merely a collection of them.

Even before Schlözer, Gatterer[13] had used the concept of system in order to describe uniformity and connectedness of reflections on universal history. In his understanding, 'system' was an internally structured nexus of mutually dependent factors. Their dependence was created by cause and effect. Gatterer thus called for historical facts not to be enumerated according to years, locations, and themes, as they had been in the older universal histories, but to be narrated in terms of a causal connection. In other words, 'the causes come first; the effects follow'.[14] Enlightenment pragmatism[15] looked for connections in the events themselves, in the 'system of occurrences'.[16] The early pragmatism of the 1760s concentrated primarily on the level of events in order to create connections. The intention to demonstrate a connection between individual events led historiography to universal history just as, conversely, the programme of universal history presupposed a pragmatism of this sort. The aim of universal historical pragmatism was 'to discover a universal connection between events'.[17] 'The highest degree of pragmatism in history

---

Universalhistorie muß uns zeigen, wie sie [die Welt] das . . . ward, was sie vordem war, und itzo ist; sie soll die vergangene Welt an die heutige schließen.' For Schlözer's criticism of traditional universal history, see now Johan van der Zande, 'August Ludwig Schlözer and the English Universal History', in Stefan Berger, Peter Lambert, and Peter Schumann (eds), *Historikerdialoge: Geschichte, Mythos und Gedächtnis im deutsch-britischen kulturellen Austauch, 1750–2000* (Göttingen, 2003), pp. 135–56.

[13] On Gatterer, see esp. Peter H. Reill, 'History and Hermeneutics in the Aufklärung: The Thought of Johann Christoph Gatterer', *Journal of Modern History*, 45 (1973), 24–51.

[14] Johann Christoph Gatterer, 'Vom historischen Plan und der sich darauf sich gründenden Zusammenfügung der Erzählung', *Allgemeine historische Bibliothek*, 1 (1767), 15–89, at 87.

[15] See, in addition to Gudrun Kühne-Bertram, 'Aspekte der Geschichte und der Bedeutungen des Begriffs "pragmatisch" in den philosophischen Wissenschaften des ausgehenden 18. und des 19. Jahrhunderts', *Archiv für Begriffsgeschichte*, 27 (1983), 158–86, now esp. Fulda, *Wissenschaft aus Kunst*, pp. 59ff., and Thomas Prüfer, *Die Bildung der Geschichte: Friedrich Schiller und die Anfänge der modernen Geschichtswissenschaft* (Cologne, 2002), pp. 101ff.

[16] ' . . . System der Begebenheiten'. Gatterer, 'Vom historischen Plan', 86.

[17] ' . . . universalen Zusammenhang der Ereignisse aufzufinden'. Hans Jürgen Pandel, *Historik und Didaktik: Das Problem der Distribution historiographisch erzeugten Wissens in der deutschen Geschichtswissenschaft von der Spätaufklärung zum Frühhistorismus (1765–1830)* (Stuttgart, 1990), p. 54.

would be the idea of a general connection between the things in the world (*nexus rerum universalis*).'[18]

For Schlözer, the notion of 'system' achieved a heightened claim to reality at a higher level of abstraction. It conveyed large and small causes, which turned world history itself into 'philosophy'.[19] Above all, however, this systematic approach took great care to distinguish the 'real connection' between events from their 'temporal connection', ensuring that one was not reduced to the other, although they presupposed each other.[20] Chronological and synchronistic points of view, or, in modern parlance, diachrony and synchrony, had to supplement each other in order to structure universal history according to immanent criteria.

Although universal historical system-building was generally described in categories drawn from mechanics, for Gatterer and Schlözer there was always a particular meaning that made a system into a system. This step—a development which goes back to Schlözer—concerned the shift from the 'system of events' objectively present in history to system as a construct of the 'philosophical' understanding. The historian's gaze no longer fell only on the system of events, but also on the system of knowledge.[21]

Schlözer called the process of systematic arrangement of historical events 'method'. Any arrangement according to a particular principle had to make visible the connection between all the individual events. They had to form a 'chain'. As the men of the Enlightenment saw it, historians writing universal history in which the individual facts were closely connected had a much more difficult task than poets.[22] However, an Enlightenment universal historian such as Schlözer recognised the importance of the historian having supreme control of the material of history in the form of independent selection and treatment.

Enlightenment universal history expressed the universality of historical experiences by expanding the concept of history in terms of contents and temporal, geographical, and thematic scope. And it was precisely this

[18] 'Der höchste Grad des Pragmatismus in der Geschichte wäre die Vorstellung des allgemeinen Zusammenhangs der Dinge in der Welt (Nexus rerum universalis).' Gatterer, 'Vom historischen Plan', 85.
[19] See e.g. Schlözer, *Vorstellung seiner Universal-Historie*, p. 30; on the context, see Blanke, *Historiographie als Historik*, pp. 165ff.
[20] Schlözer, *Weltgeschichte*, i, pt 1, p. 71.
[21] On this, see the brief summary in Fulda, *Wissenschaft aus Kunst*, pp. 60ff.; on the dissolution of the opposition between *res fictae* and *res factae* in the eighteenth century, see Reinhart Koselleck, *Vergangene Zukunft* (Frankfurt am Main, 1976), pp. 278–84.
[22] Schlözer, *Vorstellung seiner Universal-Historie*, ii, p. 337.

universalisation of historical experience, giving rise to an explosion in knowledge, which made it necessary to attempt to restructure a 'general view', as Schlözer put it. To this extent, the 'system' in Schlözer's argument corresponded to the 'general view', which encompassed the whole: 'This powerful gaze turns an "aggregate" into a "system"; joins all the states in the world to a unit.'[23] Thus Schlözer, picking up on suggestions by Gatterer and Herder, and preparing the way for Kant, went one step further and criticised the old universal historical 'sum of all special histories' as a 'mere aggregate', in order to create space for a new 'system of world history'.[24]

This statement, 'system instead of aggregate', became a widely quoted programmatic slogan that was used for the next thirty years to describe attempts to find a context for historical knowledge. It became one of the most important points of contact and a major connection between philosophy and historiography during the Enlightenment. Against the background of transcendental philosophy, however, Schlözer's system–aggregate formula acquired a quality which took it beyond cause-and-effect pragmatism.[25] These deliberations about universal history were based on reflections concerning a fundamental problem of historical knowledge which constitutes modern historiography and was expressed here for the first time: the question concerning the part and the whole.

The notion that the human race is a unit construed history as context. Only in relation to this unit could historical tradition be sensibly selected, ordered, and presented as universal history. The process of building a universal historical system, therefore, was simultaneously a process of selection. A 'system is a selection'.[26] 'In fact, it is the history of major occurrences, of revolutions', according to Gatterer. 'They may concern individuals and peoples themselves, or their relationship with religion, the state, sciences, the arts, trade and commerce; they may have happened long ago or more recently.'[27] In order to be able to select, Schlözer iden-

---

[23] 'Dieser mächtige Blick schafft das "Aggregat" zum "System", bringt alle Staaten des Erdkreises auf eine Einheit.' Schlözer, *Vorstellung seiner Universal-Historie*, pp. 18f.

[24] Ibid., p. 21.

[25] On the context of contemporary argument, see Pandel, *Historik und Didaktik*, pp. 60ff.

[26] 'System ist ein Auszug.' Heinrich Martin Gottfried Köster, Article 'Historie' in *Deutsche Encycloplädie*, 15 (1790), 648–57, at 656.

[27] 'Eigentlich ist sie die Historie der größeren Begebenheiten, der Revolutionen: Sie mögen nun Menschen und Völker selbst oder ihr Verhältnis gegen die Religion, den Staat, die Wissenschaften, die Künste und Gewerbe betreffen: Sie mögen sich in älteren oder neueren Zeiten zugetragen haben.' Johann Christoph Gatterer, *Einleitung in die synchronistische Universalhistorie* (Göttingen, 1771), pp. 1f.

tified two classes of empirically proved and real facts of history: events of partial value, and those of universal significance. According to Schlözer, not all events and all individuals were part of universal history, but only 'major facts' and names of 'universal-historical significance'.[28] Inevitably, therefore, the events that caught the attention of Schlözer and his contemporaries were those that in the language of a later time would be called cultural history events. They were the ones which, it could best be demonstrated, concerned more than one state or country. Thus in his *Vorstellung seiner Universal-Historie* of 1772, Schlözer had encouraged systematic examination of the work of economically active individuals, and promoted economic history and the history of technology as subjects of research.[29] The question of what was considered an event of world history was not ultimately decided at the level of events, but at the level of history-writing. Universal history, if it wanted to be 'system', had to limit itself to those peoples 'who, so to speak, set the tone in society at large'.[30] This latter selection criterion also served it as an 'ethnographic' principle of order.[31] The image of different peoples taking over the leading position from each other like a 'chain of ancient mountains',[32] or a 'world historical stream of peoples',[33] or, as Hegel put it, the world spirit moving down along the line, so that world history always coincided with the history of one of these peoples for a time, was, in essence, already contained in this structuring technique, with the difference that, after the turn of the century, the ordering scheme that Schlözer had seen explicitly as Linnean began to transform itself into a natural, ontological one.

---

[28] Schlözer, *Vorstellung seiner Universal-Historie*, ii, p. 27.

[29] See ibid., i, p. 27, where Schlözer states that universal history is 'weder Stats-, noch Religions-, noch Handels-, noch Kunst- und Gelehrtengeschichte; sondern aus allen zusammen borget sie, ihrer Bestimmung getreu, Begebenheiten, die den Grund erheblicher Revolutionen des menschlichen Geschlechts enthalten' (the history neither of states, nor religion, trade, art or scholars; rather it borrows events true to their nature from all of them together, events which contain the cause of major revolutions in the human race). See Blanke, *Historiographie als Historik*, pp. 122f.

[30] '...die in der großen Gesellschaft sozusagen den Ton gegeben'. Schlözer, *Vorstellung seiner Universal-Historie*, p. 19.

[31] This supplements the 'synchronistic' principle. Already to be found in Johann Christoph Gatterer, *Handbuch der Universalhistorie* (Göttingen, 1760), pp. 68ff.; then idem, 'Vom historischen Plan', pp. 15ff.

[32] 'Urgebirgskette'. Heinrich Luden, *Allgemeine Geschichte der Völker und Staaten* (Gotha, 1814), vol. 1, p. 30.

[33] '... weltgeschichtlichen Völkerstroms'. Friedrich Schlegel, *Philosophie der Geschichte* (1828), Kritische Friedrich Schlegel Ausgabe (1971), vol. 4, p. 55.

Schlözer, claiming to write universal history as the history of humanity, brought the academic discourse of German historians up to the level of the philosophical thinking that dominated his times.[34] Yet at the same time he distanced himself from their view of history. The 'history of humanity', Schlözer wrote confidently, had, 'unfortunately, mostly been written by philosophers, although it is the real property of the historian'.[35]

To think of universal history, which became the main type of work produced by Enlightenment historiography, as a causal, mechanical system, as the Göttingen school did, provoked criticism. At the centre of Herder's criticism was the traditional conceptualisation of universal history as a systematic unit comprising all special histories.[36] He was the first to develop a future-orientated synthesis of the universal-historical and anthropological approaches in that he answered the question concerning the 'meaning of history' by reference to the point of human existence, and vice versa. As far as Herder was concerned, Schlözer lacked a convincing concept of progress. In 1774 he rejected all universal-historical interpretations which saw history only as a chaotic sequence of upheavals, whose circular movement left behind a meaningless landscape of ruins. But Herder also sharply criticised the naive concept of progress held by Iselin, for example. For Herder, there had to be a guiding thread with whose help 'the labyrinth of history' could be negotiated. That is why in his *Ideen zur Philosophie der Geschichte der Menschheit* he could, without denying the unknowableness of the whole of history and its *telos* which he had proclaimed in 1774, define 'humanity' as the 'obvious purpose' of human nature, which lay in itself.[37] This excluded the possibility that the purpose and *telos* of history would mediate its diversity and degrade man into a 'blind machine'. Released from the system of pragmatic universal history, the epochs seemed to Herder to be 'immediate to God', as Ranke was to put it later.[38] However, the late Herder of the *Ideen zur Philosophie der Geschichte der Menschheit* and the idealistic philosophers of history had

---

[34] See e.g. Johann van der Zande, 'Popular Philosophy and the History of Mankind in Eighteenth-century Germany', *Storia della Storiografia*, 22 (1992), 37–56.

[35] 'Geschichte der Menschheit . . . leider meist von den Philosophen bearbeitet worden, da sie doch Eigentum des Historikers ist'. Schlözer, *Vorstellung seiner Universal-Historie*, p. 30.

[36] See e.g. Fulda, *Wissenschaft aus Kunst*, pp. 195ff.

[37] Johann Gottfried Herder, *Ideen zur Philosophie der Geschichte der Menschheit*, ed. Martin Bollacher, in Johann Gottfried Herder, *Werke* (Frankfurt, 1989), vol. 6.

[38] '. . . unmittelbar zu Gott'. Leopold von Ranke, *Über die Epochen der neueren Geschichte*, Historisch-kritische Ausgabe, ed. Theodor Schieder and Helmut Berding (Munich, 1971), p. 59.

not yet drawn this potential theoretical conclusion. For them, it was over-shadowed by the attempt first to conceive of the unity of the entire course of world history, and then to understand it in its continuity.

Schiller can stand for this universal history which had received a boost from philosophy, and for which the progressive education of mankind was not just a subject, but also its mission.[39] He brought together not only the traditions of historical anthropology and anthropological history, but also the different types of historical thinking represented by Kant and Herder. Schiller's special achievement was to have combined the academic historical discourse of pragmatic universal history with the cultural dis-course of an idealistic history of humankind. Yet, unlike the Göttingen historian Schlözer, Schiller saw the history by which the present had come about as a process of continuous progress. This notion was based on an idealistic view of history, which interpreted the history of humanity in terms of its inner meaning.

Despite all their differences, the universal-historical writers agreed that it had only become possible to write such a history at the end of the eighteenth century. Europe's expansion across the globe had made 'world affairs' ever more complex. As a result, it was no longer possible to write the history of individual states, as the real connections showed through everywhere.[40] In 1783 Niklas Vogt, a young historian from Mainz, began his reflections on universal history by stating that 'history', like the 'human race', was now 'a large whole', 'which is animated by one spirit'. If history—universal history—included the whole of the human race, then, according to Vogt, 'humanity' was defined by 'two limits', between which it 'progressed through history on the grand time scale' from 'human being' to 'citizen of the world'.[41] As history could only become a true, that is, a comprehensive history through this historical process, Vogt could state that the 'cause' of the development of the historical genre of world history 'lay in history itself'.[42]

---

[39] See now esp. Thomas Prüfer, *Die Bildung der Geschichte: Friedrich Schiller und die Anfänge der modernen Geschichtswissenschaft* (Cologne, 2002), and Otto Dann, Norbert Oellers, and Ernst Osterkamp (eds), *Schiller als Historiker* (Stuttgart, 1995).

[40] See Johann Georg Büsch, *Encyclopädie der historischen, philosophischen und mathematischen Wissenschaften* (Hamburg, 1775), pp. 123, 133, 165.

[41] Niklas Vogt, *Anzeige, wie wir Geschichte behandelten, benutzten, und darstellen werden* (Mainz, 1783), pp. 3ff.; see Ursula Berg, *Niklas Vogt (1756–1836): Weltsicht und politische Ordnungsvorstellungen zwischen Aufklärung und Romantik* (Stuttgart, 1992).

[42] '. . . selbst in der Geschichte ihren Grund hat'. Vogt, *Anzeige*, p. 4.

The *topos* of the unity of the world continued to be used in the post-revolutionary period, for example, by Johann Gottfried Eichhorn, who, in his *Weltgeschichte* of 1799–1800, described political history from the point of view of unity. 'The connection between people, tribes, and peoples is, of course, the best strand of unity upon which everything can be threaded. . . . The history of the old and the new world therefore falls into two main parts: the unconnected and the connected world.'[43]

The universal-historical conceptualisations of the eighteenth century were designed as secular histories. Schlözer's universal history, for example, was based on a secular concept of world history whose contents included religion among many other things.[44] Thus, dispensing with transcendence, the Enlightenment concept of universal history had declared the human race to be the presumptive subject of its own history in this world.[45] In the *Deutsche Encyklopädie* we read: 'But there is another universal history . . . which is called general world history. Its subject is the human race and the earth its field of action.' It shows 'why the human race has become what it really is, or what it was at each period of time'.[46]

The universal-historical perspective was clearly orientated towards the present; it was intended 'to connect the past world to the present one, and to teach both their relationship with each other'.[47] Thus this relationship was nothing more than an analysis also of the contemporary system for interpreting the world. In the fact that the account looked only at what explained the relationship between the present and history, universal history functioned as a medium of Enlightenment self-education. For

---

[43] 'Verbindung der Menschen, Stämme und Völker ist natürlich der beste Faden der Einheit auf welchen man alles reihen kann. . . . Die Geschichte der alten und neuen Welt zerfällt daher in zwei Hauptteile: in die unverbundene und die verbundene Welt.' Johann Gottfried Eichhorn, *Weltgeschichte: Erster Teil, welcher die alte Geschichte von ihrem Anfang bis an die Völkerwanderung enthält* (Göttingen, 1799), p. viii. See now Giuseppe D'Alessandro, *L'Illuminisario Dimenticato: Johann Gottfried Eichhorn (1752–1827) e il suo tempo* (Naples, 2000).

[44] See Schlözer, *Vorstellung seiner Universal-Historie*, p. 148.

[45] See esp. Reinhart Koselleck, article on 'Geschichte, Historie', in Brunner, Conze, and Koselleck (eds), *Geschichtliche Grundbegriffe*, pp. 593–717, at pp. 688f.

[46] 'Es gibt aber noch eine andere Universalhistorie, so schlechtweg so genannt, welche man die allgemeine Weltgeschichte nennt. Sie handle von dem Menschengeschlecht und vom "Erdboden" als seinem Aktionsfeld.' It shows 'warum das menschliche Geschlecht das geworden ist, was es wirklich ist, oder es in jedem Zeitraum war'. Heinrich Martin Köster, article on 'Geschichte', in *Deutsche Encyclopädie* (1787), vol. 12, p. 654.

[47] '. . . soll die vergangene Welt an die heutige anschließen und das Verhältnis beider gegeneinander lehren'. Schlözer, *Vorstellung seiner Universal-Historie*, p. 217.

Schlözer and his contemporaries, therefore, universal history was history 'with the intention of creating world citizens'.[48]

III

Both Gatterer and Schlözer conferred a new significance upon the traditional distinction between 'historia specialis' and 'historia universalis'[49] in that they criticised the traditional understanding of universal history as a mere addition of special histories, and contrasted this 'aggregate of all special history' with a synthetic connection between events in a 'system, in which world and humanity form a unit'.[50] This had implications for the relationship between the general and the particular, the whole and the part. According to Gatterer, the ideal of this pragmatic universal history was the 'notion of a general connection between things in the world (*nexus rerum universalis*)'.[51] For, as Gatterer emphasised, 'no event in the world is, so to speak, insular. Everything depends on, causes, generates, is caused by, or generated by other things, and goes on causing and generating.' The natural, that is, the causal connections of history had to be maintained, he claimed. In this sense, Gatterer stated that a 'special history', that is, the various subject-based, systematic areas of history which, taken together, constituted the concept of the history of civilisation, always tears 'a piece off a well connected whole'. Gatterer demanded that the writer of such histories should, 'from time to time', show the reader the 'ends by which the torn-off piece is connected to the whole'.[52] To this extent, every 'special history', that is, the history of one or more nations, one or more regions, sciences, arts, etc., was always a 'fragment' of a universal history.[53] Universal history was composed of all these 'special histories', which formed its subordinate parts. Thus, for Gatterer, 'patriotic history as a special history' was necessarily merely an extract of universal

---

[48] 'weltbürgerlicher Absicht'. See the brief summary in Pandel, *Historik und Didaktik*, pp. 103ff.: '"Weltbürgerliche Absicht" as a point of view'.

[49] On the early history of this opposition, see esp. Ulrich Muhlack, *Geschichtswissenschaft im Humanismus und in der Aufklärung: Die Vorgeschichte des Historismus* (Munich, 1991), pp. 97ff.

[50] 'System, in welchem Welt und Menschheit eine Einheit ist.' Schlözer, *Vorstellung seiner Universal-Historie*, p. 86.

[51] 'Vorstellung des allgemeinen Zusammenhangs der Dinge in der Welt (nexus rerum universalis)'. Gatterer, 'Vom historischen Plan', 85, 87.

[52] 'von Zeit zu Zeit die Enden zeigen, mit denen das abgerissene Stück an das Ganze verbunden ist'. Ibid., 76.

[53] Ibid., 74.

history; as an early form of national history, it was necessarily permitted on the horizon of universal history.

Schlözer referred the universal historian to special histories in two respects. First, he called on the universal historian to take the material of world history 'from the already pre-worked material of innumerable special histories'.[54] And, second, he declared that world history was 'the basis' of a future study of special histories: 'No special history of whatever sort is conceivable unless its elements are in this general history.'[55] Special history, therefore, was to precede, not follow, universal history. According to Schlözer, however, this dual functionalisation of universal history by special history must not lead to world history becoming a 'mere aggregate of all special histories'. As Schlözer pointed out, the relationship between special and universal history was recursive. 'World history grows out of special histories; merely by ordering these into an illuminated whole, it thankfully casts a new brightness over each one of these parts.' Thus all special histories were subsumed in universal history, and there were no special histories 'whose elements were not to be found in this general history'.[56] Universal history consisted of a large number of histories which it preserved as a unit; it arranged and coordinated individual histories into universal history. To this extent Schlözer applied to history Aristotle's statement that the whole was more than the sum of its parts. Schlözer must be seen as a 'systemic' historian, who brought the history of individual countries together into a unity, order, and divine harmony of a higher level. He bundled the special histories so that 'universal history' was a special history of the general; at the same time he initiated a change of perspective in history, so that a historical analysis could, conversely, also be a world history of the particular.[57]

Universal history as an encyclopaedic overview was intended to deliver the framework, so to speak, into which special histories could then

[54] 'aus dem bereits vorgearbeiteten Stoff unzähliger Specialgeschichten'. Schlözer, *Vorstellung seiner Universal-Historie*, p. 13.
[55] 'Keine Specialgeschichte, von welcher Art sie auch wäre, muss sich denken lassen, deren Elemente nicht in dieser allgemeinen Geschichte lägen.' Ibid., p. 31.
[56] 'Die Welthistorie erwächst aus den Spezialgeschichten; allein indem sie diese in ein lichtes Ganzes ordnet, so breitet sie dankbar über jeden dieser Teile eine neue Helle aus.' '. . . der Elemente nicht in dieser allgemeinen Geschichte lägen'. Ibid., pp. 34 and 31.
[57] On this, see Jörn Garber, 'Selbstreferenz und Objektivität: Organisationsmodelle von Mensch- und Weltgeschichte in der deutschen Spätaufklärung', in Hans Erich Bödeker, Peter H. Reill, and Jürgen Schlumbohm (eds), *Wissenschaft als kulturelle Praxis* (Göttingen 1999), pp. 137–85.

be fitted. With a place on the horizon of universal history, 'special history' was by no means neglected by pragmatic German Enlightenment historiography.[58] Enlightenment history-writing was well able to combine the 'point of view of the world citizen' with an account of German or patriotic history. Schlözer, who had undertaken to produce a 'national historiography' as early as 1764,[59] had a voluminous scholarly output, of which attempts at universal history formed only a part.[60] None the less, the nature of the 'special histories' which he wrote illustrates the hopelessness even of the best history produced by the German Enlightenment, rather than providing evidence of the fruitful coexistence of a universal-historical approach and concrete history-writing.

Thus neither Gatterer, nor Schlözer, nor Johannes von Müller,[61] saw special history and universal history as mutually exclusive. Von Müller's interest in history, too, had had a fundamentally universal-historical orientation from the start. Even while working on his history of Switzerland as an attempt to exclude the national past, his interest was always dictated by an overarching framework of reference. These interests come through in many parts of his history of Switzerland. Universal history was his real subject, and its earlier versions were entirely dictated by Schlözer's pragmatism.

In opposition to this pragmatic concept of universal history which subsumed empirical facts under the general conditions governing all culture, Herder developed a completely different concept, in particular, in his disagreement with Schlözer.[62] Herder was not concerned about individual data or 'facts'. Rather, he penetrated to a number of fundamental questions concerning how history was viewed and presented. Herder's central objection to pragmatic universal history was probably the way in which universal history brought together all parts into a whole. For Schlözer, the unity of universal history was derived from the fact that it was based on a uniform subject, the human race. He did not see, however, that the definition of the historical subject could say nothing about the form in which changes took place in historical time. And, finally, Schlözer did not see

---

[58] See Blanke, *Historiographie als Historik*, pp. 176ff.
[59] See Peters, *Altes Reich und Europa*, pp. 92ff.
[60] See, somewhat exaggerated, Fulda, *Wissenschaft aus Kunst*, p. 181
[61] See Michael Gottlob, *Geschichtsschreibung zwischen Aufklärung und Historismus: Johannes von Müller und Friedrich Christoph Schlosser* (Frankfurt am Main, 1989), pp. 67ff., and idem, 'Friedrich Schiller und Johannes Müller', in Dann, Oellers, and Osterkamp (eds), *Schiller als Historiker*, pp. 309–33.
[62] See Fulda, *Wissenschaft aus Kunst*, pp. 175ff.

that the unity of universal history had to relate to its diachronic extent, not to its synchronic breadth. In the disagreement that Herder and Schlözer had on this point, we see precisely that replacement of structures by processes which Hayden White and Ernst Cassirer recognised as Herder's major contribution to nineteenth-century historical thinking.[63]

Herder placed a higher value on the individual than on the general, and this reorientation was of fundamental significance for the further development of historical thinking. First, he assumed that no individual existed in isolation, postulating that every person built on individuals who had existed previously, and in turn provided the foundation for future individuals. Thus Herder developed a diachronic connection between individuals. Second, he related all individuals to the unity of mankind, based on the common human trait towards diversity.[64] Herder's new concept of individuality thus provided a model for how the particular and the general could be related to each other in a new way. This was no longer classificatory by subsuming the individual under humanity, or the event under a structure, or national history under universal history. Rather, it was dialectical in that the preconditions for the general were found in the particular, the most important being the uniqueness of the particular. This gave the historian options for how structures could be narrated and depicted by using key situations. This rehabilitation of historical particularity, which prepared an academic point of departure for the subsequent discovery of nationality, was also redefined logically at the same time.[65]

In addition to Herder, Lessing, and Kant, it was also the idealistic philosophers who no longer thought of universal history as a causal mechanical system like the Göttingen school, but as a diverse yet progressive form of educating and shaping, as they said, human nature common to all. In this view, universal history no longer needed to be comprehensively recapitulated. It could assume the forms of individual national histories which, in microcosm, pointed to the whole by presenting the character of individual peoples as different aspects of a common human nature. Moreover, not even these individual national histories had

---

[63] See Hayden White, *Metahistory: The Historical Imagination in Nineteenth-century Europe* (Baltimore, MD, 1973), p. 103.

[64] On the context, see esp. Martin Bollacher (ed.), *Johann Gottfried Herder: Geschichte und Kultur* (Würzburg, 1994) and Regine Otto (ed.), *Nationen und Kulturen: Zum 250. Geburtstag Johan Gottfried Herders* (Würzburg, 1996).

[65] See Reill, 'Das Problem des Allgemeinen und des Besonderen', and Oexle, '"Der Teil und das Ganze" als Problem'.

to obey the old law of comprehensiveness. Rather, the new 'individualising gaze' at history discovered even smaller, clearly definable units within
national histories. Thus this new, theoretical development of historical
universality conferred a particularising direction on the identity-creating
criterion of humanity. It located humanity, as a general point of reference
for historical identity-creation, within particularity, in which it found, in
each case, a culturally concrete manifestation of the 'creative power' of
the human spirit. The unity of mankind was made visible in the diversity
of its cultural forms, the general in the particular.[66] Wilhelm von
Humboldt, in particular, defined the principle of individualising history
for generations in his later writings on world history, and especially in
'Über die Aufgabe des Geschichtsschreibers' (1821).[67]

IV

In 1767 Gatterer had declared the unity of history to be the basis of pragmatic historiography.[68] He identified a number of variants of historiography, and as many grades of context. For him, a 'patriotic history' was
necessarily only an extract of universal history. For Gatterer, it followed
from this that it had to expose itself to universal criticism. Thus for reasons of rationality, the nexus of events, in its capacity for truth, dominated national history. These events were clearly elements of the whole of
history. This is precisely what characterised Enlightenment historiography until the early eighteenth century. Even if Gatterer's ambition was to
find a plan for universal history modelled on Herodotus, Polybius, and
Livy, his main passion was patriotic historiography and the history of the
Reich, whose disparity was roundly condemned.[69]

---

[66] See e.g. Wilhelm von Humboldt, 'Über die Aufgabe des Geschichtsschreibers', in idem,
Werke, ed. Andres Flitner and Klaus Giel (Darmstadt, 1960), vol. 1, pp. 585ff., at p. 595, where
Humboldt concedes 'dass die vollständige Durchschauung des Besonderen immer die Kenntnis
des Allgemeinen voraussetzt, unter dem es begriffen wird. In diesem Sinn muss das Auffassen des
Geschehenen von Ideen geleitet seyn' (that a complete understanding of the particular
always presupposes a knowledge of the general, under which it is subsumed. In this sense the
understanding of what has happened must be led by ideas).
[67] See most recently Thomas Prüfer, 'Wilhelm von Humboldts "rhetorische Hermeneutik":
Historische Sinnbildung im Spannungsfeld von Empirie, Philosophie und Poesie', in Daniel
Fulda and Thomas Prüfer (eds), *Faktenglaube und fiktionales Wesen: Zum Verhältnis von
Wissenschaft und Kunst in der Moderne* (Frankfurt am Main, 1996), pp. 187–96.
[68] See Gatterer, 'Vom historischen Plan'.
[69] See e.g. Ernst Ludwig Posselt, *Ueber teutsche Historiographie* (Karlsruhe, 1786), pp. 30f.

To the extent that there was a 'Geschichte der Teutschen' (history of the Germans)—this title was used, for example, by Jacob Mascov in 1726[70]—it was 'Reichs-Historie',[71] that is, the legal and constitutional history of the Reich, traditionally cultivated by lawyers as an auxiliary subject. Its point was to investigate the peculiarities of the German Reich as a state. As a 'special history of the Germans', *Reichs-Historie* differed markedly from 'older forms' of historiography. Thus *Reichs-Historie*, initially no more than a methodologically unregulated form of confidence-boosting, became a form of historical knowledge, embedded in the academic context of, for example, Göttingen university.[72] Given this background, *Reichs-Historie* provided a strong boost for the incipient discipline of historiography. It undoubtedly had great significance for the development of history as an academic subject. The use of documents as sources and the development of technical auxiliary subjects to clarify questions of authenticity, dating, and assessment prepared the ground for future generations of historians. *Reichs-Historie* was strongly problem-orientated. Ultimately, its core was political in terms of the understanding and practice of the Holy Roman Empire of the German Nation as protecting legality and the administration. Of course, *Reichs-Historie* did not have to be restricted to legal or constitutional history in the narrow sense; in fact, it could not be. As many things in the Reich had to be settled by traditional means, this history also had to include customs and practices and the conditions which governed them, such as climate, geography, the agrarian economy, the character of the peoples, etc. This was not always necessary but, in theory, it was possible at any time, for after all, 'every republic has its own special structure. Therefore we no longer look at the *principia generalia*, but at the *ordinem specialem*'.[73]

Johann Stefan Pütter's definition of *Reichs-Historie* outlined all the features of this genre: 'The point of German *Reichshistorie*, or the history of the German Empire, is to recognise in context those events which allow

---

70 Johann Jakob Mascov, *Geschichte der Teutschen bis zum Anfang der fränkischen Monarchie* (Leipzig, 1726); idem, *Geschichte der Teutschen bis zum Abgang der Merovingischen Könige* (Leipzig, 1737).

71 See esp. Notker Hammerstein, 'Reichs-Historie', in Hans Erich Bödeker, Georg J. Iggers, Jonathan B. Knudsen, and Peter H. Reill (eds), *Aufklärung und Geschichte: Studien zur deutschen Geschichtswissenschaft im 18. Jahrhundert* (Göttingen, 1986), pp. 82–104.

72 See Hammerstein, 'Reichs-Historie', *passim*.

73 '. . . eine iede republique eine besondere Structur. Daher sehen wir da nicht mehr auf die principia generalia, sondern auf den ordinem specialem'. Disc Cocceji, Cap. I, § 5, quoted from Notker Hammerstein, *Jus und Historie: Ein Beitrag zur Geschichte des historischen Denkens an den deutschen Universitäten im späten 17. und 18. Jahrhundert* (Göttingen, 1972), p. 220.

us to understand the reasons for current conditions in the German Reich.'[74] To the extent that Pütter drew any distinctions within this definition, they relate to conditions that take us into completely different contexts. Thus he distinguished between *Reichs-Historie* and 'general history'.[75] His *Handbuch der deutschen Reichshistorie* marked both the climax and the final product of the discipline of *Reichs-Historie*. In it, *Reichs-Historie* had, in fact, reached its final and highest stage. It was unable to achieve, out of itself, a new, different, and deeper justification for historical interest. After 1806, Pütter's achievement, generally highly valued by contemporaries, was considered obsolete. After all, the need for *Reichs-Historie* had passed with the Holy Roman Empire itself. Moreover, the fact that this was a history of princes and Estates, but not of the people, was criticised. In addition, the experience of the French Revolution, the knowledge of German idealism, of German classicism—for its part a response to French events—which partially grew out of other roots, had found a more profound continuation in legal and constitutional history.

Reichs-Historie took its place next to French national history, centred on the monarchy, and British national history, which developed around the poles of monarchy and parliament. From the middle of the eighteenth century, however, *Reichs-Historie* had less and less claim to be considered the sole or exclusive history of the Germans. 'The history of Germany is to be distinguished from German *Reichs-Historie*', wrote the Göttingen historian Johann David Köhler. 'The former is wider in scope than the latter, and tells everything worth noting that has happened to the German peoples from the beginning, in their original freedom, about and under the Romans, similarly under the Franks, and finally, under their own kings, right up to the present day. German *Reichs-Historie*, by contrast, concerns only the last piece of this history, that is, a precise description of the many changes which have affected the head and limbs of Germany, since it has been a state of its own, completely separate from the Frankish Empire, or an independent kingdom.'[76]

---

[74] 'Die deutsche Reichshistorie oder die Geschichte des Deutschen Reiches hat zu ihrem Gegenstand, dass man diejenige Begebenheit in ihrem Zusammenhang erkennen lerne, welche dazu dienen, den heutigen Zustand des Deutschen Reiches aus seinen Gründen einzusehen.' Johann Stephan Pütter, *Vollständiges Handbuch der Teutschen Reichshistorie*, 2nd edn (Göttingen, 1772), p. 1.

[75] '. . . allgemeinen Historie'. See ibid., 'Vorrede'.

[76] 'Die Historie von Teutschland ist von der teutschen Reichs-Historie wohl zu unterscheiden. Jene ist von weitern Inbegriff als diese und erzählet alles dasjenige, was sich mit denen deutschen Völkern von ihrem Ursprunge an, in ihrer angeborenen Freiheit, von und unter den Römern, in gleichem unter den Franken und endlich unter ihren eigenen Königen, bis auf unsere Zeit

Thus German history was gradually assigned a subject area different
from that of *Reichs-Historie*, without the link to *Reichs-Historie* being
completely severed until the end of the eighteenth century. From the middle of the eighteenth century on, professors at the University of
Göttingen in particular recognised a legitimate interest in historical questions going beyond the scope of *Reichs-Historie*. Gatterer's much praised
historical work in particular did not fit into the tradition of *Reichs-
Historie*. The discussion of how a German history should be written,
which began at that time, was conducted in public.[77]

Mascov must certainly be named as a pioneer in the development
towards a 'German history'. He gave the process of differentiation an
important boost in his *Geschichte der Teutschen* by including in his inves-
tigations 'form of government, qualities of disposition, religion, customs,
weapons',[78] thus treating subject areas that went beyond the real field of
Reichs-Historie. Also of significance for the development of a future
'German history' were problems of methodology and the philosophy of
history which concerned research not orientated by *Reichs-Historie* much
more than *Reichs-Historie* itself, including the question of how historical
connections were to be understood. Gatterer, in particular, had worked
intensively on this subject.[79]

Given the complex demands made by a 'German history', warnings
against tackling such a project were issued openly. A historian could only
embark upon such a venture, it was claimed, when the history of every
individual territory had been written. A comprehensive history of
Germany was regarded as a project for the future. It was in this area that
one of Michael Ignaz Schmidt's remarkable achievements lay, one which
also surprised contemporaries.[80] In his historical work, he showed that a

---

merkwürdiges zugetragen. Diese aber ist nur das letzte Stück von selbiger und also nur eine
genaue Erzählung der vielen Veränderungen, welche Deutschland in seinen Haupt und Gliedern
betroffen, seit dasselbe ein besonderes und von dem fränkischen Reich gänzlich abgesonderter
Staat oder ein independentes Königreich war.' Johann David Köhler, *Kurzgefaßte und gründliche
Teutsche Reichs-Historie vom Anfang des Teutschen Reichs* (Frankfurt, 1767), p. 20.
[77] See Hammerstein, 'Reichs-Historie', p. 85.
[78] 'Regierungs-Form, Gemüts-Eigenschaften, Religion, Sitten, Waffen'. Mascov, *Geschichte der
Teutschen*, vol. 1, 'Vorrede' (no page numbers).
[79] See the brief summary in Reill, 'History and Hermeneutics in the Aufklärung'.
[80] See Michael Ignatz Schmidt, *Geschichte der Deutschen*, 5 vols plus index volume (Ulm,
1778–83); Arnold Berney, 'Michael Ignatz Schmidt: Ein Beitrag zur Geschichte der deutschen
Historiographie im Zeitalter der Aufklärung', *Historische Zeitschrift*, 44 (1924), 211–39; and
most recently Peter Baumgart (ed.), *Michael Ignaz Schmidt (1736–1744) in seiner Zeit: Der
aufgeklärte Theologe, Bildungsreform und 'Historiker der Deutschen' aus Franken in neuer Sicht*
(Neustadt an der Aisch, 1996), pp. 63ff.

'German history', taking *Reichs-Historie* as its point of departure, could be unfolded and written from the point of view of the Reich. 'My intention in this work is to show how Germany acquired its customs of the time, Enlightenment, arts and sciences, but mainly such an excellent state and church constitution; in short, how it became what it really is.'[81] For Schmidt, emphasising Germany's current cultural situation and making explicit an awareness of the high value of the present life of the state were the tools for grappling with a total history. His themes of 'efficiency of rulers', 'cultural level', and 'national happiness' were the common stock of the Enlightenment. Now they were applied to historiography in the framework of the nation.[82]

For his contemporary Herder, however, Schmidt was by no means the 'first historian of the Germans'. This rejection reflected a change in ideas about the task and scope of a 'German history' at the end of the eighteenth century. In 1795, that is, one year after Schmidt's death, Herder published an essay entitled 'Warum wir noch keine Geschichte der Deutschen haben?' (Why do we not yet have a history of the Germans?').[83] Here he emphasised an account of the German national spirit as what constituted a 'German history'. Although he rated Schmidt's achievements highly, Herder did not find this requirement fulfilled in Schmidt's work.

It was no coincidence that German thinkers and historians of the eighteenth century in particular cultivated a universal-historical perspective, for the fragmentation of the German nation seems hardly to have permitted anything but ecclesiastical history, the history of science, and art history of individual territories and Estates. The aspirations of the bourgeoisie could still best be channelled into a general history of culture in a universal history.

---

[81] 'Meine Absicht bei diesem Werk ist zu zeigen, wie Deutschland seine damaligen Sitten, Aufklärung, Künste und Wissenschaften, hauptsächlich aber seine so sehr ausgezeichnete Staats- und Kirchenverfassung bekommen habe; kurz wie es das geworden sei, was es wirklich ist.' Schmidt, *Geschichte der Deutschen*, vol. 1, 'Vorrede', p. 3.

[82] Ibid.

[83] See Johann Gottfried Herder, 'Warum wir noch keine Geschichte der Deutschen haben?', in Bernhard Suphan (ed.), *Herders Sämmtliche Werke* (Berlin, 1883), vol. 28, pp. 380–4.

V

The rehabilitation of particularity initiated by Herder, which offered a
model for how the particular and the general, the part and the whole,
could be related to each other in a new way, was an element of wider epistemological changes at the end of the eighteenth century. But even this
revaluation of the particular was not undertaken for its own sake, but in
the name of the 'general'. The general, as a condition of knowledge, had
been defined by Enlightenment history and the philosophy of history as
a historical whole, but the line of historians from Herder via Humboldt
to Ranke reverted to an understanding of it as the generic, whose relationship with historical particularity was one of exemplification not integration. And Humboldt, in his works on world history and, in particular,
in his 'Über die Aufgabe des Geschichtsschreibers' (1821) laid down the
principle of individualising history, thus creating a tradition. Ranke also
formulated an interest in the individual and the particular in his expression, directed against 'dogmatic' philosophy: 'Whereas the philosopher,
regarding history from the viewpoint of his own field, sees infinity merely
in the process, the development, the totality, history recognises an infinity
in every existence, every condition, every being; something eternal coming from God—and this its vital principle. How could anything exist
without a divine reason for its being? That is why, as we said, it prefers to
turn to the individual; that is why it likes to adhere to the conditions of
the phenomenon; that is why it pursues its particular interest.'[84]

A second innovation, also inherent in Herder's 'individualising gaze',
was later expounded by Kant.[85] In his writings on the philosophy of history dating from 1784, he made it clear that the unity of history was
based on the creative achievement of the theoretician and the history-
writer. It did not simply arise out of what had happened, but had to be

---

[84] 'Während der Philosoph, von seinem Felde aus die Historie betrachten, das Unendliche bloß
in dem Fortgang, der Entwicklung, der Totalität sieht, erkennt die Historie in jeder Existenz ein
Unendliches an; jedem Zustand, jedem Wesen; ein ewiges aus Gott kommendes;—und dies ist
ihr Lebensprinzip. Wie könnte irgendetwas sein ohne den göttlichen Grund seiner Existenz?
Darum wendet sie sich, wie wir sagten, dem Einzelnen mit Neigung zu; darum haftet sie gern an
den Bedingungen der Erscheinung; darum macht sie das partikulare Interesse geltend.' Leopold
von Ranke, 'Französische Geschichte vornehmlich im sechzehnten und siebzehnten
Jahrhundert', in idem, *Aus Werke und Nachlass*, ed. Peter Fuchs and Theodor Schieder (Munich,
1974), vol. 4, p. 77.
[85] See Immanuel Kant, 'Idee zu einer allgemeinen Geschichte in weltbürgerlicher Absicht', in
idem, *Werke, vol. 6: Schriften zur Anthropologie, Geschichtsphilosophie, Politik und Pädagogik*,
4th edn (Darmstadt, 1983), pp. 31–50.

productively reconstructed; it did not simply emerge from the events themselves, but only in the 'idea' which 'a philosophical mind (which, incidentally, must have a good knowledge of history)',[86] recognised in them. By declaring that things were dependent on knowledge, not vice versa, in stressing that while the context and progress of world history could not be demonstrated theoretically, practical reason demanded action, Kant both questioned the 'scientific' nature of history again and encouraged philosophers to have the confidence a priori to prescribe the path of history, drawing on their knowledge and practical common sense. This was the origin of the tension between the philosophy of history and the emergent academic discipline of history at the beginning of the nineteenth century.

At the same time, however, Kant opened up the possibility of basing the narrative of history on the unity of ideas instead of, as previously, on recording what had happened (which was continued as the demand for comprehensiveness, and resulted in disparateness).[87] As the account no longer of 'remarkable events', but of the 'ideas' of these events, it could achieve unity and immediacy. The creative achievement of the historian was no longer considered to be a source of error and the origin of all forgeries, but was elevated into a condition for the possibility of historical knowledge—and thus its depiction.[88]

The epistemological objectivism of Enlightenment history refuted, more thoroughly even than Kant's critical philosophy, Herder's deepening of the critique of knowledge, based on the philosophy of language. After all, Kant had bypassed the linguistic relativity of the a priori categories of knowledge, as Herder pointed out critically in his *Metakritik* (1799).[89]

Thus historians were no longer under the paralysing pressure to which they had still been subjected in Gatterer's theory of manifest narration to demonstrate that 'contemporaries [of the events narrated] had thought about it in this way' too.[90] They now achieved the freedom and the right to see history anew on the basis of critically secured empirical material.

---

[86] 'ein philosophischer Kopf (der übrigens sehr geschichtskundig sein müsste)'. Kant, 'Idee', p. 50.

[87] See Süssmann, *Geschichtsschreibung oder Roman?*, pp. 71ff.

[88] See esp. Fulda, *Wissenschaft aus Kunst*, and Prüfer, *Die Bildung der Geschichte.*

[89] See esp. Ulrich Gaier, *Herders Sprachphilosophie und Erkenntniskritik* (Stuttgart-Bad Cannstatt, 1988), pp. 183–209.

[90] '. . . die Zeitgenossen (des erzählten Geschehens), so davon gedacht haben'. Johann Christoph Gatterer, 'Von der Evidenz in der Geschichtskunde', in *Die allgemeine Welthistorie die in England durch eine Gesellschaft von Gelehrten ausgefertigt worden. In einem vollständigen und pragmatischen Auszuge hrsg. von Friedrich Eberhard Boysen*, Alte Historie, 1 (Halle, 1767), pp. 1–38, at p. 27.

The imagination, previously spurned despite Gatterer's and Schlözer's attempts to raise its value, now played the key role in historical knowledge and historiography. It was not to be long before somebody recognised this opportunity, and used it to create a new type of history-writing.

What Kant passed on to a whole generation of people with historical interests as an epistemological principle had been expressed much earlier as an insight gained in practice in a number of historiographical accounts. Thus J. J. Winckelmann wrote in 1764, in the preface to his *Geschichte der Kunst des Altertums*: 'Conjecture, but of a sort which is attached to something solid at least by a thread, can as little be removed from writing of this sort as hypothesis can be banished from scientific work; it is like the structure of a building.'[91] These words were immediately taken up and their implications extended by Justus Möser. Only if a historian, like Winckelmann, made 'the history of an ideal into a major campaign', if he selected his point of view with care, drew up a plan, risked a hypothesis, could he elevate his account, through 'the unity of plot, into a historical epic'.[92] And, indeed, the historiography of the future announced itself first in the territorial histories of J. Möser and Ludwig Timotheus Spittler.[93]

This epistemological turn was summed up by Wilhelm von Humboldt in his essay, 'Über die Aufgabe des Geschichtsschreibers' (1821). According to Humboldt, the historian had to follow 'two paths' at the same time in order to achieve his task. By working on the sources he obtained the 'material' of history, but this was 'not history itself'. Therefore the second path was more important, namely, 'connecting what has been researched', and 'guessing what cannot be found out by those means' using intuition and the ability to connect things. These capacities are directed towards ideas, for ideas, 'by their very nature, lie outside the circle of finiteness, but rule and dominate world history in all its parts'. For Humboldt, therefore, 'all history' is 'only the realisation of an idea'. The task of the history-writer, therefore, 'reduced to its simplest form', is

---

[91] 'Mutmaßungen, aber solche, die sich wenigstens durch einen Faden an etwas Festem halten, sind aus einer Schrift dieser Art ebenso wenig als Hypothesen aus der Naturlehre zu verbannen; sie sind wie das Gerüste zu einem Gebäude.' Johann Joachim Winckelmann, *Geschichte der Kunst des Altertums*, ed. Ludwig Goldscheider (Vienna, 1934), p. 18.
[92] '. . . die Geschichte eines Ideals zur Haubt-Action . . . die Einheit der Handlung zur historischen Epopee'. Justus Möser, *Briefe*, ed. Ernst Beins (Hanover, 1939), p. 189, see also pp. 150, 168, 183, and 184f.
[93] See Hans Erich Bödeker, 'Landesgeschichtliche Erkenntnisinteressen der nordwestdeutschen Aufklärungshistorie', *Niedersächsisches Jahrbuch für Landesgeschichte*, 69 (1997), 247–79.

to 'describe the striving of an idea to achieve existence in reality'. Of course, the 'ideas can only be recognised by the events themselves'. Pursuit of the ideas, therefore, reveals the 'individual event in its true light', and gives 'the whole thing shape'.[94]

In summing up Schiller's idea of historiography, as it were,[95] Humboldt laid the foundations for the historicist theory of history. Schiller discovered the form which historiography found for itself in the principle of description, and Humboldt turned this into a principle of knowledge. Carefully but emphatically, he moved Schiller's idea on from historical writing to historical knowledge, upon which the former was based. To this extent Humboldt in retrospect underlined Schiller's historiography with a theory of knowledge. And at this point, it was no longer possible to keep the critical and the philosophical components of history apart.

This insight into the constructivity of historical knowledge, finally, was first consistently developed by Johann Gustav Droysen.[96] In the meantime, a poetological constructivism had emerged in the creative aesthetic of the Storm and Stress (*Sturm und Drang*), and especially in the classical and early Romantic aesthetic of autonomy. During the same period, historiography turned away from the encyclopaedic principle in favour of the perspectivist principle, which was aware of particularity.

Barthold Georg Niebuhr's lectures on Roman history were epoch-making because in them he presented a new view of early Roman history and the agrarian history of Rome which went against all the narrative sources.[97] Taking his favourite subject of classical education, which had a contemporary resonance because of the discussion of the emancipation of the serfs, Niebuhr demonstrated that it was possible to attain qualitatively new historical knowledge without recourse to new sources, merely by restructuring the material on the basis of new ideas. Only in the mode

[94] Humboldt, in idem, *Werke*, ed. Flitner and Giel, vol. 1, at pp. 585, 586f., 590, 601, and 604f.
[95] This rather exaggerated claim in Süssmann, *Geschichtsschreibung oder Roman?*, pp. 80ff.
[96] See Johann Gustav Droysen, *Historik: Rekonstruktion der ersten vollständigen Fassung der Vorlesungen (1857), Grundriss der Historik in der ersten handschriftlichen (1857/1858) und in der letzten gedruckten Fassung (1882)*, ed. Peter Leyh (Stuttgart, 1977); stimulating on Droysen, Uwe Barrelmeyer, *Geschichtliche Wirklichkeit als Problem: Untersuchungen zu geschichtstheoretischen Begründungen historischen Wissens bei Johann Gustav Droysen, Georg Simmel und Max Weber* (Münster, 1995), pp. 32ff.
[97] See the following according to Gerrit Walther, *Niebuhrs Forschungen* (Stuttgart, 1993), pp. 94–113, 186ff., 200–16, 482–7.

of speculative practical reason, he argued, was qualitative progress in history possible from now on, and its price was abstraction. Instead of presenting historical material, Niebuhr discussed possible interpretations; instead of describing history, he constructed its main ideas. Niebuhr himself felt this as a painful lack. Although he was a pioneering researcher, he valued history-writing far above research.

And in his famous and consistently misunderstood phrase from the foreword, namely, that he merely wanted to say 'wie es eigentlich gewesen',[98] Ranke meant the same thing. He was not referring to facts, but to the connections hidden in them; not to a presumably unconditional empiricism, but to the historian's construction of empirical material; not to how it was in reality, but to how it was in essence. And this essence of history, this 'it' that Ranke presents, consisted of historical ideas. Only based on this theoretical premiss can Ranke's history-writing be understood. Only this casts light on its immense ambition.

And the emergent awareness of a scholarly mission of the Germans, finally, was also based on these epistemological innovations.[99] One of the first to make the German mission for historiography into a major theme was Wilhelm von Humboldt, who, in 1796–7, during a visit to Paris, criticised the French for their inability to interpret historical phenomena.[100] Subsequently, building on Humboldt, a trend developed to see the new historical thinking as a German mission. And at the beginning of his *Historik* (1857), Johann Gustav Droysen, referring to Humboldt, expressed the hope that 'the Germans will accomplish the task of developing a theory of history'.[101]

The close connection between emergent disciplinary independence and a growing national self-confidence is obvious. This scholarly nationalism points strongly towards the cultural constitution of the German nation during the Enlightenment. Naturally, there was a strongly compensatory element in the conceptualisation of the German historiographical mission. However, the two developments appear to be directly connected to the extent that in the most important cultural field of schol-

---

[98] Leopold von Ranke, *Geschichten der romanischen und germanischen Völker von 1494 bis 1535* (Leipzig, 1824) , vol. 1, pp. vf.

[99] Muhlack, 'Universal History and National History', pp. 38ff. is concise and to the point on this.

[100] Humboldt, 'Das achtzehnte Jahrhundert', in idem, *Werke*, ed. Flitner and Giel, vol. 1, pp. 376–501, at pp. 456f.

[101] Droysen, *Historik*, p. 53.

arly activity, history took over the role of a quest for finding the national self.[102]

The emphasis on particularity logically resulted in the practice of researching historical life mainly in the statements of individuals and particularities, that is, in the actions of great individuals, as 'men make history', and in the articulations of collective individuals, such as nations. Comprehensive units of such individuals, namely, peoples and nations, could be interpreted by Humboldt, for example, as 'super-individuals'. Emergent historiography related to the nation as its main guiding idea. To be sure, the term 'nation' was understood in many very different ways. For some it contained an earthy-*völkisch* element, which could be traced as an entity until well into the Middle Ages (this notion gave rise to the national undertaking of the *Monumenta*); for others, such as Ranke, for example, the concept of nation was tied to a concrete political structure such as the Prussian state.[103]

VI

Historians began to distance themselves from pragmatic universal history mainly because of epistemological progress in the subject. History began to define itself as a scholarly discipline in the late eighteenth century, and a definitive breakthrough in historiographical practice was achieved from about the 1820s on. The publication of Niebuhr's *Römische Geschichte*, for example, whose methodological standards Ranke transferred to the new history a good ten years later, coincided with the Wars of Liberation. For Niebuhr, it was simply no longer possible to write history not based on a complete review and critical assessment of the sources without some explanation.[104]

Universal history could not easily ignore this progress in knowledge; indeed, it was in danger of falling victim to it. 'Only history that has been critically researched can count as history', Ranke was later to write in the preface to his *Weltgeschichte*.[105] But what historian could honestly claim to have critically researched history in its totality? 'Historical science is

---

[102] See e.g. Becker, *Zeit der Revolution, passim.*
[103] See Blanke, *Historiographie*, pp. 205ff.
[104] Despite all their differences, contemporary historians agreed on this.
[105] 'Nur kritisch erforschte Geschichte kann als Geschichte gelten.' Quoted from Ranke, *Historische Meisterwerke* (1928), vol. 1/2, p. 20.

not yet ready to reconstruct universal history on new foundations', Ranke himself stated around 1867.[106]

The problems faced by historiography in establishing itself as a scholarly discipline were not limited to those of dealing critically with the inflated mass of source material. Even if these heuristic and critical preparatory tasks for an academic world history had been completed—which they had not—it was still not clear how the wealth of established facts could be combined in a literary synthesis. After all, the 'scientification' of history corresponded to its 'literarisation'.

The fundamental principle of working closely with the sources necessarily resulted in a restriction to partial areas of history—particular periods, institutions, states, individuals, etc.—and practically demanded the abandonment of the philosophically inspired universal concept of world history. Historiographically, the unity of history could no longer be achieved under the changed methodological points of view. The rejection of universal history was justified by pointing to the inadmissible influence of philosophy, but it is easy to overlook the fact that this was not a renunciation, but an exchange in the philosophical system of reference.

The demand for a total knowledge of history was increasingly withdrawn. Heeren, the last of the great universal historians at Göttingen, whose career had begun only shortly before the revolutionary period, stated in 1795, with reference to Herder and his emphasis on individual peoples, that history as a discipline was empirical and tried to understand events in their pragmatic connections.[107] Ranke considered it 'impossible' to establish a 'causal nexus'; universal history seemed to him too complex for the inductive method of the historian,[108] who could not resolve its contradictions. Emergent historicism surrendered the quest for a knowledge of the whole back to God; according to Ranke its specific method, understanding, could grasp 'the meaning of every period in and of

[106] 'Zur Rekonstruktion der Universalgeschichte auf neuen Grundlagen ist die geschichtliche Wissenschaft noch nicht reif.' Leopold von Ranke, 'Vorlesungseinleitungen', in idem, *Aus Werk und Nachlaß*, ed. Volker Dotterweich and Walter Peter Fuchs (Munich, 1975), vol. 4, p. 463.

[107] See Arnold Hermann Ludwig Heeren's review of K. H. L. Pölitz, *Grundlinien zur pragmatischen Kultgeschichte als ein Versuch, sie auf Ein Prinzip zurückzuführen* (Leipzig, 1795), in *Göttingische gelehrte Anzeigen* (1795), pp. 264ff.; on this, see Christoph Becker-Schaum, *Arnold Hermann Ludwig Heeren: Beitrag zur Geschichte der Geschichtswissenschaft zwischen Aufklärung und Historismus* (Frankfurt am Main, 1993).

[108] Ranke, 'Idee einer Universalhistorie', in idem, *Aus Werk und Nachlaß*, vol. 4, pp. 72–85, at p. 83.

itself'. Consequently Droysen, too, could concede only an 'inkling of the whole'.[109]

To have withdrawn the epistemological claims of historiography was not a loss for the historicist theory of history, but grew out of a reassessment of the relative values of the particular and the whole. The particular no longer derived its value solely from the contribution it made to the whole, but 'every age'—and we could add, every people, and, ultimately, every individual—'is immediate to God, and its value rests not upon what grows out of it, but resides in its existence itself, in its own self'.[110] In Ranke as in Droysen, 'surmising' and 'understanding' were contrasting methods of achieving historical knowledge, different in terms of mode, degree, and extent. This methodological distinction, however, meant that historians, in their research work, were directed to the revalued 'middling' entities of history, that is, states, peoples, periods. The renunciation of the universal dimension of representation, but not necessarily of the epistemological dimension, followed from this. This was undoubtedly easier for the patriotic German nineteenth century in general than it was for Ranke personally.

However, expressions such as a 'separation from the general' offer an inadequate description of the process of shaping this awareness which, at first glance, seemed to implicate the end of the universal-historical epistemological interest.[111] Anyone who remembers what not only Humboldt and Ranke, but also Gervinus and Droysen, wrote about the historian's duty, if not to grasp, then at least to suspect, the general in the particular, and if not to express it, then at least to hint at it, will hesitate to contradict so crassly such a decidedly inductionist epistemological intention which was universalist after all. Not separation, but a respectful distancing was intended, and this only as a negative circumlocution of an approach that was essentially affirmed, was hampered by various misgivings.

Despite its appeals to empiricism and particularity, and its professional rivalry with philosophy, history ultimately shared philosophy's conviction that the individual historical phenomenon could not stand alone as an epistemological object, but needed the support of the 'general'. The meaning of history adheres to its totality. In the still teleologically

<hr/>

[109] Droysen, *Historik*, p. 38.

[110] '. . . ist unmittelbar zu Gott, und ihr Wert beruht gar nicht auf dem, was aus ihr hervorgeht, sondern in ihrer Existenz selbst, in ihrem eigenen Selbst'. Ranke, 'Idee einer Universalhistorie', p. 78.

[111] 'Absonderung vom Allgemeinen'. See Gerhard Schneider, *Absonderung vom Allgemeinen: Ursprung und Wesen der Staatsideologie des historischen Nationalismus* (Düsseldorf, 1973).

coloured language of historians, this means that only the whole sum of
events constitutes a subject unit that can represent the indispensable
standard of reference for every individual phenomenon.

History can use any event to show the general, the 'form of history'.[112]
Every work of history treats its particular subject 'in relation to the whole
of humanity'.[113] In addition to external-objective universality, there was
a 'subjective' universality, and this was the one that counted: 'There is
no historical masterpiece that does not, even in the smallest space, reflect
the history of humanity.'[114] 'Every special moment in time is a revelation
of God',[115] every individual period 'is highly worthy of observation',[116] as
is also every individual people. 'The history of humanity appears in the
nations';[117] in their state organisations they represent the 'thoughts of
God'.[118]

Ranke's central epistemological problem, for example, was the relationship between the particular, that is, the special individual event, the
individual actor, the particular thought, which the historian encountered
in his sources, and the general, that is, the conditions, contexts, and
developments of which they were part and in which they could alone be
understood, but which were not expressed explicitly and adequately in
the sources. This was, in fact, the central problem of all historical
knowledge. In Ranke's view, historical research, unlike the philosophy of
history, concentrated 'by its nature on the individual'. But it would not
be fulfilling its purpose if that was all it did; rather, it had to concentrate
on the 'live moments of a general development'.[119] 'One must keep the

[112] 'Form der Geschichte'. Humboldt, 'Über die Aufgabe des Geschichtsschreibers', p. 593.
[113] '. . . im Bezuge auf die ganze Menschheit'. Georg Gottfried Gervinus, *Grundzüge der Historik* (Leipzig, 1827), p. 366.
[114] 'Kein historisches Meisterwerk, das nicht im engsten Raume die Geschichte der Menschheit widerspiegelt.' Wilhelm Roscher, *Leben, Werk und Zeitalter des Thakydides* (Berlin, 1892), pp. 19f.
[115] 'Jeder besondere Moment der Zeit ist Offenbarung Gottes.' F. W. J. Schelling, 'Vorlesungen oder die Methode des akademischen Studiums (1803)', in *Die Idee der deutschen Universität: Die fünf Grundschriften aus der Zeit ihrer Neubegründung durch klassischen Idealismus und romantischen Realismus* (Darmstadt, 1956), p. 67.
[116] '. . . der Betrachtung höchst würdig.' Leopold von Ranke, *Über die Epochen der neueren Geschichte*, ed. Alfred Dove (Berlin, 1888), pp. 4f.
[117] 'In den Nationen erscheint die Geschichte der Menschheit.' Ibid., p. 15.
[118] '. . . Gedanken Gottes'. Ibid., p. 27.
[119] '. . . lebendigen Momente einer allgemeinen Entwicklung'. Leopold von Ranke, *Zwölf Bücher Preußische Geschichte*, 'Vorrede', quoted from *Gesamtausgabe der Deutschen Akademie, 1. Reihe, P. Werke*, ed. Georg Reinhart (1930), vol. 1, p. 87. See Rudolf Vierhaus, 'Ranke und die Anfänge der deutschen Geschichtswissenschaft', in Bernd Faulenbach (ed.), *Geschichtswissenschaft in Deutschland* (Munich, 1974), pp. 17–34 and 168–71.

general and the particular equally in mind in order to be able to understand both the effect which is achieved, and the repercussions that flow from it.'[120] Ranke considered it impossible to deduce history from general principles; however, he believed that one could progress from observing the individual to the general. He recognised principles in the actions of people; he saw their actions as led by ideas, pressures, and necessities, which went beyond their intentions and means. 'The general movement of the world consists in the conflict between the general and the personal, or in their combination.'[121]

Ranke's vague and inconsistent terminology makes it extraordinarily difficult to decide what is meant by the general and the particular in each case. As the general was not 'world history', 'humanity', 'society', or 'material conditions', so the particular was not only the individual person or event. Ranke always recognised the mutual reciprocity and interdependence of both.

Around the middle of the nineteenth century, Droysen referred to the exact point at which historicism both continued the universalisation of the specifically historical identity-building which the Enlightenment had begun, and gave it a new direction. For Droysen, the problem of the part and the whole could not be understood and discussed in an absolute sense, but only in a relational one, as he explained in his *Historik* lectures of 1857: 'We understand the whole only out of the parts, and again, the parts make sense only in terms of the whole, although an absolute and complete totality can, of course, never be achieved. For human understanding grasps only the middle, not the beginning, not the end.' Thus the starting point is 'the foundation of the whole procedure . . . only a relative general, . . . not the general as such, . . . only a relative own, not the one itself. The spirit has recognised how much it has now recognised; understanding piece by piece, it supplements what it has understood piece by piece to create a totality, and out of this it understands itself and the many.'[122] But Droysen's *Historik* long had no impact at all on the

---

[120] 'Man wird das Allgemeine und das Besondere gleichmäßig vor Auge behalten müssen, um das eine und das andere zu begreifen: Die Wirkung, welche ausgeübt, die Rückwirkung, welche erfahren wird.' Leopold von Ranke, *Geschichte Wallensteins*, 'Vorrede', quoted from idem, *Sämtliche Werke*, 4th edn (1880), vol. 23, p. viii.

[121] 'In dem Konflikt des Allgemeinen und des Persönlichen, oder ihrer Verbindung, besteht die allgemeine Bewegung der Welt.' Ranke, *Englische Geschichte vornehmlich im 17. Jahrhundert*, vol. 5, quoted from idem, *Sämtliche Werke*, 4th edn (1877), vol. 28, p. 209.

[122] 'Nur aus den Teilen verstehen wir das Ganze, und wieder, erst aus dem Ganzen die Teile', wobei eine absolute und vollkommene Totalität freilich nie erreichbar sein kann. 'Denn das Begreifen des Menschen fasst nur die Mitte, nicht den Anfang, nicht das Ende.' '. . . die

discussion of the theory of historical knowledge, as the first (incomplete) edition was not published until 1937.[123]

Despite this development, the genre of universal history, which must always be considered in all its different forms, was still not finished by the early nineteenth century. It had to fulfil the needs of schools and to satisfy a broad educated public's appetite for popular editions. It was therefore at first seriously affected by neither the methodological nor the nationalist turn taken by German historiography in the early nineteenth century. The only question was whether it was still methodologically at the cutting edge of the subject and abreast of its times. In his *Geschichte der historischen Forschung und Kunst* of 1818, Ludwig Wachler could still state: 'Thus participation in world history is not merely widespread but generalised in schools, at universities, and in business, among high and low, and is the major means of educating the people in the widest sense.'[124] It is perhaps obvious to relate this comment to the overall balance-sheet of the eighteenth century, the century of universal history. More critical and more sceptical comments could be cited from later centuries. Although philologists such as F. A. Wolf and historians such as Wachler held on to the idea that with the concept of universal history they were giving everyone an overview of the whole of history, these attempts increasingly receded into the background in the early nineteenth century.[125]

VII

The rehabilitation of historical particularity, initiated by Herder and other theoreticians, did not result directly in historians developing a particular interest in German history. Thus Humboldt, for example, had by

---

Grundlage des ganzen Verfahrens ... nur ein relatives Allgemeines, ... nicht das Allgemeine selbst, ... nur ein Relativ eigenes, nicht das eine selbst. Der Geist hat erkannt, wieviel er denn jetzt erkannt hat; stückweise verstehend ergänzt er das stückweise Erfasste zu einer Totalität, und aus dieser versteht er sich und das Viele.' Droysen, *Historik*, pp. 30f., 32.

[123] On this, see ibid., pp. xivf.

[124] 'So ist in Bürger- und Gelehrtenschulen, auf Universitäten und im Geschäftsleben, bei Hohen und Niederen, die Teilnahme an Weltgeschichte nicht bloß verbreitet, sondern schon verallgemeinert und nimmt unter den Bildungsmitteln des Volkes im weiten Sinne eine Hauptstelle ein.' Ludwig Wachler, *Geschichte der historischen Forschung und Kunst seit der Wiederherstellung der litterärischen Cultur in Europa*, 2 vols (Göttingen, 1818), vol. 2, p. 874.

[125] See Pandel, *Historik und Didaktik*, pp. 225ff.

no means given up the idea of world history, but had reformed it via the concept of individuality. In other words, for him, humanity manifested itself via the individual. In fact, the universalist attitude of German historians first led them to look outward in their search for the general. They called for foreign cultures and nations to be researched so that a balanced picture of human development could be shown, but ultimately also in order to push ahead a new interpretation of universal history.

As a topic of historical research in the late eighteenth and early nineteenth century, the German nation played, if any part at all, only a subordinate one. Contemporary publications by historians reflect this view. Thus in his research on the Greeks, Friedrich August Wolf was essentially interested in a 'history of humanity'.[126] And in his work on Roman history, Barthold Georg Niebuhr focused on the 'great world revolution' in 'world history'.[127] These universalist traditions of early German national historiography were still alive in Droysen's work.

The rising tide of nationalisation, however, eventually also reached the historians. Academic and political–cultural nationalism finally converged. The beginnings of the idea of the nation-state, which was later developed in greater detail by historicism, can already be found in late Enlightenment patterns of argument. Yet there can be no quibbling that, under the impression of the events of 1813, German historiography discovered the dimension of national history for the first time, and devoted itself to it wholeheartedly. The idea of individuality logically resulted in historical life being researched, particularly in terms of the expressions of individuals and particularities, that is, in the actions of great individuals and the articulations of collective individuals such as nations. The result was a strict polarity: universality and nationality split; international society and the fatherland separated. The national rising of that time was the space from which German historiography drew new life, and the national idea was the driving force behind it. Probably all nineteenth-century historiographical directions would, in fact, have subscribed to the 'connection between historiography and the nation',[128] even if they would not have interpreted it in exactly the same way, and in it we find the basic consensus which, however questionable, is the basic signature of the German

---

[126] Friedrich August Wolf, *Darstellung der Altertumswissenschaft nach Begriff, Umfang, Zweck und Wert (1807)*, ed. Johannes Irmscher (Berlin, 1985), p. 134.

[127] Berthold Georg Niebuhr, *Römische Geschichte* (Berlin, 1811), vol. 1, p. 15.

[128] '. . . Zusammenhang der Geschichtswissenschaft mit der Nation'. Becker, *Zeit der Revolution*, p. 14.

nineteenth century. There is no doubt that the nationality mentioned in the label 'German historiography' intended a *differentia specifica*.

The fact that the nation became the central unit in the historical paradigm and came to stand for the real process of history long remained obscured by the shadow of this paradigm. When Luden, for example decided to publish a general history during the war with Russia, it was still in the universal-historical tradition. History was human progress, and, as such, the history of progressive culture and freedom. It took place in a chain of civilised peoples, among whom the Germans did not, at first, have any particular place reserved for them. Only when Luden published the continuation of his history for the Middle Ages in 1821, did he have an opportunity to bring an interest in national and universal knowledge together and reduce them to a common denominator: 'German life and the German way is the next subject of history, and the progress of the history of humanity is to be found in it.'[129]

For many historians, academic work and political conviction agreed on essential points. This was the case so long as the creation, justification, maintenance, and further development of national unity were seen as the main task of history. In all countries, history entered into such a close connection with the national movement that it became the national and political discipline *par excellence*.

To be sure, still at the peak of its self-confidence, German historiography took pride not only in its patriotic mentality and national rootedness, but also in its universality. In his Inaugural Lecture at the University of Königsberg in 1858, which graced the first volume of the *Historische Zeitschrift* in the following year, Wilhelm Giesebrecht, for example, explained that since the Wars of Liberation, German historiography had 'with the full seriousness of the German nature [thrown itself] into studying the history of the Fatherland. But it did not therefore give up the universal points of view which the discipline had so early picked up on.'[130]

The historical theory and the historiography of incipient historicism by no means abandoned the ideal of universality in the extensive–integral sense as radically as the existing reconstructions would like to suggest.

---

[129] 'Teutsches Leben und teutsche Art ist der nächste Gegenstand der Geschichte, und in ihm das Fortschreiten der Geschichte der Menschheit zu suchen.' Heinrich Luden, *Allgemeine Geschichte der Völker und Staaten des Mittelalters* (1821), vol. 1, pp. 4f.

[130] '. . . mit dem ganzen Ernst der deutschen Natur auf das Studium der vaterländischen Geschichte (geworfen). Aber die universellen Gesichtspunkte, welche die Wissenschaft so früh ergriffen hatte, gab sie deshalb nicht auf.' Wilhelm Giesebrecht, 'Die Entwicklung der modernen deutschen Geschichtswissenschaft', *Historische Zeitschrift*, 1 (1859), 1–17, at 9.

For Ranke, God was most visible in 'the context of big history',[131] and Humboldt had thought so too, not even to mention Droysen's sharp-edged plea for the 'right of world historical contemplation'.[132] That the whole history of humankind, if it did not aim for one particular *telos*, yet displayed a comprehensive 'trend', was one of the background convictions of German historical thinking in the early nineteenth century which was hardly disputed. There was no question in any case of any fundamental renunciation of the claim to universal-historical knowledge.

The conclusion that, strangely, seemed to follow from this was that although world history should always be kept in mind, it was not actually to be written. Ranke, too, for decades observed the principle of reading about universal history,[133] but not writing it. Another temporary solution to universal-historical thinking suggested itself under changed political and epistemological conditions: cooperation between specialists, such as Heeren and Ukert had organised in their thematically limited *Geschichte der europäischen Staaten*, published from 1829, which was modelled on the English 'world history' of the eighteenth century.[134] Once again, it seemed that universal history could be written, if at all, only in the form of an aggregate of specialist histories, at the expense of the large context which, it became clear after earlier misunderstandings, Ranke was as passionately concerned about as his opposites on the spectrum of the philosophy of history.

However, this universal-historical interest on the part of historicists not only picked up the late Enlightenment concept of the history of mankind, but sometimes also expressly denied it, which simply lay in the logic of the situation relating to the history of the subject and the political culture.

---

[131] '. . . Zusammenhang der großen Geschichte'. Eberhard Kessel, 'Leopold von Ranke: Idee der Universalgeschichte', *Historische Zeitschrift*, 1978 (1954), 269–308, at 301.

[132] 'Recht der weltgeschichtlichen Betrachtung'. Droysen, *Historik*, p. 269; for the strongly universalistic tradition of the national idea in the *Vormärz* period, see also Wolfgang Hardtwig, 'Von Preußens Aufgabe in Deutschland', in *Deutschlands Aufgabe in der Welt, Historische Zeitschrift*, 231 (1980), 265ff., at 297ff.

[133] Gunther Berg, *Leopold von Ranke als akademischer Lehrer. Studium zu seinen Vorlesungen und zu seinem Geschichtsdenken* (Göttingen, 1968).

[134] The foreword (vol. 1, 1829) emphasises, 'dass ein Einzelner unmöglich jetzt das leisten könne, was man erwartet und verlangt' (that it is impossible for an individual to achieve what is expected and demanded), namely 'aus Quellen selbst soll, ohne Vorliebe für eine Partei, für einen Stand, die Geschichte der Regenten wie der Regierten dargestellt werden' (the history of the rulers and the ruled is to be presented from the sources themselves, without any preference for political party or social status).

The temporal and spatial limitations placed on historicist universal history had been followed immediately by a retreat from cultural history to the history of the state. This trend, too, arose at least as much from methodological pressures as from ideological preference. According to the prevailing view of the early nineteenth century, the subject of world history was no longer simply mankind itself, but its state organisation, whether it was conceived in the Kantian tradition as a genre-wide process of politigony, or as by Ranke, who sought traces of 'God's thoughts' in the purposeless 'life' of the states.[135] Schlosser had tried to hold tight to the full idea of Enlightenment universal history as against 'world history' in this reduced sense.[136] His student Gervinus, and especially Droysen,[137] also committed themselves to this project, which Ranke himself abandoned only when he turned from theory to practice.[138]

VIII

Multi-layered Enlightenment universal history was not immediately displaced by a German national history. In fact, if we look at the balance-sheet of the nineteenth century, it did not achieve the national-historical synthesis any more easily than the universal-historical one. If German history was written, then it was mostly by writers of the second rank, who explicitly apologised for the provisional nature of their undertaking. Enlightenment universal history was gradually replaced by a concern with the history of individual periods of German national history. In this process, epistemological causes (that is, the increased value placed on the individual and the contructivity of historical knowledge), the dimensions of the discipline (that is, the establishment of history as an academic subject), and political and cultural factors (that is, nationalisation) all mutually presupposed each other in a way that could be separated out only analytically.

---

[135] Ranke, 'Idee einer Universalhistorie', p. 282.
[136] See Friedrich Christoph Schlosser, *Universalhistorische Übersicht der Geschichte der alten Welt und ihrer Cultur* (1826), vol. 1/1, 'Vorwort'.
[137] See Droysen, *Historik*, p. 259.
[138] See Leopold von Ranke, *Weltgeschichte: Vollständig in neun Teilen* (Leipzig, 1881–8).

Views of the Past in Irish Vernacular
Literature, 1650–1850

VINCENT MORLEY

A BOOK BY THE PIONEERING FOLKLORIST THOMAS CROFTON CROKER published in 1824 contains the following description of a typical schoolmaster
in the province of Munster:

> He praises the Milesians—he curses 'the betrayer Dermod'—abuses 'the
> Saxon strangers'—lauds Brian Boru—utters one sweeping invective against
> the Danes, Henry VIII, Elizabeth, Cromwell 'the Bloody', William 'of the
> Boyne,' and Anne; he denies the legality of the criminal code; deprecates and
> disclaims the Union; dwells with enthusiasm on the memories of Curran,
> Grattan, 'Lord Edward,' and young Emmet; insists on Catholic emancipation;
> attacks the Peelers, horse and foot; protests against tithes, and threatens a
> separation of the United Kingdoms![1]

Croker intended the above sketch, not as a portrait of any particular individual, but as a summary of attitudes which were typical of a key social
group—the 'philomaths' who presided over the unofficial 'hedge schools'
on which a large section of the Irish population relied for whatever education they received.[2] Croker's teacher believed implicitly in traditional
accounts of the common racial origin of the native Irish, whom he
described as 'Milesians'—that is, as descendants of Milesius, the mythical ancestor of the Gaels. His view of the Irish past incorporated a
rogues' gallery populated by foreign tyrants (Henry VIII, Elizabeth I,
Oliver Cromwell, William III) and an Irish traitor (the 'betrayer Dermod'
was Diarmait Mac Murchada, king of Leinster, who solicited the Anglo-
Norman invasion of 1169), as well as a pantheon of Irish patriots ranging
in period from Brian Bóruma, king of Munster and high king of Ireland
who defeated the Norse of Dublin at the battle of Clontarf in 1014, to
Robert Emmet, leader of an unsuccessful republican rebellion in 1803.

---

[1] T. Crofton Croker, *Researches in the South of Ireland* (London, 1824), p. 328.
[2] See P. J. Dowling, *The Hedge Schools of Ireland* (Cork, 1968).

Proceedings of the British Academy, **134**, 171–198. © The British Academy 2006.

Employing both local and national perspectives, Croker's representative teacher repudiated both English law and the body responsible for enforcing it, the County Constabulary, a paramilitary force colloquially known as the 'Peelers'; denounced the collection of tithes on behalf of the established Anglican church; condemned the legal disabilities to which Catholics were subject; and, last but by no means least, rejected Ireland's constitutional position since 1801 as part of the United Kingdom. Clearly, an unequivocally nationalist interpretation of Irish history had been elaborated and was being propagated through the schools by the 1820s at the latest.

A substantial body of evidence supports the view that the historical perspective described by Croker enjoyed considerable popularity in the early nineteenth century. For example, the *Irish Magazine*, published monthly between 1807 and 1815, was perhaps the earliest periodical to articulate a consistently nationalist view of the Irish past and by 1813 its print-run had reached 5,000 thousand copies per issue, giving it the largest circulation of any periodical in the country.[3] Edited by Watty Cox, a veteran of the republican United Irish movement of the 1790s, the *Irish Magazine* described itself as a 'monthly asylum for neglected biography' and devoted a great deal of space to historical topics. The following passage from its issue of May 1810 gives an accurate idea of the views promoted in its columns:

> . . . the history of the Universe contains nothing more atrocious than the persecutions of the Irish by the English; nothing more repugnant to civilisation; nothing more base or more flagitious; nothing more blasphemous or more profane; bidding a bold defiance to every attribute by which the Creator has distinguished the human species from the ravening beasts of prey.[4]

Several of the historical villains and heroes who featured prominently in the pages of the *Irish Magazine* have already been mentioned: Henry VIII was a 'memorable brute' with a penchant for 'broiling young ladies, and murdering his wives';[5] Elizabeth I was described as 'burning with unquenchable desires', even in her old age when, 'vain of her haggard and cadaverous form', she 'sought to allure her many lovers';[6] while William III was portrayed as a 'gloomy and fanatical Dutchman' who treacher-

---

[3] *Irish Magazine*, April 1813, 163.
[4] Ibid., May 1810, 236–7.
[5] Ibid., May 1812, 215.
[6] Ibid., February 1809, 51–2;

ously dethroned his uncle and father-in-law.[7] On the other hand, a visit by the editor of the *Irish Magazine* to the site of Brian Bóruma's victory over the Danes occasioned the following reflections:

> I set out on foot, and passed through Clontarf. This ancient village so renowned in our History, for the defeat and expulsion of the Danes, and the death of the illustrious Brian Boirhome, who distinguished himself on that remarkable event, excited the most lively sentiments in my bosom, of gratitude and affection for the heroes, who taught us to detest the government of a stranger, and whose impatience at the weight of his yoke, gave existence to an event which forms one of the greatest features in Irish History, for the valour which the Irish displayed and the glorious and decisive victory which crowned it.[8]

Likewise, Cox's discussion of the character and objectives of Robert Emmet could hardly have been more laudatory or outspoken, given that it was published in 1808, only five years after Emmet's execution and in the midst of a European war:

> Young Emmet and his College companions were soon distinguished for Anti Anglo opinions, and in 1798 he was expelled [from] the University with several other young men accused of entertaining a taste for French politics . . . Some time in the beginning of the year 1803 his ardent and impetuous mind, impatient at what he conceived to be the degraded condition of his country, contemplated the possibility of throwing off the English government, and erecting in its place an Irish republic. We regret to say, (because his country has lost one of her best children,) that his judgment, did not keep pace with his rapid fancy, great mind and honest thinking.[9]

Thomas Moore's *Irish Melodies* also achieved immediate and extraordinary popularity on their first appearance in 1808. The elevated tone and genteel language of Moore's finely crafted lyrics could hardly have been further removed from the robust polemics and scabrous abuse of Cox's journalism. Yet the glaring contrast in form should not obscure an underlying similarity in content. Unlike Cox, Moore had never been a member of the United Irishmen but he had sympathised with the movement and his *Irish Melodies*, as much as Cox's *Irish Magazine*, furnished an eager public with nationalist representations of key episodes in Irish history. Thus Brian Bóruma's victory at Clontarf was celebrated in Moore's 'Remember the glories of Brien the brave':

---

[7] *Irish Magazine*, June 1808, 307.
[8] Ibid., April 1814, 164.
[9] Ibid., November 1808, 512.

> Remember the glories of Brien the brave,
> 　Tho' the days of the hero are o'er;
> Tho' lost to Momonia [Munster] and cold in the grave,
> 　He returns to Kinkora [his palace] no more!
> That star of the field, which so often has pour'd
> 　Its beam on the battle is set;
> But enough of its glory remains on each sword,
> 　To light us to victory yet![10]

Likewise, Moore commemorated the martyred Robert Emmet in 'Oh!
Breathe not his name':

> Oh! breathe not his name, let it sleep in the shade,
> Where cold and unhonor'd his relics are laid:
> Sad, silent and dark, be the tears that we shed,
> As the night-dew that falls on the grass o'er his head!
>
> But the night-dew that falls, though in silence it weeps,
> Shall brighten with verdure the grave where he sleeps,
> And the tear that we shed, though in secret it rolls,
> Shall long keep his memory green in our souls.[11]

Yet merely to recognise the real and undoubted influence of the *Irish
Magazine* and the *Irish Melodies* in the early nineteenth century is not to
explain their influence. It is to leave the most important question unan-
swered: that is, *why* did Cox's essays and Moore's songs evoke such a
strong response from the Irish public? Was their popularity merely the
Irish reflection of a wider European *Zeitgeist*—an early manifestation of
the romantic nationalism that would be so ubiquitous a generation later?
I think not. It will be argued in this essay that the interpretation of the
Irish past espoused by Croker's schoolteacher was not primarily the product of contemporary cultural influences, whether originating in Ireland
itself or elsewhere in Europe, but was, on the contrary, a central feature
of an indigenous tradition of historical writing that originated in the
mid-seventeenth century.

　To trace this historiographic tradition back to its source we must turn
from writing in English to writing in Irish and from printed works to
manuscript sources. We must leave the bourgeois 'public sphere' behind
and enter a very different forum for the exchange of ideas: a forum associated more with rural taverns and fairs than with urban coffee houses
and reading rooms; a forum in which the discourse was oral rather than

---

[10]　Thomas Moore, *Irish Melodies and Miscellaneous Poems* (Dublin, 1833), p. 4.
[11]　Ibid., p. 7.

written, and was conducted through the medium of a vernacular tongue ignored by the state and shunned by the upwardly mobile. In assessing the importance of this alternative, demotic, 'public sphere', a well known quotation from a Scottish writer, Andrew Fletcher of Saltoun (d. 1716), is likely to be more pertinent than the writings of Jürgen Habermas. In Fletcher's words, 'if a man were permitted to make all the ballads, he need not care who should make the laws of a nation'.[12]

Some knowledge of the linguistic situation in early nineteenth-century Ireland is required for a proper appreciation of the importance of the vernacular sources. In the most substantial study of the subject, Garret FitzGerald found that at least 80 per cent and 77 per cent of the children born in Connacht and Munster respectively in the period 1801–11 were Irish speakers. Even in the more anglicised provinces of Ulster and Leinster, where the corresponding figures were 15 per cent and 11 per cent respectively, Irish remained a common vernacular in counties Donegal, Tyrone, Armagh, Monaghan, Cavan, Louth, Meath, and Kilkenny. In Ireland as a whole, FitzGerald calculated that at least 41 per cent of the children born in the first decade of the nineteenth century were Irish speakers.[13] These data were, however, abstracted from the returns of censuses conducted in the aftermath of the famine of 1845–9 in which mortality was highest among the poor of the south and west—precisely the demographic group that was most strongly Irish-speaking. For this reason, among others, Dr FitzGerald argued that the census figures underestimated the true extent of Irish speaking and concluded that 'something approaching half—perhaps even half or more—of the children in Ireland at the start of the nineteenth century spoke Irish'.[14] As the language was already giving way to English in some areas—in north Leinster and south Ulster for example—the proportion of Irish speakers among the adult population would have been higher still.

---

[12] *The Oxford Dictionary of Quotations*, 4th edn (Oxford, 1992), p. 287.
[13] Garret FitzGerald, 'Estimates for Baronies of Minimum Level of Irish-speaking among Successive Decennial Cohorts: 1771–1781 to 1861–1871', in *Proceedings of the Royal Irish Academy*, 84c (1984), 127.
[14] Ibid., 126.

Keating

It is hardly possible to open a discussion of historiography in Irish without referring to the synthetic history of Ireland entitled *Foras Feasa ar Éirinn* ('A basis of knowledge about Ireland') written by Geoffrey Keating, a Catholic priest of Old English descent, around the year 1634. Keating's history is widely regarded as the most influential historical text to have been written in Ireland before the emergence of cheap print and mass literacy in the nineteenth century. Professor Pádraig Ó Fiannachta, himself a Catholic priest, memorably described Keating's history as 'Aeneid na hÉireann, nó dá mba áil liom é a rá, Geinisis nó Pentatúc na hÉireann' ('the Irish Aeneid or, if I cared to say it, the Irish Genesis or Pentateuch').[15] Professor Breandán Ó Buachalla, one of the foremost students of seventeenth-century Irish literature, numbered the history among what he termed 'téacsaí bunúis an náisiúin Chaitlicigh Éireannaigh' ('the foundation texts of the Irish Catholic nation').[16] Bernadette Cunningham, in her recent monograph on *Foras Feasa ar Éirinn*, has also stressed its 'prolonged and profound influence on perceptions of Irishness'.[17] I have no wish to dissent from the views of these scholars. On the contrary, I fully accept that *Foras Feasa ar Éirinn* marked a novel departure in the history of Irish letters and thought, and that its influence on the outlook of later generations was considerable. I do, however, wish to draw attention to a number of factors—I might say, to a number of impediments—which, taken together, limited the direct influence of Keating's history on the Irish-speaking population.

The first of these impediments lay in Keating's use of a conservative language which retained features of the literary dialect employed by the *aos dána* (the hereditary learned caste in traditional Irish society) from the thirteenth century until the overthrow of the native social and political order at the beginning of the seventeenth century. This is not to suggest that Keating's prose was intelligible only to a few elderly graduates of the bardic schools, but rather that his archaising style, while greatly admired by the literati, may have been disconcerting for the unlettered masses. The practical difficulties of disseminating a book of some

---

[15] Pádraig Ó Fiannachta, 'Stair finnscéal agus annála', in *Léachtaí Cholm Cille*, 2 (1971), 7.
[16] Breandán Ó Buachalla, *Aisling Ghéar: na Stíobhartaigh agus an tAos Léinn 1603–1788* (Dublin, 1996), p. 98.
[17] Bernadette Cunningham, *The World of Geoffrey Keating: History, Myth and Religion in Seventeenth-century Ireland* (Dublin, 2000), p. 226.

150,000 words constituted a second impediment. As *Foras Feasa ar Éirinn* remained unpublished until the nineteenth century, its circulation depended on the time-consuming and laborious process of transcription, a process requiring skills and materials that must often have been in short supply. Furthermore, given the length of the work, the numerous manuscript copies that were produced would have been more suitable for individual perusal at leisure than for reading aloud in company. In short, it seems reasonable to conclude that the influence of Keating's history was strongest among a literate elite who had sufficient material resources to produce or to commission manuscript copies of their own.

One further limitation of Keating's history must also be mentioned— a limitation which lay in its content rather than in its form. With the exception of a historiographical preface in which he took issue with the arguments of earlier writers who had criticised the native Irish, Keating discussed no event more recent than the arrival of the Anglo-Normans in the twelfth century. Whatever factors may have shaped the attitudes of Croker's teacher towards Henry VIII, Elizabeth I, Cromwell 'the bloody', and William 'of the Boyne', not to mention more recent figures such as Henry Grattan, Lord Edward Fitzgerald, and Robert Emmet, Keating's history cannot be numbered among them.

It seems clear, therefore, that the influence of *Foras Feasa ar Éirinn* on the historical perspective of the Irish-speaking population was mainly an indirect one. Rather than itself shaping the historical outlook of the illiterate masses, Keating's history was a ready compendium of historical episodes and mythological tales from which the authors of later works that were more popular in form could draw. The most comprehensive of these vulgarisations was the long historical poem variously entitled *Tuireamh na hÉireann* ('Ireland's dirge') or *Aiste Sheáin Uí Chonaill* ('Seán Ó Conaill's composition'). Practically nothing is known about Seán Ó Conaill. A tradition that he was bishop of Ardfert, a diocese roughly coterminous with County Kerry, cannot be correct, but internal evidence suggests that the poem was composed in Kerry around 1655, while its use of Latin phrases from the *Pater noster* and *Ave Maria* is consistent with the view that its author was a Catholic clergyman.[18]

[18] For a discussion of Seán Ó Conaill, see Cecile O'Rahilly (ed.), *Five Seventeenth-century Political Poems* (Dublin, 1952), pp. 50–4.

Tuireamh na hÉireann

None of the factors that would have hindered the propagation of Keating's history applied to *Tuireamh na hÉireann*. It is true that literary scholars are not entirely agreed in their characterisation of the poem's language: although Cecile O'Rahilly, who prepared the modern scholarly edition of the work, referred to its 'bare simplicity of language',[19] Breandán Ó Buachalla has more recently argued that Ó Conaill's language cannot be assigned to either the highest or lowest linguistic registers.[20] This divergence is, I feel, more apparent than real. While it is true to say that the language of *Tuireamh na hÉireann* was closer to the speech of contemporary educated gentlemen than to that of the illiterate masses, it is equally the case that Ó Conaill eschewed the obsolescent literary forms favoured by Keating.[21] The linguistic register of *Tuireamh na hÉireann* was sufficiently elevated to lend the composition an air of learning and authority but it was also sufficiently colloquial and contemporary to ensure that its accessibility for the general population was not compromised. At the present day, the work is still readily intelligible to those who have no familiarity with early modern Irish—something that cannot be said of Keating's history. Languages do not evolve at uniform rates, and comparative estimates of intelligibility are always highly subjective, but the Irish of *Tuireamh na hÉireann* bears comparison with the English of Milton's *Paradise Lost* in its ease of comprehension for a modern audience, while Keating's Irish might be said to fall about midway between the English of Shakespeare and that of Chaucer.

Furthermore, *Tuireamh na hÉireann* is a poem—a long poem which runs to 496 lines in the standard edition—but none the less a poem which could be committed to memory and recited in any company. The metre used, a minimalist form of *caoineadh*, is one of the simplest in Irish prosody and requires only that each line has the same vowel sound in its final stressed syllable. The resulting text is at once natural, almost prosaic in its diction and syntax, yet strongly cadenced. The poem's clarity and metre facilitated its transmission through oral routes that demanded neither a high standard of literacy nor material resources.

---

[19] O'Rahilly, *Five Seventeenth-century Political Poems*, p. 59.

[20] Ó Buachalla, *Aisling Ghéar*, p. 122.

[21] For a commentary on these, see Osborn Bergin (ed.), *Sgéalaigheacht Chéitinn: Stories from Keating's History of Ireland*, 3rd edn (Dublin, 1981), pp. xii–xxvii.

Apart from these important differences in form, the content of *Tuireamh na hÉireann* differed from that of *Foras Feasa ar Éirinn* in one crucial respect: whereas Keating concluded his narrative in the twelfth century, Seán Ó Conaill brought the story down to his own generation. His account of early Irish history closely resembles Keating's: the migration of the Milesians from Spain; their victory over Ireland's previous inhabitants, the Tuatha Dé Danann; the descent of the principal Irish lineages from the various sons of Milesius; the mythical champion Fionn mac Cumhail and his warrior band, the Fianna; the arrival of St Patrick on a mission mandated by Pope Celestine; the fame of early-Christian Ireland as the 'island of saints'; the depredations of the Norse and their ultimate defeat by Brian Bóruma; the sexual immorality of 'the betrayer Dermod' and his introduction of the Anglo-Normans—all these are recounted. However, the historical narrative becomes more detailed as it approaches the mid-seventeenth century. The most salient episodes of the previous hundred years are described, and unambiguous positions are adopted in relation to them. Ó Conaill's condemnation of the Reformation was unrestrained:

> Cailbhín coitcheann is Lúter craosach,
> dias do thréig a gcreideamh ar mhéirdrig
> 's i n-aghaidh na heaguilse sgríobhaid go héigneach.
> Prionnsaí Saxan—olc dearbh an sgéil sin—
> an t-ochtú Hénrí is Élizabétha,
> Rí na Breataine 's Alban Séamus,
> Lúter leanaid 's an eaglais séanaid.[22]

> (Promiscuous Calvin and voracious Luther, a pair who abandoned their faith for a harlot and wrote violently against the church. The princes of England—sad but true the story— Henry VIII and Elizabeth, and James, king of Britain and Scotland, they followed Luther and deserted the church.)

Conversely, Ó Conaill justified the rebellion of O'Neill and O'Donnell, earl of Tyrone and lord of Tyrconnell respectively, against the centralising and anglicising regime of Elizabeth I:

> Dlí beag eile do rinneadh do Ghaelaibh,
> *surrender* ar a gceart do dhéanamh.
> Do chuir sin Leath Cuinn trí na chéile,
> glacaid a n-airm gé cailleadh iad féin leis.

---

[22] O'Rahilly, *Five Seventeenth-century Political Poems*, p. 72.

An t-iarla Ó Néill fuair bárr féile
's an tighearna Ó Domhnaill ba mhór géille.[23]

(One further law was passed against the Irish, that they should
surrender their rights. This threw the north of Ireland into turmoil, they took up arms but were lost thereby: Earl O'Neill of
great generosity and Lord O'Donnell of great authority.)

Ó Conaill's only regret in relation to the rising of 1641 and the protracted
war which followed was that it ended in the defeat of the Confederate
Catholics—a defeat caused, not by the strength of their opponents, but
by their own internal dissensions and their failure to heed the advice of
the papal nuncio Giovanni Battista Rinucinni:

Ag so an coga do chríochnaig Éire
's do chuir na mílte ag iarra déarca.
An uair do díbreadh an Nuntius naofa
do rith pláig is gorta ortha i n-aonacht.
Tógaim finné Risdird Béiling
nach díth daoine, bíg ná éadaig
ná neart námhad do bhain díobh Éire
acht iad féin do chaill ar a chéile.[24]

(This was the war that finished Ireland off and sent thousands
out begging for alms. When the holy nuncio was expelled,
plague and famine beset them simultaneously. I accept the tes-
timony of Richard Bellings that neither want of men, food nor
clothing, nor the enemy's strength caused the loss of Ireland,
but their own failure to support each other.)

The fatal consequences of dissension among the Irish would become a
frequent theme in vernacular historical verse. Ó Conaill described the
most recent calamity to befall Ireland, the Cromwellian conquest of
1649–53, at length:

'S iad do chríochnaig *conquest* Éireann,
do ghabh a ndaingin 's a mbailte le chéile
ó Inis Bó Finne go Binn Éadair
's ó Chloich an Stacáin go Baoi Béarra.
. . .
Cá ngeabham anois nó créad do dhéanfam?
Ní díon dúinn cnoc ná coill ná caolta.

---

[23] O'Rahilly, *Five Seventeenth-century Political Poems*, p. 74.
[24] Ibid., p. 75.

Níl ár leigheas ag liaig i n-Éirinn
acht Dia do ghuí 's na naoimh i n-aonacht.[25]

(It was they who completed the *conquest* of Ireland, and seized
its fortresses and towns together, from Inishbofin [west] to
Howth [east] and from the White Lady [north] to Dursey
[south] . . . Where will we go now or what will we do? We have
no shelter from hill, wood or marshes. The physicians of
Ireland cannot heal us, we can only pray to God and the saints
in unison.)

Seán Ó Conaill's view of the Irish past was anti-Protestant and anti-
English. He condemned Luther, Calvin, Henry VIII, Elizabeth I, and
Cromwell, among others, and furnished the Catholic population with a
narrative summary of Irish history in metrical form that was vivid, lively,
and inspiring—a narrative, moreover, that could be easily understood,
memorised, and recited.

Propagation

While passages from a long prose work such as Keating's *Foras Feasa ar
Éirinn* might be read aloud on occasion, this was impossible without a
manuscript. Shorter metrical works, in contrast, could be propagated by
purely oral routes—by public recitation or, in the case of songs, by public
singing. Where poems and songs are concerned, the surviving manuscript
copies should therefore be seen more as an effect than as a means of their
dissemination. None the less, an analysis of the geographical and temporal distribution of extant manuscripts provides one means, however
crude, by which the popularity of a work can be gauged: quite simply,
scribes would not have bothered to record works that were of no interest
to them. It must, however, be borne in mind that the general level of manuscript production varied between regions (high in Munster, lower in
north Leinster and south Ulster, sporadic elsewhere) and between periods
(rising throughout the seventeenth and eighteenth centuries to peak in the
early nineteenth century and fall sharply after 1850).

In view of the exceptionally large number of extant copies of
Tuireamh na hÉireann there can be no doubt that the work enjoyed a
phenomenal popularity in the two centuries following its composition.
Indeed, it would appear that the number of extant copies is greater than

---

[25] O'Rahilly, *Five Seventeenth-century Political Poems*, pp. 76 and 79.

for any other Irish-language poem or song of any period.[26] In a survey of
the catalogues of the principal manuscript collections, I identified 248
copies of the work dating from the nineteenth century or earlier.[27]
Although published catalogues are now available for most of the major
collections of Irish literary manuscripts (Royal Irish Academy, NUI
Maynooth, British Library, Trinity College Dublin, Cambridge), publication of the catalogues of some important collections is still in progress
(National Library of Ireland, University College Cork, Oxford) or has
yet to commence (University College Dublin, NUI Galway).[28] In addition, a considerable number of manuscripts are held in minor collections
or in private hands. The true number of extant copies of *Tuireamh na
hÉireann* must exceed 248 but there can be no doubt that a large majority
of the extant copies were enumerated in this survey. The size of the
sample is sufficiently large to provide assurance that more complete data

[26] The largest collection of Irish literary manuscripts, that of the Royal Irish Academy, contains
eighty-nine copies of *Tuireamh na hÉireann*. The second most numerous work, with seventy-nine
copies in the same collection, would appear to be an Ossianic dialogue attributed to St Patrick
and Oisín (*A Oisín is fada do shuan*).
[27] The following catalogues were consulted: Morris Mss in *Irisleabhar na Gaedhilge*, 14 (1905)
(UCD Morris); O'Laverty Mss in *Irisleabhar na Gaedhilge*, 16 (1906) (O'Laverty); *Catalogue of
the Irish Manuscripts in the Library of Trinity College, Dublin* (Dublin, 1921) (TCD); *Catalogue
of Irish Manuscripts in the British Museum*, 3 vols (Oxford, 1926–53) (BL); *Catalogue of Irish
Manuscripts in the Royal Irish Academy*, fascicules 1–27 (Dublin, 1926–70) (RIA);
Lámhscríbhinní Gaeilge Choláiste Phádraig, Má Nuad, fascicules 1–7 (Maynooth, 1943–72)
(NUIM); Liverpool Mss in *Celtica*, 4 (1958) (Liverpool); *Catalogue of Irish Manuscripts in the
National Library of Ireland*, fascicules 1–13 (Dublin, 1961–96) (NLI); Drumcondra Mss in
Studia Hibernica, 1 (1961) [no ms. found]; *Clár na Lamhscríbhinní Gaeilge i Leabharlann Phoiblí
Bhéal Feirste* (Dublin, 1962) (Belfast Public Library); *Manuscript Sources for the History of Irish
Civilisation*, vol. 3 (Boston, 1965) (Ennis, Harvard, State of Victoria); Limerick Mss in *Éigse*, 12
(1967–8) (Limerick); *Catalogue of Irish Manuscripts in the Franciscan Library, Killiney* (Dublin,
1969) (UCD Franciscans); *Catalogue of Irish Manuscripts in King's Inns Library Dublin* (Dublin,
1972) [no ms. found]; *Clár Lámhscríbhinní Gaeilge Choláiste Ollscoile Chorcaí: Cnuasach Thorna*
(Dublin, 1972) (UCC Torna); *Catalogue of Gaelic Manuscripts* (Boston, 1973) (NLS); Roscrea
Mss in *Éigse*, 17 (1977–9) (Roscrea); *Clár Lámhscríbhinní Gaeilge: Leabharlanna na Cléire agus
Mionchnuasaigh*, 2 vols (Dublin, 1978–80) (Armagh, Fermoy, Longford, Waterford); Mullingar
Mss in *Éigse*, 19 (1982–3) (Mullingar); *Catalogue of Irish Manuscripts in the Cambridge Libraries*
(Cambridge, 1986) (Cambridge); *Catalogue of Irish Manuscripts in Mount Melleray Abbey Co.
Waterford* (Dublin, 1991) (Mount Melleray); *Clár Lámhscríbhinní Gaeilge Choláiste Ollscoile
Chorcaí: Cnuasach Uí Mhurchú* (Dublin, 1991) (UCC Ó Murchú); Dunnington Mss in *Éigse*, 25
(1991) (Dunnington); *Catalogue of Irish Language Manuscripts in the Bodleian Library at Oxford
and Oxford College Libraries*, pt 1 (Dublin, 2001) (Bodleian). I did not refer to the manuscripts
themselves.
[28] I have, however, consulted the unpublished catalogues of the Ferriter collection in UCD compiled by Eibhlín Ní Ógáin (UCD Ferriter), of the Hyde collection in NUIG compiled by Áine
de Búrca (NUIG Hyde), and of the UCC collection compiled by Máire Eibhlín Ní
Dhonnchadha (UCC Lyons, UCC Gaelic).

would be unlikely to alter significantly the broad outlines of the results detailed below.

The manuscript catalogues did not always provide sufficient information to allow me to determine with certainty when and where a particular copy of *Tuireamh na hÉireann* was written. I therefore had recourse to a number of approximations. Manuscripts that were compiled over a number of years and straddled two time intervals were assigned to the earlier or later period in accordance with the poem's position towards the front or back of the manuscript. When watermarks provided the only means of dating, the year of the latest watermark was taken as the date of the manuscript. In cases where no place or date of writing was specified in a manuscript but the scribe's home district or floruit could be ascertained from other sources, the manuscript was assigned accordingly. Whenever manuscripts consisted largely of material composed in the Ulster–Leinster border region, I assumed that the manuscript originated in the same region—a region designated 'Oriel' in the tables below.[29] All of these assumptions are likely to be true but may be mistaken in particular instances: loose sheets were not always bound in the order in which they were written; paper sometimes lay unused for several years; scribes occasionally relocated from one region to another; and some manuscripts containing material of Oriel provenance were copied in Dublin city. None the less, with all of the above caveats, scribal colophons, other internal evidence, and background information about the scribes allowed the extant copies of *Tuireamh na hÉireann* to be assigned to a specific twenty-five-year interval in a large majority of cases (233 of 248).[30] Most of these manuscripts in their turn (196 of 233) could also be assigned to particular counties or regions (see Figure 1 showing map of places mentioned in this essay).

An analysis of the manuscripts' temporal and regional distribution produced some results that might not have been expected. For example, although it is clear from dialect forms used in the poem and from local references that *Tuireamh na hÉireann* was written by a Munster author, and although the internal evidence points to a date of composition around

---

[29] A convenient practice suggested in Breandán Ó Buachalla (ed.), *Peadar Ó Doirnín: Amhráin* (Dublin, 1969), p. 8.

[30] The information in the catalogues was insufficient to allow fifteen copies of *Tuireamh na hÉireann* found in the following manuscripts to be assigned to a particular twenty-five-year interval: RIA Mss 23 I 35 (ii), 24 M 30, 23 M 45, 24 C 56 (a composite manuscript containing three copies of the poem); NUIM Mss C 16, C 92 (b), C 93 (f), C 102 (d); NLI Mss G.423, G.663; UCC Torna Ms. iii; Roscrea Ms. 3; O'Laverty Ms. G.

Figure 1. Ireland, showing places mentioned in the text.

1655, I found only two copies of the work dating from the seventeenth century and neither is of Munster provenance. See Table 1.

Both copies were made towards the end of the century: BL Ms. Egerton 187 in or after 1686 and RIA Ms. A ii 5 in 1699. Furthermore, the scribes, Uilliam Ó Loingsigh and Seán Ó Súilleabháin respectively, were members of a Dublin literary coterie, although Ó Súilleabháin was a native of Munster.[31] The absence of earlier copies requires explanation. One must acknowledge, of course, that the chance of survival decreases with age, but the number of seventeenth-century manuscripts is so small that natural attrition is unlikely to provide a sufficient explanation in this case. It would seem that the very factors which won the poem its popularity in the oral tradition—its colloquial language and simple metre— caused it to be neglected for some time by scribes whose main focus of attention in the late seventeenth century continued to be the bardic poetry of earlier centuries. A comparatively recent propagandist work written for a popular audience lacked the necessary literary cachet to secure a place in the manuscript anthologies of the period.

With the passage of time, however, *Tuireamh na hÉireann* acquired a patina of age and, with it, increased literary respectability, as is evident from the data for the first quarter of the eighteenth century. See Table 2.

Table 1.   Copies dating from the seventeenth century

Co. Dublin	2 copies	BL Egerton 187; RIA A ii 5
total	2 copies	

Table 2.   1701–25

Co. Dublin	3 copies	RIA 23 D 30; TCD H.3.23; NUIM M 86(b)
Co. Meath	2 copies	RIA 23 D 13, 23 M 18
Co. Cork	1 copy	NUIM C 88
Co. Down	1 copy	NLI G.869
Co. Galway	1 copy	O'Laverty Ms. E
Co. Roscommon	1 copy	RIA 23 M 23
Unknown	2 copies	TCD H.4.13, H.5.1
total	11 copies	

[31] See the poem by Tadhg Ó Neachtain beginning 'Sloinfead scothadh na Gaeilge grinn' in Alan Harrison, *Ag Cruinniú Meala* (Dublin, 1988), p. 135.

At least eleven extant copies date from this period and they include examples from all four provinces, indicating that knowledge of the poem had already spread throughout the country from its apparent region of origin in the extreme south-west. The numbers for the second quarter of the eighteenth century differ little from those for the first quarter. See Table 3.

The geographical distribution of manuscripts is also similar to that in the previous quarter, and the slight increase in the number does not suggest that any significant change in scribal activity occurred. However, the data for the third quarter of the century reveal a sharp increase in the number of manuscripts as well as a shift in the main centre of production from Dublin and the north-east to the south. See Table 4.

These findings are more likely to reflect a general expansion of scribal activity in Munster than any sudden increase in the popularity of

Table 3. 1726–50

Co. Dublin	3 copies	TCD H.4.19; BL Egerton 166; NLI G.82
Co. Clare	2 copies	RIA E iv 3, 23G 4
Co. Cork	2 copies	RIA 12 F 7; NLI G.148
Co. Down	1 copy	Cambridge Add. 3085
Queen's Co.	1 copy	NUIG Hyde 7
Co. Wexford	1 copy	RIA 23 D 8
Unknown	2 copies	RIA 23 D 31; NLI G.140
total	12 copies	

Table 4. 1751–75

Co. Cork	8 copies	RIA A iv 2, 23 I 20, 23 I 28, 23 N 21; UCC Torna xliii, Torna lxvi; Fermoy PB 9; Longford ML 8
Co. Clare	7 copies	RIA 23 C 16, 23 C 24, 24 L 24; NUIM C 70(g), M 111; NLI G.296; Liverpool 12051 M
Co. Dublin	3 copies	NLI G.38, G.171; RIA 23 I 35
Co. Limerick	3 copies	NLI G.350; BL Egerton 150; Longford ML 3
Co. Galway	1 copy	RIA 23 O 35
Co. Kerry	1 copy	UCC Lyons V
Co. Meath	1 copy	RIA 23 K 24
Co. Tipperary	1 copy	NLI G.363
Co. Waterford	1 copy	NUIM M85
Unknown	5 copies	RIA 12 E 22, 23 D 24, 24 C 34; TCD H.4.24; NUIM C102(h)
total	31 copies	

Tuireamh na hÉireann. None the less, the large number of extant copies from counties Cork and Clare establishes that the poem had achieved considerable popularity in the southern province by the third quarter of the eighteenth century at the latest.

The final quarter of the eighteenth century is commonly seen as a time of unprecedented popular politicisation. The era of the American and French revolutions was a period of turmoil in Ireland: it witnessed the agrarian violence of the Whiteboys throughout much of Munster and Leinster; popular mobilisations in favour of free trade, parliamentary reform, and Catholic relief; and the emergence of the earliest mass revolutionary organisations (the Defenders and United Irishmen)—a process which culminated in the rebellion of 1798 in which an estimated 20,000 people lost their lives. Surprisingly, however, it would appear that the copying of *Tuireamh na hÉireann* increased little if at all during this period. See Table 5.

While forty-one copies dating from the final quarter of the century can be identified, the modest increase over the preceding twenty-five-year interval may reflect nothing more than the better survival rate of later manuscripts. I cannot pretend to have a ready explanation for the failure of an evidently popular and strongly anti-English historical poem to attract greater attention during a period of heightened political activity. One might, however, speculate that the political optimism of the 1780s and 1790s may have focused men's minds more on the future than on the past. Alternatively, the strongly religious perspective of the poem may

Table 5.   1776–1800

Co. Cork	10 copies	RIA F v 1, 23 A 28, 23 B 38, 23 I 25, 23 I 36, 24 B 9; NLI G.70; BL Add. 18,951; UCC Torna x; NLS 50.3.12
Co. Clare	6 copies	RIA 23 L 31, 23 L 35; NUIM C 18, C 40, M 52; UCD Franciscans A 33
Co. Limerick	6 copies	RIA 23 L 28, 24 L 4; NLI G.233, G.641; BL Add. 31,877; Mount Melleray 1
Oriel	4 copies	RIA 23 D 23; NLI G.227; BL Egerton 155 and Egerton 161
Co. Dublin	2 copies	RIA F v 5; BL Egerton 129
Co. Kilkenny	2 copies	RIA 4 A 46; TCD H.6.24
Co. Tipperary	2 copies	NLI G.123; Bodleian Ir.e.3
Co. Galway	1 copy	NUIM C 11
Co. Roscommon	1 copy	RIA 23 Q 18
Co. Waterford	1 copy	RIA 23 I 18
Unknown	6 copies	TCD H.6.9, H.6.10, H.6.21; NUIM M 54 (b), M 58 (b); NLI G.976
total	41 copies	

have been uncongenial to many at a time when political radicals were stressing secular objectives and seeking to minimise sectarian divisions.

Be that as it may, perhaps the most striking result to emerge from this analysis of the manuscripts is the dramatic increase in the number of copies of *Tuireamh na hÉireann* which date from the first quarter of the nineteenth century. See Table 6.

It is evident that the failure of the republican rebellion of 1798 and the subsequent Act of Union had not diminished public interest in the Irish past. If the evidence of the manuscripts can be trusted, it would appear that the Catholic and anti-English message of *Tuireamh na hÉireann* was enjoying unprecedented popularity in the early nineteenth century, just as similar views were beginning to be articulated through English and in print. Indeed, at least three translations of *Tuireamh na hÉireann* had been made by the 1780s and they subsequently appear in the literary

Table 6.   1801–25

Co. Cork	28 copies	RIA 23 A 14, 23 A 29, 23 C 10, 23 E 15, 23 N 3, 23 O 74, 24 A 11 (3 copies), 24 A 21; NLI G.84, G.180, G.360, G.366, G.596; UCC Ó Murchú 59, Torna xi, Torna xiii, Torna xlii; NUIM M 5, M 6, M 94; Fermoy CF 28; Longford ML 2; UCD Franciscans A 52; BL Add. 33,567; Roscrea Ms. 5; Mullingar Ms. 7
Co. Clare	12 copies	RIA 23 B 9, 23 G 41, 24 I 9; NLI G.208, G.314, G.376; NUIG Hyde 6, Hyde 21; NUIM M 112; UCC Torna xliv; Ennis Ms. 3; State Library of Victoria Ms. 091
Co. Waterford	6 copies	RIA 23 C 13, 23 I 17, 23 L 5, 23 L 9, 23 O 68; Waterford CE 16
Co. Tipperary	5 copies	RIA 23 B 4, 23 K 3; NLI G.642; Cambridge Add. 6474; Dunnington Ms. 2
Co. Limerick	4 copies	RIA 23 M 21, 24 L 23; NLI G.210, G.494
Co. Dublin	3 copies	BL Egerton 139, Egerton 154; NLI G.36
Co. Kerry	3 copies	NLI G.400; NUIG Hyde 17; BL Egerton 169
Oriel	3 copies	NLI G.532; NUIM MF 8; UCD Franciscans A 40(a)
Co. Louth	2 copies	UCD Morris 6; Armagh Don. 3(c)
Co. Meath	1 copy	RIA 23 O 79
Co. Antrim	1 copy	Belfast Public Library XXXVI
Co. Cavan	1 copy	RIA 23 O 1
Co. Kilkenny	1 copy	NLI G.472
Co. Leitrim	1 copy	NLI G.436
Unknown	16 copies	RIA 23 L 1, 24 L 30, 24 P 19; NLI G.219, G.648; UCC Ó Murchú 32, Torna xii, Torna lxv, Lyons I; TCD H.6.23; NUIG Hyde 2; UCD Ferriter 21; Belfast Public Library VIIII; Cambridge Add. 4206; Harvard Ir.10, Ir.23
total	87 copies	

manuscripts, often alongside copies of the original.[32] Likewise, the poem made a belated appearance in print, being privately printed on a small hand press in Cork city around 1820 by Denis O'Flynn, who was himself an active scribe. O'Flynn probably distributed the unbound sheets in small quantities to his acquaintances and only one copy of his printing is known to survive.[33]

In 1827, *Tuireamh na hÉireann* was published in Dublin in an edition which also included an original English translation in verse and extensive historical notes provided by the editor, Michael Clarke. The translation succeeded in keeping tolerably close to the sense of the original poem while reflecting the contemporary mood, as can be seen from its opening verse:

> Whene'er I think on Erin's hapless fate,
> Her ruin'd sons, her clergy's banished state;
> Her tortur'd children, still with woes opprest,
> My throbbing heart still aches within my breast.[34]

The editor entered fully into the spirit of his text. For example, when describing the career of Diarmait Mac Murchada—the 'betrayer Dermod' as Croker's schoolteacher described him—Clarke assured his readers that:

> This execrable wretch died a shocking spectacle to insatiable and vicious ambition; his body became covered with foetid sores; he was attacked with the Morbus Pedicularis, and he died in the greatest misery, without friends, pity or spiritual comfort![35]

The size of this edition is not known but it attracted some 300 subscribers, mainly from counties Dublin, Meath, and Louth. In 1855 *Tuireamh na hÉireann* again appeared in print, along with a literal English translation, as the principal work in an anthology edited by Martin O'Brennan, who was both a schoolteacher and a promoter of the Irish Tenant League.[36] When a second edition of the anthology appeared in 1858, O'Brennan claimed that the first edition of 1,000 copies had sold

---

[32] See 'When the Irish heroes I behold dismayed' in RIA Ms. 24 P 6, copied in 1780–3; 'Irish heroes when I remind' in Mount Melleray Ms. 1, copied in 1785; and 'When the brave Irish chiefs I call to mind' in RIA Ms. 23 L 28, copied in 1788.

[33] Bound in NLI Ms. G.522.

[34] Michael Clarke (ed.), *Ireland's Dirge, an Historical Poem, Written in Irish* (Dublin, 1827), p. 7.

[35] Ibid., p. 98.

[36] Martin A. O'Brennan (ed.), *Ancient Ireland* (Dublin, 1855).

out in less than two months, a pleasing circumstance from which he drew
the following conclusions:

> First—That there are at least one thousand nationalist readers to be had.
> Second—That there still exists an indestructible flame of nationality never to
> be wholly subdued. Third—That an active politician, besides attending to his
> ordinary business, without losing a moment from it, (as can be ascertained from
> pupils) can think, write and produce a work, as well as talk, for his country.
> Fourth, that such a man can compose a work, having vitality in it—not an
> emasculated one, not a crude narration of facts, perhaps omitting unpalatable
> ones. Fifth—That everything Irish is not a failure. Sixth—That a man does not
> suffer by placing confidence in the public, if he gives value. Seventh—and,
> though last, not least, that the heart of Ireland is yet pure, and loves liberty.[37]

The second edition itself had a distinguished list of more than 700 subscribers who included all four Catholic archbishops of Ireland as well as
twenty-seven other bishops.

The appearance of printed editions of *Tuireamh na hÉireann* may have
contributed to the decline in the number of manuscript copies which is
evident in the second quarter of the nineteenth century. I have identified
only thirty-five copies, less than half the number for the first quarter. See
Table 7.

It is likely, however, that the retreat of Irish in the face of English
(especially in Oriel), a fall in manuscript production as printed material
became readily available, and the appearance of alternative nationalist literature also contributed to this decline. The excess mortality associated
with the great famine of 1845–9, together with the increased rate of emi-

Table 7. 1826–50

Co. Cork	13 copies	RIA 23 C 8, 23 C 26, 23 D 19, 24 M 4; NLI G.101, G.422, G.667; NUIM M 89; UCC Torna i, Gaelic 112; Fermoy CF 3; Waterford CE 9; Limerick Ms. K
Co. Clare	5 copies	RIA 24 A 8, 24 A 19; NLI G.492; NUIM R 69, R 70
Co. Kerry	5 copies	RIA 12 G 15, 23 O 63, 24 P 54, 24 P 57; NLI G.480
Co. Galway	2 copies	NLI G.473, G.479
Co. Limerick	2 copies	RIA 24 P 49; Limerick Ms. I
Co. Waterford	2 copies	RIA 24 L 27; NLI G.365
Co. Dublin	1 copy	RIA 24 B 33
Co. Kilkenny	1 copy	NUIG Hyde 29
Unknown	4 copies	RIA 23 M 6; NLI G.209, G.666; UCD Ferriter 23
total	35 copies	

[37] Martin A. O'Brennan (ed.), *O'Brennan's Antiquities* (Dublin, 1858), vol.1, p. 7.

gration in subsequent decades, accelerated the process of language change and sent the production of Irish-language manuscripts into sharp decline. I have traced only fourteen copies of Ó Conaill's poem dating from the second half of the nineteenth century. See Table 8.

It may be noted in passing, however, that the work was still being copied in the early twentieth century.[38]

Table 8.   1851–1900

Co. Cork	3 copies	NLI G.669; UCD Franciscans A 48; NUIG Hyde 41
Co. Clare	2 copies	RIA 23 L 40; UCC Torna lii
Co. Waterford	2 copies	RIA 23 O 71; NLI G.658
Co. Armagh	1 copy	UCD Franciscans A 49
Co. Dublin	1 copy	UCC Torna lxxx
Co. Galway	1 copy	NLI G.485
Co. Kerry	1 copy	NUIM DR 4
Co. Mayo	1 copy	NUIG Hyde 67
Unknown	2 copies	UCD Ferriter 33; UCC Gaelic 113
total	14 copies	

Later Historical Poems

I have so far considered only one historical poem, but much of the significance of *Tuireamh na hÉireann* lay in its ability to inspire similar compositions in later generations—compositions which updated the historical narrative by including more recent events without, however, departing from the historical perspective of the original. The works I will now consider were composed in different parts of Ireland and at widely separated periods, yet they strongly resemble *Tuireamh na hÉireann* and each other in both form and content.

Seán Ó Gadhra (1648–*c.* 1720), a poet from County Sligo, composed two poems in which the influence of *Tuireamh na hÉireann* is evident.[39] The first, entitled *Tuireadh na Gaeilge agus teastas na hÉireann* ('The dirge of Irish and the description of Ireland'), focused on Irish historiography and followed Keating's *Foras Feasa ar Éirinn* in denouncing writers who

[38] UCD Ferriter Ms. 1 was written in New York by an emigrant from Co. Kerry in 1912; NUIG Hyde Ms. 54 was typed in Philadelphia by an emigrant from Co. Cork in 1915.
[39] Line 489 of *Tuireamh na hÉireann* is echoed in both of Ó Gadhra's poems; line 493 is echoed in the second of his poems.

were hostile to the native Irish or to Catholicism.[40] Those who aroused Ó Gadhra's ire included Giraldus Cambrensis, William Camden, James Ussher, George Buchanan, Richard Stanyhurst, and Hector Boece. On the other hand, he praised authors who had vindicated the country's reputation as *oileán na naomh* (the island of saints). The latter group comprised Keating, John Lynch, James Ware (a Protestant, but one who took a sympathetic view of Irish antiquity), John Colgan, Peter Walsh, and Roderick O'Flaherty. The second poem by Ó Gadhra might be described as an addendum to *Tuireamh na hÉireann* and has been edited under the title *Staid nua na hÉireann 1697* ('Ireland's new condition 1697'). In it, Ó Gadhra painted a grim picture of the plight of the population in the aftermath of the Williamite conquest:

> Is cosmhail a gcás le pláigh na hÉigipt,
> nó leis an mbroid do chuir Turgésius
> maor Lochlann, sa bhfothram dá gcéasadh,
> nó an connradh do chuir Cromaill is Értoin.[41]

> (Their case is like the plague in Egypt, or the bondage inflicted by the Norse commander Turgesius, torturing them in the tumult, or the settlement imposed by Cromwell and Ireton.)

But, unlike Seán Ó Conaill, Ó Gadhra also conveyed a message of hope. Irish history clearly showed that the Milesians and the true religion had both vanquished powerful enemies in the past:

> Minic do saoradh ó dhaoirse Éire,
> Tuatha Dé Danann do scaipeadh le hÉibhear;
> . . .
> is é Pádraig theagaisc creideamh do Ghaedhlaibh,
> is ní fada mhair smacht Oilibhérus.[42]

> (Ireland was often freed from bondage, the Tuatha Dé Danaan were routed by Éibhear [a son of Milesius] . . . Patrick taught religion to the Gaels, and transient was the dominion of Oliver [Cromwell].)

By implication, a similar radical transformation for the better could occur again.

About the year 1714, Aodh Buí Mac Cruitín (*c.* 1680–1755), a native of County Clare and one of the most prolific Irish-language poets of the

---

[40] Edited in An tAthair Mac Domhnaill (ed.), *Dánta is Amhráin Sheáin Uí Ghadhra* (Dublin, 1955), pp. 11–18.

[41] Ibid., p. 19.

[42] Ibid., p. 20.

eighteenth century, composed *A Bhanba is feasach dhom do scéala* ('Oh Ireland, I know your story'), a long historical poem which resembles Ó Conaill's composition so strongly as to be itself entitled *Tuireamh na hÉireann* in some of the manuscripts.[43] Indeed, one of the earliest extant copies of *Tuireamh na hÉireann* is in Mac Cruitín's hand.[44] Mac Cruitín had a particular interest in Irish history and in 1717 he published a history of the country in English which was closely modelled on Keating's *Foras Feasa ar Éirinn*.[45] Mac Cruitín's poem placed greater emphasis on legendary accounts of the prehistoric period than *Tuireamh na hÉireann* had done, but it did not ignore recent history and its account of the sixteenth and seventeenth centuries was as anti-Protestant and as anti-English as anything in *Tuireamh na hÉireann* itself. Mac Cruitín described the Anglo-Norman invasion and the Reformation in the same sentence:

> Teacht na nGall tar cheann an éigin
> le Diarmuid don iath seo mar aon ris
> teacht Chalvin ler aistríodh na léacsa
> do bhain sealbh na bhflaitheas de chéadta.[46]

> (The arrival of the foreigners for the sake of violence, along with Diarmuid to this land, as well as the advent of Calvin who translated the law which deprived multitudes of the enjoyment of heaven.)

This juxtaposes references to 'the betrayer Dermod'—seen as a traitor to his country—and Jean Calvin—seen as a traitor to the Catholic religion. Mac Cruitín juxtaposed another pair of historical villains, 'Cromwell the Bloody' and 'William of the Boyne', as follows:

> A dtarla d'ár in áras Éibhir
> le linn Cromwell ler folmhadh aoltúir,
> tar taoide chuir fuíollach an éaga
> ar uireasba bídh is dí is éadaigh.
> Teacht Uilliam i ndiaidh gach péine,
> do fuair ár bhfearaibh 's ár bhfearannta daoradh,
> do fuair ár mbailte is ár leathan túir aolta,
> do fuair ár n-eachra 's ár n-arm gan aonta.[47]

---

[43] Lines 242, 185–92 and 241 of *Tuireamh na hÉireann* are echoed in Mac Cruitín's poem.

[44] NUIM Ms. M 86 (b), copied in 1714.

[45] Hugh MacCurtin, *A Brief Discourse in Vindication of the Antiquity of Ireland* (Dublin, 1717). For an account of Mac Cruitín's life and work, see Vincent Morley, *An Crann os Coill: Aodh Buí Mac Cruitín, c. 1680–1755* (Dublin, 1995).

[46] RIA Ms. 23 C 8, p. 133.

[47] Ibid.

(All the slaughter which happened in Ireland in Cromwell's
time, who emptied splendid mansions, and expelled overseas
the remnant not killed, in need of food and drink and clothing.
The arrival of William [III] after every torment, who condemned
our men and our estates, took our dwellings and our fine great
mansions, and found our cavalry and army disunited.)

Here again, dissension among the Irish was presented as the cause of
their defeat—though the factual basis for such an explanation of William
III's victory was less obvious than it had been in the case of Cromwell.

The *caoineadh* metre was commonly used for elegies in the seventeenth
and eighteenth centuries—indeed, the word *caoineadh* means 'elegy'.
Possibly under the influence of *Tuireamh na hÉireann*, some of the elegies
composed in *caoineadh* metre not only praised the personal virtues and
distinguished ancestry of the deceased but also incorporated summary
accounts of Irish history. Examples of what might be termed 'historical
elegies' include *Tuireamh Shomhairle Mhic Dónaill* ('Sorley MacDonnell's
dirge'), composed by the County Louth poet Séamas Dall Mac Cuarta
(*c.* 1647–1733) for an officer in the army of James II who fell at the battle
of Aughrim (1691);[48] *Tar éis mo shiúil fríd chúigibh Éireann* ('Having
walked through the provinces of Ireland'), a lament for an undistinguished
descendant of the O'Neills of the Fews composed around 1769 by the
County Armagh poet Art Mac Cumhaigh (*c.* 1738–73);[49] and *Tuireamh
an Bhráthar Seán Ó Néill* ('Friar Seán Ó Neill's dirge'), composed by
Patrick Ward around 1772.[50] The second of these will be considered here.

Although a certain Ulster bias is discernible in Mac Cumhaigh's composition, his political and religious sympathies are indistinguishable from
those of the Munster authors discussed previously. Here, for example, is
his account of the earl of Tyrone's rebellion in the reign of Elizabeth I:

Bhí Iarla mór Thír Eoghain in éifeacht,
rí na leon ó Bhóinn go hAontroim,
's dá bhfaigheadh cuidiú mar chóir ó chóigibh Éireann
Essex 's a shlóite go leonfadh an tréanfhear,
Elizabeth mhór 's a trón go mbuairfeadh,
is gheobhadh clann Mháirtín bás go héascaidh.[51]

---

[48] Edited in Seán Ó Gallchóir (ed.), *Séamas Dall Mac Cuarta: Dánta* (Dublin, 1971), pp. 63–9.
[49] Edited in Tomás Ó Fiaich (ed.), *Art Mac Cumhaigh: Dánta* (Dublin, 1981), pp. 118–26.
[50] Edited in Cuthbert Mhág Craith (ed.), *Dán na mBráthar Mionúr* (Dublin, 1967), vol. 1, pp.
307–11.
[51] Ó Fiaich, *Art Mac Cumhaigh*, p. 122.

> (The great earl of Tyrone was powerful, the king of the war-
> riors from the Boyne to Antrim, and had he received due help
> from the [other] provinces of Ireland the champion would have
> crushed Essex and his host, he'd have shaken mighty Elizabeth
> and her throne and the progeny of Martin [Luther] would have
> quickly perished.)

In this case also, the absence of national unity had led to ultimate defeat after initial successes. Unlike Seán Ó Conaill, a southern author, Mac Cumhaigh emphasised the role of the commander of the Ulster Catholic army, Eoghan Rua Ó Néill, when discussing the war of the 1640s and claimed—inaccurately—that Ó Néill had defeated Oliver Cromwell. Like Ó Conaill, however, Mac Cumhaigh associated the causes of Ireland and Catholicism. Protestantism was not merely a heretical doctrine, it was also a foreign doctrine:

> Chuir Cromail chun sodair 's gach bodach dar ghéill dó,
> sciúirse thug greadadh do chreideamh Liútérians,
> Scotia is Sacsain gur chreathnaigh sé in éineacht,
> nó gur chloígh 's gur chreapall 's gur threascar an t-éag é.[52]

> (He [Eoghan Rua Ó Néill] routed Cromwell and all the churls
> who obeyed him, a scourge who flailed the Lutherans' religion,
> he made Scotland and England tremble together, until death
> vanquished, tramelled and destroyed him.)

The province of Connacht lacked the active scribal tradition of Munster and Oriel. This might lead one to expect that *Tuireamh na hÉireann* would not have diffused as readily in the west as in other regions. However, a historical poem of 404 lines entitled *Seanchas na sceiche* ('The history of the bush') composed by the blind County Galway poet Antaine Raiftearaí (1779–1835) around 1822 contains unmistakable echoes of *Tuireamh na hÉireann*, a fact which establishes that the author was familiar with Seán Ó Conaill's work.[53] Given the absence of a strong scribal tradition in the west, as well as Raiftearaí's blindness, one can hardly avoid the conclusion that *Tuireamh na hÉireann* formed part of the oral repertoire in Connacht by the early nineteenth century. Indeed, fragments of the poem survived in the oral tradition in County Galway until the middle of the twentieth century.[54] Raiftearaí's view of

---

[52] Ó Fiaich, *Art Mac Cumhaigh*, p. 122.
[53] Tomás Ó Concheanainn, 'Nótaí ar "Sheanchas na Sceiche"', *Éigse*, 12 (1967–8).
[54] Ibid., 270 (footnote).

Irish history is indistinguishable from Seán Ó Conaill's. Once again, the identity of the Catholic and Irish causes were stressed:

> Isibéal tháinig i gcoróin 'na déidh sin,
> nár phós fear is nar throisc gan chéile.
> Chuir a cúl is a droim le cuing na cléire,
> chuir ruaig ar easpaig is ar an eaglais Ghaelach.[55]

> (Elizabeth succeeded to the crown after her [Mary], she wed no man but never abstained for want of a husband. She turned her back on the obligations of the clergy, and banished the bishops and the Irish church.)

Raiftearaí's identification of the Catholic church as the church of the Irish people is particularly noteworthy. As Art Mac Cumhaigh had done in the previous century, Raiftearaí lauded the achievements of the Ulster Catholic commander Eoghan Rua Ó Néill in the 1640s:

> Eoghan Rua a tháinig i ndiaidh an scéil sin,
> maiseach, fearúil, barrúil, béasach,
> cleasach, súgach, lúfar, éasca,
> a bhain léim leataoibh as *Cromwellians*.[56]

> (Eoghan Rua [Ó Néill] arose after that episode, graceful, gal-lant, genial, courteous, wily, spirited, active, quick, and he made the *Cromwellians* leap aside.)

The emphasis placed on the achievements of an Ulster commander in a poem by a Connacht author provides further evidence that a pantheon of national heroes had been elaborated and accepted by the early nineteenth century.

A generation later, around the year 1850, Nicholas Kearney (*c.* 1802– *c.* 1865), a native of County Louth and a contributor to *The Nation*, organ of the nationalist Young Ireland movement, composed a 500-line poem entitled *Crua-ghorta na hÉireann* ('Ireland's cruel famine') in *caoineadh* metre on the subject of the great famine of 1845–9.[57] While Kearney dealt at length with the human consequences of the subsistence crisis, he situated it in an old and familiar historical context and por-trayed the enormous mortality as the latest manifestation of England's constant malevolence towards Ireland. The similarity between Kearney's

---

[55] Ciarán Ó Coigligh, *Raiftearaí: Amhráin agus Dánta* (Dublin, 1987), p. 146.
[56] Ibid., p. 147.
[57] For Kearney, see S. Ó Dufaigh and D. Ó Doibhlin, *Nioclás Ó Cearnaigh: Beatha agus Saothar* (n.p., 1989).

treatment of earlier historical episodes and the outlook expressed in *Tuireamh na hÉireann* is striking:

> Is iomdha ceannfort clamprach claonmhar,
> d'fhear pláigh is gorta orainn go léanmhar;
> Siobal bhaothmhar, éigneach, náireach,
> is Oliver péisteach, bréagach, gráinneach.[58]

> (Many were the hostile prejudiced rulers, who sadly brought plague and famine on us; ignorant, violent, disgraceful Elizabeth, and monstrous, deceitful, horrible Oliver [Cromwell].)

Kearney attributed the same anti-Irish malevolence to the English rulers of his own day—to John Russell, the prime minister, and to Earl Clarendon, the lord lieutenant:

> Seán beag Ruiséal pocán gan éifeacht
> bhí'n t-an 'na cheannfort os na réigiúin;
> fear ionaid an rí 'n Áth Cliath níorbh fhearr é—
> Clarendon ciapach, cíosach, scléipeach.[59]

> (Little John Russell, an ineffectual billy-goat, was at that time ruler over the countries; and the viceroy in Dublin was no better—vexatious, well-heeled, ostentatious Clarendon.)

It is hardly coincidental that a copy of *Tuireamh na hÉireann* penned by Kearney is extant.[60]

Conclusion

Nicholas Kearney's composition could not command the same degree of public attention as the earlier historical poems discussed above. By the time it was composed, English was replacing Irish as the vernacular language throughout most of Ireland; public recitation was giving way to private reading as literacy rates increased; and newspapers—including the phenomenally successful *Nation*—had supplanted literary manuscripts as the principal reading material in even the remotest regions. None the less, Kearney's poem demonstrates that a genre of demotic historiography which emerged in the mid-seventeenth century continued for

---

[58] National Library of Ireland, Ms. G.545, p. 3.
[59] Ibid., p. 13.
[60] UCD Morris Ms. 6, copied in 1819.

200 years. A tradition which originated in the era of the wars of religion persisted throughout the revolutionary era of the late eighteenth century and provided a fertile substrate for the romantic nationalism of the nineteenth century.

English-language writers of the early nineteenth century such as Watty Cox and Thomas Moore were important, but their originality lay more in their medium than in their message. Their role was to facilitate the successful translation of a long-standing interpretation of Irish history from a declining oral and manuscript-based vernacular culture into an emerging culture based on print and the English language. Notwithstanding the impact of French revolutionary ideals, a failed republican rebellion, and parliamentary union with Great Britain, Irish popular culture in the early nineteenth century was, I would submit, characterised more by gradual evolution and the blending of traditional and innovative elements than by sudden transformations and ruptures with the past.

Unity and Diversity in European Culture, *c.* 1800: Summary of Discussion

Music and the Visual Arts

Professor James Sheehan (Stanford University): 'Art and its Publics, *c.* 1800'

Professor Silke Leopold (Heidelberg): 'Towards the Idea of National Opera, *c.* 1800'

Professor John Deathridge (King's College London): 'The Invention of German Music, *c.* 1800'

EMMA WINTER OPENED THE FIRST DISCUSSION SESSION by suggesting that the replacement of traditional patronage by the market place and the gravitation of the centre of the art world from Rome to Paris were more contested than would appear from James Sheehan's paper. Rome revived and retained its significance for the art world throughout the first half of the nineteenth century and continued to attract artists from all over Europe in what Winter also described as a very anti-French movement. In addition, she asked whether the state acted as mediator in the development from classical forms of patronage to the emerging art market. Sheehan agreed that Rome indeed retained some significance or developed a different kind of importance in the nineteenth century, but argued that it ceased to be an active centre and became much more a place of training and a museum where people went to learn about the ancient world. Sheehan also agreed that, especially in the field of architecture and public sculpture, the state, but also municipalities and other bodies became important sources of patronage. He conceded that he should have gone into more detail concerning the differences between quantity and quality. In terms of quantity, the state and other forms of public patronage remained very important, but it did not produce the art we do now value. Winter, however, argued that art which is not considered of particularly high quality today was at times highly influential in the past.

Proceedings of the British Academy, **134**, 199–206. © The British Academy 2006.

With reference to John Deathridge's paper, Siegfried Weichlein suggested a connection between the rise of German idealism and Germany's retrospective identification with abstract symphonic music, with which Deathridge agreed. However, he stressed that the links between philosophy and the composers of music are not strong. If one looks at what composers say in their letters, matters do become much more interesting and complicated, but also less philosophical and impressive. Silke Leopold added that symphonic music became identified with Germany because there had been a tradition of orchestras in this country since the eighteenth century. In contrast to France and Italy, Germany had a relatively large number of orchestras which could play symphonic music and provide a setting for the composition of such music. Asked whether it was the reception of an opera which turned it into a 'national opera', Leopold agreed completely and stressed that this was the only way of defining an opera as 'national'. After all, as she later added, the Belgian revolution in the nineteenth century was started by a French opera, *La Muette de Portici*, on an Italian subject.

Coming back to Sheehan's paper, one participant pointed out the irony that in the eighteenth century the opera was quintessentially Italian while at the same time uniquely cosmopolitan. Another paradox was fascist Italy's reinterpretation of Verdi's move to Paris as the conquest of France by Italian music, while Verdi and Rossini had to become to some extent French composers at that time in order to further their respective careers.

Another questioner emphasised the importance of the collective private patron as an intermediate and transitional stage between the individual patron and full public participation in the arts through the market in the first two decades of the nineteenth century. Deathridge agreed, but thought that a combination of collective or personal patronage and the market was even more characteristic in 1800. Market relationships and patronage were initially mixed, and this mixture took different forms all over Europe. As to whether Bach should be seen as completing a tradition invented around Beethoven rather than vice versa, Deathridge confirmed that Beethoven's contemporaries had felt the need to invent an impressive origin for what they considered German music, and to which Beethoven measured up. Richard Wagner, by contrast, eventually treated Beethoven as the origin in order to deflect attention from the fact that the modern orchestra had been invented by Berlioz. Deathridge stressed that the contradiction between construct and practice was a constant theme in the history of so-called German music.

One participant wondered whether it is necessary to be quite so sceptical about the concept of national art. After all, towards the end of the eighteenth century there was a serious attempt to create a British school of painting which defined itself in opposition to what French painters were doing and which was recognised as distinct by contemporaries. Sheehan agreed on the danger of being too sceptical, but responded that the debate about the nature of British art must be separated from discussion about the formation of a British art school. Much of the clarity on what constitutes British art begins to evaporate when the works of art themselves are examined.

Faced with the question of whether the idea of German music was carried on in practice after 1945 under internationalist rhetoric, Deathridge responded that the Darmstadt school indeed continued Schoenberg's ideology, but in the guise of one of his students, Anton Webern, who took the idea of infusing the construct with Darmstadt practice even further than Schoenberg had done. Another participant then raised the question of what constituted 'Germany' when people search for and talk about German music, to which Deathridge responded that this construct had very powerful and aesthetic implications precisely because there was no such place as 'Germany'. This made the construct of German music so potent. Tim Blanning then closed the session by pointing out that Wagner had famously said: 'If I am German, I carry Germany around inside me.'

Political Culture

Professor Peter Alter (Duisburg): 'The Impact of Napoleon'
PD Dr Siegfried Weichlein (Humboldt, Berlin): 'Cosmopolitanism, Patriotism, Nationalism'
Dr Peter Mandler (Gonville and Caius, Cambridge): 'Art in a Cool Climate: The Cultural Policy of the British State in European Context, *c.* 1780 to *c.* 1850'

John Breuilly started the second session by questioning Peter Alter and Siegfried Weichlein about how the discourse of the nation could become so universal and polymorphic and serve so many purposes. He suggested that it might be useful to examine how this dominant rhetoric of the nation was used in different political structures by different kinds of groups in different areas operating under different circumstances. By going back to structures and interests, Breuilly argued, one could give meaning back to a rhetoric which, by becoming universal, also becomes utterly meaningless. In addition, he wondered whether the pursuit of the national sometimes leads to the neglect of the non-national. Peter Mandler was then asked whether by arguing that cultural policy is about secular culture, he covered only a small part of the story. In addition, Breuilly highlighted the role of voluntary associations in financing art galleries.

In response, Alter argued that the concept of the nation became more and more attractive at the beginning of the nineteenth century because it contained the promise of a new society in which everybody was equal and had the same chances. For that reason, French rule in occupied parts of Europe was not resisted by the people until after 1806–7, when they realised that it had become oppressive and a form of despotism. In this situation, the concept of the nation again held out a promise, of the nation as free and self-determined. The concept became increasingly popular over the years and developed from an elite to a mass movement in the 1840s. However, it was a long process, and it took more than 100 years, for example, to create the French nation.

Weichlein stressed that the patriotic discourse was more flexible than constitutionalism, especially in the pre-revolutionary phase. Instead of issuing provocative demands to the monarchies, the patriotic discourse empowered them and worked as an *Ermächtigungsformel*, not as a *Verpflichtungsformel*. When constitutionalism and parliamentarism developed, nationalism became a less flexible concept. Weichlein cautioned against identifying nationalism or nationalistic interests with particular social interests. Rather, the rise of social interests within the nationalist movement should be examined.

Mandler agreed that alternative discourses of mobilisation and organisation in the nineteenth century have sometimes been pushed aside by the obsession with the nation, especially in the twentieth century. Especially in the British case, he suggested, the language of civilisation and the language of Christianity were at least as important as the language of the nation. Mandler explained that when he had spoken of philanthropic activities, he had meant this to include voluntary associations. Nevertheless, he expressed the opinion that their significance for the funding of art museums had been exaggerated. Most of the big provincial museums in Britain were created by acts of individual patronage after the 1840s.

Volker Sellin suggested that Napoleon hampered rather than fostered German nationalism by abolishing many of the smaller free imperial cities, ecclesiastical territories, and so on in favour of modern states. These states, like Bavaria, became the new reference point for the patriotism of their inhabitants, a development which impeded the creation of a German national state. Weichlein agreed that the creation of a German nation-state had not been a foregone conclusion and that, up to the 1840s and 1850s, the situation was still undecided. There was disagreement on these remarks from Alter, although he concurred that, in the very early stages of German nationalism, its point of reference had been open. Nevertheless, Fichte, for example, did not mention Prussia or the Prussian king in his *Speeches to the German Nation*, and we can speak of a Bavarian or Prussian nation only from 1848 on. At that time, however, nation-building efforts in Bavaria by the state bureaucracy responded only to a regionalism that affiliated itself with a larger nationalism at sub-state level.

Sheehan asked Weichlein what people around 1800 meant by patriotism and whether their loyalty was to their cities or towns rather than to the state. Sheehan added that one of the central problems of state patriotism and nationalism was the transition of scale from a political set of loyalties built on relatively face-to-face relationships to something which had, in Anderson's phrase, to be imagined. Weichlein responded that he had wanted to point out that there was no linear development from small-scale to large-scale. There was also a change from large-scale to small-scale points of reference in Germany after Napoleon's defeat.

Another commentator pointed out that, between the French Revolution and 1814, people in Germany were unsure about their identity and what their fatherland was. The concept of the nation filled that void when it appeared. Eric Hobsbawn asked how the German Swiss or the Baltic Germans, to whom the concept of the German fatherland was not very relevant, were affected by this. Weichlein also pointed to the importance of religion, for example, the success of the Catholic counter-mobilisation against nationalism and the French Revolution in the rural areas because of its strategy of religious identity-building and its credibility at local level. It was also pointed out that the Swiss were indeed worried about the tendency to define the extent of the German fatherland in cultural terms.

Like others before him, Michael Rowe expressed scepticism about the notion that the period under scrutiny saw the rise of modern nationalism and argued that one problem was the language of resistance and collaboration. Napoleon was resisted, but he also represented institutions such as the Civil Code, which received a great deal of support in many parts of Germany throughout the nineteenth century. Rowe suggested looking at the revolutionary Napoleonic period as a debate on whether state power should be exercised freely or constrained, a question which is still highly relevant. As nationalism turned out to be so successful, historians have to explain why it happened, when it started, and how the little bits and pieces of its origin became a larger image later on in the nineteenth century. In response, Weichlein said it would be a gross misrepresentation if one were to refer only to nationalism, as it emerged along with liberalism and modernisation in the nineteenth century. The latter two were not always welcomed by the people. For example, they were regarded as a threat in rural areas and in southern Germany. Rejection was part of the package, as, for example, the rise of anti-Semitism showed. The increasing degree of internal integration simultaneously fostered nationalism and reaction, such as anti-liberalism and anti-emancipatory movements.

Clarissa Campbell Orr pointed out to Peter Mandler that, while the royal family in England could not build palaces because of limited financial means, the Bank of England was built in London as a palace of public credit. Mandler agreed, although the original Bank building was much more modest than the current one, which was built in the early twentieth century. Mandler added that Parliament was not shy of aggrandising itself in public, especially in the new Houses of Parliament.

Benedikt Stuchtey asked Weichlein for his view on why, given the centrality of the concept of nation at that time, no German historian of the nineteenth century wrote a *Meistererzählung* of German history before Teicher, Zeber, or Lamprecht. Weichlein responded that Hegel had, in a way, filled that need. In addition, historiography was more occupied with the history of smaller regional German states and the history of dynasties and monarchs. Any author writing a national master-narrative in the early nineteenth century would also have encountered problems with his own government.

The Written Word

Professor Otto Dann (Cologne): 'The Invention of National Languages'
Professor Marilyn Butler, FBA (Exeter College, Oxford): 'Cosmopolitan Europe: A View from Ireland in 1798'
Dr Vincent Morley (Mícheál Ó Cléirigh Institute for the Study of Irish History and Civilisation, University College Dublin): 'Views of the Past in Irish Vernacular Literature, 1650–1850'

Ted Royle opened the third session by asking Vincent Morley whether he would agree that two things happened at once: first, the emergence of the demotic tradition which was cultivating language and a culture and ideas which were not immediately influential on elites; and, second, the discovery of this demotic tradition towards the end of the eighteenth century by those who rationalised, formalised, standardised, and increasingly politicised it. Morley agreed, but stressed that Irish popular culture had existed independently of the urban intellectuals before the latter rediscovered it. They did not carry this culture back to the grass roots, but had to go to the people if they wanted to lead them. Morley said Ireland was an interesting case because its national language was cultivated only by the lower people and a small linguistic elite. Asked by Stuchtey about the existence of Protestant poetry that could be identified with colonial nationalist ideas, Morley replied that such popular poetry was printed in newspapers around the periods of the American and French revolutions, but declined afterwards, when Irish Protestants reassessed their political loyalties in the wake of 1798. It existed only in English, not in Irish, because of the close correlation between language, community, ethnic origin, religion, and politics.

Michael Sullivan pointed out that not only Maria Edgeworth, but also a number of contemporary publications picked on the ragged appearance of Irish people. Marilyn Butler replied that, throughout her work, Edgeworth frequently referred to similar people in other places. Butler emphasised the connection between this sort of writing and these sorts of images and the expeditions undertaken by German scholars within the Russian Empire in the mid-eighteenth century. There was quite an interest in 'savage' people, as they were sometimes called, and the scholars' travel accounts were still being published by the *Edinburgh Review* in the early nineteenth century.

Weichlein shifted the discussion to national languages by pointing out that they could be associated with state-building and standardisation, but at the same time also with the break-up of empires and secession projects. In addition, he stressed the connection between national languages and religion in many cultural nations (*Kultur-Nationen*), for example, Ireland. Otto Dann agreed and emphasised again the problems which official state languages posed for multinational empires. John Breuilly commented on England's uniqueness in having a *Volkssprache* (people's language) which is also the *Schriftsprache* (written language) and the *Staatssprache* (official language). He identified the state, the intellectuals, and socio-economic developments as the agencies which tried to bring these three together, and suggested that their interaction and mutual support could help to explain the different degrees of success in achieving this goal.

Breuilly then asked Morley whether there was a political programme embedded in the Irish tradition of what political form Ireland might have taken without English rule, if it were not to be a confederation of ancient kingdoms or the like. According to Morley, there was a political strategy, but not a political programme. Until the death of Bonnie Prince Charlie in 1788 and the beginning of the French Revolution, this was the Jacobite project, that is, the restoration of the Stuarts. Later on, hopes rested on Napoleon, and after 1815 on Daniel O'Connell. The hope was that Ireland would achieve equality with the other two kingdoms of England and Scotland and be linked with them through personal union of the crowns. Asked by Sheehan why, in contrast to Poland, the national language of Ireland did not become a marker of independence and national self-consciousness, Morley pointed towards the famine, which especially hit monoglot Irish speakers. Many of them died or emigrated, while the bilingual Irish were under pressure to speak English as the language of upward social mobility. Claire Connolly closed the session with a comment on the link between the tradition of demotic historiography in the Irish language and the emerging English-language literature of Romanticism in the period around 1800. She pointed to Edgeworth as an intellectual writer trained in the Enlightenment tradition who, through a romantic interest in the politics of orality, gave voice to a perspective that was otherwise alien to a British novel-reading audience. According to Connolly, literary studies now show that Romanticism and romantic nationalism did not just reject the present and look back to a misty past, but also tried to localise and nationalise the transition to modernity.

Index

Compiled by Vera Nohl